Murders in the Mist

Also by Nicholas Gordon

IVORY KNIGHTS

Murders in the Mist

WHO KILLED DIAN FOSSEY?

NICHOLAS GORDON

Hodder & Stoughton
LONDON SYDNEY AUCKLAND

British Library Cataloguing in Publication Data

Gordon, Nicholas
Murders in the Mist: Who Killed
Dian Fossey?
I. Title
364.1

ISBN 0-340-59880-8

First published in Great Britain 1993

Published by Hodder and Stoughton,
a division of Hodder and Stoughton Ltd,
Mill Road, Dunton Green, Sevenoaks, Kent TN13 2YA
Editorial Office: 47 Bedford Square, London WC1B 3DP

Photoset by Rowland Phototypesetting Ltd,
Bury St Edmunds, Suffolk

Printed in Great Britain by
St Edmundsbury Press Ltd, Bury St Edmunds, Suffolk

Author's Note

Rwanda is the smallest country in Africa, yet, unlike its larger neighbours, it managed to keep its secrets from the white man for far longer. Surrounded by mountains, defended by a well-organised warrior force, for centuries it remained isolated from the West, retaining its independence and excluding the colonists until barely a hundred years ago. Even the great Stanley never set foot on Rwandan soil. It is a place that is difficult to come to terms with. Rwandans speak in riddles. There is an art form to elliptisism. Nothing is simple and that includes the war. By African standards it is not a particularly "big" war. It has spluttered on like a damp fuse for three years, occasionally bursting into savagery and then dying down. Thousands have been killed. Over a million have been made homeless. The war is being fought out on ethnic lines, between the former ruling class, the Tutsi, and their one-time vassals and now rulers, the Hutu. Yet this is to over-simplify, because there are many Hutu fighting alongside the Tutsi in the rebel army, the FPR.

I knew the war was going to make my investigation difficult. People were vanishing overnight, and those opponents of the regime who were not killed were being tortured or imprisoned or both. Despite this, many were courageous enough to risk their lives and freedom and talk, and curiously I think the fact that the war was raging and their colleagues and friends and family were dying prompted those who could have remained silent to reveal what was going on.

There are many people I must thank for making my investigation possible. Most of them still live in Rwanda and I dare not name them. Where I have used names, I have in many cases changed them to protect the source. But I can thank all those at A.D.L., the human rights organisation based in Kigali, Rwanda's capital, the former Minister of Justice M. Stanilas Mbonampeka, Enno Bussmann, who was attached to Orinfor, the state news agency, at the time I was researching, Colonel Charles Uwihoreye, who was brave enough to go on the record, Alphonse Nkubito, Ros Carr and Dr Quaestiaux.

In America, I received invaluable background help from former Ambassador Frank Crigler and from his wife Betty, Jim Foster, Judy Kessler Hayes, widow of Harold Hayes, the author of *The Dark Romance of Dian Fossey*, who gave me access to the Hayes archive at Wake Forest University, North Carolina. I would like to thank Farley Mowat for his encouraging words, Richard Rombach, Shirley McGreal, Stacey Coil, Sandy Harcourt, David Watts, Dr Elton Wallace, and Ruth and Tom Keesling.

In Europe, Peter van der Bunt, Denis Newson, Kathleen Austin, Filip Reyntjens, Jackie Holland, John Bakker, Adrian Warren, Alexie Forrester, Alan Goodall, Ian Redmond, Dr Iain West of Guy's Hospital, Cornelia Van Brussel, Lesley-Ann Jones and Vivienne Schuster.

Lastly, I could not have written this book without the help of two dear friends, François Misser who started off giving me a background briefing in Brussels and ended up accompanying me on two journeys to Rwanda, and Abdul Perera, who from the very beginning in the south of the Sudan right through until my last journey this February acted as my eyes and ears, and gave me the sort of advice that keeps you alive.

June, 1993

Prologue

IN THE HEART of Africa, beyond the sunset, beyond Mpororo, past the slick waters of Muta Ngize, there is a graveyard. It is a dismal place, damp, and green, dripping with lushness, a place of shadows. A single twisted Hagenia tree, standing sentry over the solitary black, marble tombstone, looks down on a land that is at war.

Behind the graveyard, the fractured peak of a volcano lours. It is cold and breath does not come easily, because, though the equator runs nearby, the sun rarely appears and the altitude is 12,000 feet. This is Dian Fossey's last resting place. She was buried here on Tuesday, December 31 1985, four days after she had been found murdered, apparently hacked to death, in her cabin in Karisoke.

Today, seven years after her murder, I read the inscription on her grave and suppressed an instinct to laugh out loud. They, her few friends, her enemies, for she had many, and those who continue her research into mountain gorillas and her work in trying to save them, couldn't even get this last tribute right.

It reads:

NYIRMACHABELLI
Dian Fossey
1932–1985
No one loved gorillas more
Rest in peace, dear friend
Eternally protected
In this sacred ground
For you are at home
Where you belong

They thought it fitting to inscribe on her grave this name Nyirmachabelli. They thought it described her exactly, they thought it meant "the woman who lives alone on the mountain". But it doesn't. It means "the small woman who moves fast" and though

Dian Fossey moved fast, she was never a small woman. Nor could they spell the word properly. Someone has Italianised the sound. It really should be Nyaramicibili.

These may appear to be insignificant errors or innocent mistakes, but they are diagnostic, because they set the mood for a story which is spattered with hypocrisy, evasion, chicanery, lies, half-truths, subterfuge, greed, and murder. Not one murder, that of Dian Fossey, but, to my knowledge, three others.

When I first decided to find out what really happened to Dian Fossey that December night in 1985, I faced a barrage of hostility from those who had worked with her. They were incredulous that I wanted to learn the truth. They agreed, well most of them agreed, that the man who had been convicted of her killing, the American research student Wayne McGuire, was innocent. They thought, well most of them thought, that his alleged accomplice, the Rwandan Emmanuel Rwelekana, who was found hanged in his prison cell while awaiting trial, was innocent too. Yet when I asked for their help, they told me to leave the bones of Fossey alone. They said that no one would ever find the truth. They warned me that to go looking for it would jeopardise their research work. They even played the gorilla card, saying that all I would do would be to stir up a dust-storm, and that the gorillas' chances of survival would be damaged.

When I pointed out that they were scientists and their entire lives were devoted to finding out truth, they looked blankly at me. When I explained that there was more than a scientific truth to be discovered at the end of a microscope, they ignored me. When I played my moral card, and talked about justice and right, they scoffed at me.

You know something: I got the impression that no one really cared about Dian Fossey. They didn't care enough to get her tombstone right. They didn't care enough to see that justice was done.

Of course, this made me all the more determined to go through with it. But the story doesn't really begin here, in this graveyard, 12,000 feet up in the Virungas, and I didn't feel this way until well after the beginning. And, anyway, there would not have been a beginning if I hadn't heard about witchcraft and *sumu*, about poison and *pangas*.

But that was before I met Abdul.

Sudan: March 1991

I WAS LYING under a tree, a sparse umbrella that was shielding me from the sun, and wondering when the convoy would move again. It was three o'clock now and, even though my eyes were closed tight, I could feel the sun printing its image on to my eyelids.

This wasn't the sort of place to stick around for long, despite the heat of the afternoon. There were bandits in the purple mountains that frowned down either side of the thin, brown dirt road. They had attacked the last convoys through here and there was plenty of evidence of fire-fights even around the meagre shadow that I was sheltering in. As I lay there, under the spindles and thorns, my fingers had taken an idle wander in the dirt and picked up enough empty cartridge cases to start some sort of cottage industry: brass tubes, manufactured to carry inside them a dose of death, could quite easily be fashioned into genuine rebel bracelets, pendants to swing from girls' ears, lucky charms to stroke a woman's skin, made by and for Kalashnikov in the USSR and sold only in the Sudan.

I wouldn't have put it past Abdul to start up a business here, by the side of this dusty strip of stones and ruts and potholes that swallowed the wheels of the thirty-four-tonners carrying grain deep across the Other Side. But Abdul shook his head, or at least the towel that covered it shook, and from inside the makeshift tent he had made for himself, murmured that there would never be tourists here; only wars, only men like him, men from the UN, and journalists like me, foolish enough to cover them.

Abdul was the convoy leader. I had met him in Kampala a week before, on the eve of the convoy's departure for the Other Side. The drivers, the UN monitors, the logistics men, the radio boys, the mechanics, the contractors, the grain dealers, never addressed their destination as the Sudan. Always, it was the Other Side, almost as if they believed they were stepping out of the real world for a couple of weeks and exploring another planet. I thought it an overstatement, a dramatisation of the task ahead of them, an attempt, perhaps, to portray themselves as heroes to me, the man from London who was going to write about them, but then I was still in Kampala and I hadn't crossed to the Other Side.

I thought about that night in Kampala, the night before the convoy left, when Abdul had finally checked the lorries, all twenty-eight of them, had supervised the loading of the grain, all 600 tons of it, a donation from the Austrian government, had walked the length of the convoy, inspecting the tyres of each of the massive Fiat and Mercedes trucks, had pushed his hand into the treads of quite a few, and shook his head and despaired aloud to me how lorries like this would ever make the journey.

"We are," he said, rolling his black eyes, "going to be on the road for fourteen days. That's if the rains don't beat us. That's over 1,500 kilometres and the road runs out at Gulu."

"How far is that? Is it on the Other Side, Gulu?" I asked.

"No, it's still in Uganda. The rest is terrible."

The way he said the word spelt out the journey ahead as clearly as a satellite mapping. His tongue bumped and ground over every consonant, torturing the letters until they screamed with pain.

"Terrr-i-bulll." He repeated it. And broke off to show me his hand disappearing up to his elbow inside a tyre. He looked rather like a vet bending over a stricken cow, except he wasn't wearing gumboots and his arms were bare. "Look at this. They told me these tyres were all good. Thirty-two ply. See for yourself."

I too bent down and pushed my hand into the rubber.

Now, one week later, 330 tyre bursts or punctures later, so Abdul's log-book recorded, I was on the Other Side, sitting, lying, rolling, itching, searching for saliva, opening my shirt and flapping it to kindle a breeze on my stomach, and wondering whether the bandits, the Tupamos, would attack this afternoon.

"If they do, then it is God's will," Abdul said quite calmly. And he turned on his side and stroked away the queue of flies forming around his head and adjusted the towel once more. "I would," he said, "quite like to see a gorilla."

"Tupamos? You must be joking."

This was most definitely Tupamos territory. The cartridge shells told me that. I expected to be attacked before dusk, which was in about two and a half hours, and probably be killed. I wasn't a Muslim, and I couldn't quite accept Abdul's quiet resignation.

He had already explained to me how they attack, sweeping down from the mountains, the same purple shards of rock that enclosed the road, how they were a tribe who had never been pacified, how they would work for whoever paid them more, and how the Khartoum government, the Arabs from the north, were now enjoying the lethal services of this most efficient of killing machines. Their brief, he had said, in the meeting before we set out from Kampala, was to disrupt any convoy bringing food into the south. We were a military target, despite the humanitarian purpose of our mission.

I asked why.

"Because," he said, "the food is distributed by the rebels, the SPLA, the Sudan People's Liberation Army." He explained that the SPLA had been fighting a war against the Arab north for over twenty years, and this had caused famine, brought disease, and a massive upheaval in people's lives. The food we were bringing, the 600 tons of maize, would be under the control of the rebels to give out to the starving. This is why it was a target.

"Do you mean," I said, "that it goes only to the SPLA?"

Abdul said nothing.

That was in Kampala a week before, and now, here on the Other Side, he wanted to see a guerrilla.

He threw off the towel, spreading the flies, and stood up. Now he was the size of the tree. He bent from his shoulders, set his head square on his neck, and pounded his fists against the hairs of his chest. "No, I mean a gorilla."

"Well, Abdul," I said, "you won't see one here."

"No," he said, "but still I would like to see one. I would like maybe to tune one."

Tuning was one of Abdul's great pleasures, perhaps the pleasure of his life. When Abdul tuned, he was in paradise, with perfumed dancing *houris*, who shed their veils faster than even he was capable of removing his inhibitions.

As he stood by the tree, he changed from gorilla into practised tuner, holding his hands in front of him, fingers clenched, probing them forward into the air, and then twisting them from side to side with an easy accomplishment that came to him naturally, but which he said had taken years to perfect. "I learnt to tune in the clubs of Nairobi," he had told me after a few days on the convoy. "The Florida 2000 and Buffalo Bill's, and Toys in Mombasa. I will take you there one day. We will tune together."

I didn't really know what he was talking about at first, but from the smile on his face, from the way his lips stretched the Zapata moustache and the eyes twinkled, I could see tuning would not be as acceptable in the constraints of English society as it clearly was in Toys Club.

"Why tune a gorilla?" I said. "Why not one of these women in the SPLA camp? Or some old girl on the road?"

"They are very ugly, these Sudanese women. Very, very black."

"That didn't stop you tuning in Gulu the other night. And anyway, so are gorillas."

"Come," he said, "it is time to move."

Even then, under that tree in Tupamos territory on the Other Side – and why should it have been any other way? – I did not think that for the next two years my life would be measured by these creatures and dominated by the murder of one woman, and that both Abdul and I would be drawn into another country, and on to a mountain whose forests were wreathed in mists, a mountain which nature had beheaded, and where the truth was concealed, in a dark place.

Ayod: March 1991

THE GRAIN was delivered safely to a place called Ayod, a dot on the atlas, which, like many of those dots spattered about the African continent, signifies nothing more than the optimism of the traveller who has never quite arrived. Ayod was hardly worth the effort of the cartographer. All there was to see was a large canvas marquee bending in the breeze, pinned to the dusty earth by a taut set of ropes. That was all. This had been erected by the UN to store the grain and as the convoy rumbled into the compound, thin men and women stood up. I could hear the crack of arms and backs as they flexed their bodies. There were no cranes, no fork-lifts in Ayod. These people were the hi-tech of Ayod. For each sack they heaved into the grain store, they would be paid in food.

The convoy was over. But my friendship with Abdul had grown. And with it, so his fascination for gorillas had rubbed off on me.

It was curious, the two of us, riding in his Toyota Landcruiser through hostile country, watched every day from the air by the enemy's ancient Antonov, a reconnaissance aircraft that also dropped the occasional stick of bombs on towns and villages in SPLA hands, and listened to by our own side, the bosses in Kampala and Nairobi who monitored every move we made. Curious, because while we followed the convoy, we talked about ourselves, and our work, and our countries and our families, but mostly we talked about adventure, as if we weren't in the midst of one itself.

No, this convoy was work. We slept in our boots, under the moon, hooking our mosquito nets up against the bumpers and grilles of the trucks. We ate off the land, exchanging tins of Guinness, warm and volcanic, for live chickens. We listened to the snarls of lions in the night, and drank milky Italian coffee with the Somali drivers. It was the Somalis who told Abdul and me about Fossey. Not about the murder; but about the gold.

But first Abdul. He was an easy companion on this convoy, a first-rate mechanic who was running his own transport business in Kenya. He had made his fortune carrying, in his fleet of lorries, oil-drilling equipment from Mombasa on the Indian Ocean coast hundreds of kilometres up to the prospecting areas in the north of Kenya, near the Somali border.

It is a tough, hard road to follow. After Isiolo, past Mount Kenya, on the edge of Samburu, the road, the tarmac strip the British had laid first in the thirties and then in the fifties, ends. The metal runs out as abruptly as the town itself. Isiolo, Abdul's birthplace, is a crossroads in the sand, an administrative centre that serves as a last reminder that 300 kilometres down the road, south of the equator line, there is another world, a place of law, order, regulation and taxes, called Nairobi. After Isiolo, there is the desert, where borders are cold exercises in human geometry and where the Shifta, the Somali bandits, live as they want, taking cattle and land and women with contempt for the city boys so far away.

But Abdul was no city boy. He had, it was true, been brought up in Nairobi and Mombasa where he had relations, but it was always Isiolo that he came back to. And it was here in this frontier town with its sharp tang of Boran, and Meru, and Samburu and Somali, that he learnt the ways of the bush. He learnt to handle snakes; he was paid five shillings for each one he brought to the resident herpetologist in the town, an American on exchange, and was becoming quite rich, in his contemporaries' eyes at least, until, one day, he brought in a baby black mamba and sent the herpetologist back to Nairobi on the next bus.

"It was only a small mamba," he said, "maybe this long," holding his hands apart so they made a gap of about a foot.

He learnt how to track game, how to kill, how to read the signs of the wind and the sky, and he learnt the cardinal rules of the bush: "Never give away anything, food, weapons, water, nets, pans, anything, until you are back in town. Never travel after five at night, unless you have eaten first. And always sleep with your legs wrapped around a tree."

I could understand the first two rules, but sleeping with my legs wrapped around a tree?

"You'll laugh at this, Nick," he said. "Now, I mean." He paused. "Last night, remember last night?"

I tried to. Where had the convoy got to? Somewhere between the SPLA base at Pageri and the one at Liria, the one on the edge of the Tupamos territory. "What about last night?"

"You woke up."

I nodded.

"You asked me if I could hear sheep in the night."

I had heard baa-ing in the night. "So?"

"Well, you didn't hear sheep."

A pause.

"Okay, Abdul, if I didn't hear sheep, what did I hear? Goats?"

"No, what you heard was a python."

"Rubbish."

"No, it is true. I didn't want to tell you because I knew you would be afraid. You would have kept me up all night with your fear."

"Python baa?"

"Yes, like sheep. Like this," and he baa-ed.

"So what has that got to do with sleeping with your legs around a tree?"

"So the python can't swallow you entirely," he said, with a hint of a laugh in his eyes.

"I didn't notice you with your legs around a tree, Abdul."

"No, I had mine around that SPLA girl. There was no need for me to find a tree. But you, Nick, you would have had to find one, or a girl. So I told you the python was a sheep."

It was in the bush, beyond Isiolo, beyond the limits of civil engineering, among the Shifta, that Abdul secured his reputation and his money. The story emerged, piece by piece, during the convoy, and as it took shape, I began to wonder what had made him join the UN when he could be making so much money in Kenya.

"That's easy to answer," he said. "First there is no work there now. Recession. So no oil, no drilling. Then, I felt it was time I put back something into the world. God has been good to me. Now it is my turn to repay Him."

God, indeed, had been good to Abdul. He came back from the desert, from the north, not a rich man in Nairobi terms. He did not have enough in his pocket to finance a tourist hotel in the city the way cabinet ministers do, but he built one in Isiolo. He also erected three huge warehouses where he hoped to store grain and where he could service his lorry fleet. And he supported the poor of the town for three months from his own pocket. But beneath this patina of bush saint, there was an earthiness, a humour that was irrepressible. Especially when it came to tuning, and certainly when it came to the subject of what and who to tune.

The Somali drivers were intrigued and amused by our conversations. Each night when the convoy pulled in to the side of the way, or into the haven of a rebel camp, the turn boys, the drivers' companions who sat alongside them each day in those garishly decorated cabs, each one a reminder of the faith with its Koranic exhortations leaping from the windscreen – a kind of Islamic equivalent of Kevin and Sharon – would fetch water and light the fires, lay out the straw mats alongside the vehicles, poke each of the thirty-two tyres, and return to the cookpot.

We would often wander over, through the pale rings of smoke, and sit on the mats, next to the Somalis. They were men with long, hard stories at their command. They knew Africa as well as Stanley or Tippu Tibb, the slaver from Zanzibar with the sinister flickering eyelids that gave him his nickname. They had no country, these Somalis, they belonged to the unmarked roads and the tracks of the continent. But everywhere they went, they took with them their stories, their religion and their pasta. They spoke

Arabic and Italian and Swahili, and a smatter of English, enough to call me Englishman, enough to invite me to settle alongside them, enough to ask me whether I liked the thick, coarse grains of sugar to go with my coffee. Their turn boys were their slaves. These were mostly in their teens and twenties, all of them African, and by that I mean they were not Somali, and all of them willing to please.

"Why are these boys called turn boys?" I asked one night.

"Because they tell us the way to go. They say 'Turn here and turn there' whenever we reach a crossroads."

For these drivers, it was their first Sudan convoy. They had reached the assembly point in Kampala by the most circuitous route I could imagine. I suspect that the turn boys must have earned every shilling finding the way there.

As we settled on the mats and sipped their coffee, they began talking about their journeys, about how they had driven through the continent, past lakes and through mountain passes, across the great wastes; and all with a contempt for the borders that London or Brussels or Berlin man had drawn.

"Where were you before Kampala?" I asked.

"Rwanda."

"And you drove to Kampala?"

"No, Mombasa."

"And then Kampala?"

The drivers nodded. They were smiling.

"What were you carrying?"

"Tea and coffee. This coffee you are drinking."

"Is that a good profit for you?" Abdul asked.

"We made it worth the journey. There were other things on board too."

I asked them what.

"There are many things in Rwanda that are worth carrying. There is a good trade in contraband in Rwanda."

His name was Ali and he lay on the matting, his left hand propping up his head so delicately that his eyes and mouth looked more like an ornament than flesh and bone.

"Like what?" I asked.

The drivers glanced at one another, sipped their coffee and then one leant towards the battered metal pot that was sitting on the fire. Ali shifted his bottom and shimmied his body over to it. He picked up the ladle and gave the pasta that was bubbling inside a cursory stir. The other driver pulled back his head and jerked his neck forward. A long, single piece of phlegm shot past my ear. This was a signal for everyone, his companion, the turn boys and Abdul to start hawking.

When the chorus of coughing and throat-clearing had faded so that only the bubbling of the pot and the hissing and crack of the fire could be heard, Ali resumed his position on the mat, gave me a hard look and said, "Rwanda is a country where there is no sea. It is a prisoner. And it is men like us who are freeing it."

I gave Abdul a what's-he-talking-about look. But Abdul was far too involved in the turn of the conversation to notice, or, at least, to hint to me that he had noticed. I sensed that Abdul had smelt out a business opportunity.

"Freeing it from what?" I asked.

"From what you people in the cities make men do."

I gave up, sank down on the mat alongside the drivers and sipped the dark, rich, sweet coffee. The night was clear and I saw a solitary flash of tracer light up the mountains. No one else on the mat took any notice. They were huddled, the drivers, the turn boys and Abdul in the sort of conversation that I knew from its tone and gesture and speed was not the ordinary passing of the time of day.

When, finally, the coffee was drunk and the turn boys had emptied the dregs from the pot on the sand next to the mats, and Abdul had risen from the mat and said his farewells, he motioned me back to our nets, slung over our sleeping-bags.

As he slid under and adjusted the sides of the net, tucking it beneath his body, he said, "We must go. There is a lot of money to be made in Rwanda."

"How?"

"Those drivers. They told me. They have moved gold. It comes in from Zaire, from Walikale, and they move it out on their trucks wrapped in tea or coffee."

"What did they mean about the country being like a prisoner?"

"Oh, that's the way they speak. He means it is a land-locked country. They rely on truckers. They have too many customs duties to pay. They bring in cigarettes and move out gold."

"What about gorillas?"

"Fuck gorillas," he said, laughing as he began to tune with his hands.

London: April 1992

"DEAR NICK,

How is the great city? When do you get my PASSPORT?"

A letter from Abdul, postmarked Nairobi. He had quit the UN. Too many convoys, too many shoot-ups, too much food lost, too much bureaucracy. Not enough money and too much malaria.

"Those mosquitoes," he wrote, "in Bor are the size of gunships. They bite through everything, even my overalls."

He told me about his nights in Nairobi and all the tuning he had done, and then he mentioned Rwanda . . .

"I need to get there. Business is really bad here. I have to get my lorries moving. The oil industry is broke. I thought that there might be some wells drilled near Isiolo, but it is not going to happen."

"Gorillas! Rwanda!"

Abdul.

If business was bad for Abdul, it was worse for me. I, too, no longer had a job. I had been fired, and I was wondering what to do next. The phone had not rung. There had been no big offers, and my life was regulated by a two-weekly visit to window number three at the Greenwich social security office, where I signed my name and watched men grind out cigarette butts on lino floors as they shuffled towards their window. And then, of course, there was the library. I had started reading about Rwanda, and it didn't take me long to come across the story of Dian Fossey, and how she had exchanged a career of looking after mentally handicapped children in America's mid-West to live and work with gorillas in central Africa.

It was clear that Fossey was a complex character. She was tough and determined, saw life in absolutes, didn't suffer fools; she was arrogant and contemptuous of blacks; she was foul-mouthed and did not shrink from using violence. She grew old with gorillas and, as she aged, she isolated herself from her fellow human beings. She was a jewel of a woman, a twenty-four-carat bitch who during her life made many, many enemies. It is seven years since her death yet I could see that those who had known her, her colleagues, her few friends, her biographers, could not make up their minds about her, about who had really killed her, or why.

A fellow scientist, an American researcher, who was the only white living and studying in her gorilla research centre in the Virunga Mountains, had been charged with her murder. His name? Wayne McGuire. His motive? He wanted to steal her research notes and so complete his own thesis. His weapon? A *panga*. McGuire escaped the country some months after the murder and is now living in America. He was tried in absentia and sentenced to death by a Rwandan court. But he has never been extradited. I wondered why.

I also wondered how he had managed to slip out of the country when it appeared that he was already under suspicion. Perhaps it was incompetence that let him go. Or was there something more?

As for the motive, would a man kill for scientific notes? Would the only white man in the research station not feel he would be automatically suspected? He would have to be insane to go through with the crime.

And then there was the matter of the accomplice. McGuire, it was alleged, was aided in the murder by a Rwandan tracker called Emmanuel Rwelekana. Rwelekana, like McGuire, wasn't present at the trial. This wasn't because he too had fled the country. It was because he had died. He was found, so the books stated, dead in his cell, hanged, in Ruhengeri prison, the town at the foot of the Virunga Mountains in northern Rwanda. Why did Rwelekana hang himself? The biographies all carry glowing reports of him. He was, it is said, a loyal tracker, a good man, almost a permanent fixture up there in the mountains with Fossey.

Finally, what of the American government's position? Why did the US State Department not institute its own enquiry into Fossey's death? She was a prominent American scientific figure, known throughout the world for her study of mountain gorillas. She was the focus of a worldwide conservation effort to preserve these creatures. Pictures of her talking to gorillas, stroking gorillas, playing with gorillas had touched a nerve. Fossey was a heroine, a prototype for the American Dream, a woman who had hauled herself out of the viscosity of mid-West life and forced herself upon an alien environment that she first conquered and then understood. And she had been murdered in the country for which she had achieved so much. Not only that, an American, a fellow scientist, had been convicted of her murder and his Rwandan accomplice had hanged himself in prison.

The books about Fossey concentrated very much on the making of the woman. Her lonely childhood, how her father had drunk himself away from his family, how she could not get on with her mother whose ambition was to be a model, how she disliked her stepfather, a builder from California, how she felt too tall and gangly and awkward in people's company, her failure with boy-friends, how she found a kind of fulfilment working with the handicapped, how she insisted on living as far away from her colleagues as she could – in one case over seven miles and in as isolated a cottage as she could find – how she stumbled on her new life when she heard the Kenyan primatologist Louis Leakey speak about gorillas at a lecture in Kansas City, how she pestered him to let her work with them, how she persuaded him to take her on despite the fact she had had no scientific training, how she had her appendix removed to convince him of her sincerity, how she established herself in Africa, first in Zaire, and when that blew up and she was forced out by the fighting, in Rwanda.

It is a seesaw of a tale. First the struggle to mount the plank, then that heady feeling of flying upwards, God-propelled, and finally the crash to earth.

It is also the tale of the remarkable success of an extraordinary woman who died in the most mysterious of circumstances. If McGuire, with the help of Rwelekana, had killed Fossey, then I wanted to know why. I could not believe, even at the beginning, that she would be savagely *panga*-ed to death just because a fellow scientist wanted her notes.

I had met scientists before, conservationists rather, and I had certainly found them to be, on the whole, a strange cliquey crowd, set apart from the rest of the world by their work which often took them into isolated places where the ways and manners of the real world seldom impinged. But I never realised how peculiar, freaky and outlandish they could be until I started talking to the primatologists, the men and women who had spent some of their career working with Dian.

I could see that already there were questions here to be answered: Was Dian as horrible as the testimony of her colleagues suggested? Did McGuire kill her? If so, why? What part did Rwelekana play? Why did he commit suicide? How did McGuire manage to escape so easily? Why didn't the US State Department take a more active, even investigative, role?

Why had no one tried to investigate the case before me? To be fair, one writer, the American journalist Harold Hayes, who wrote the book *The Dark Romance of Dian Fossey*, had touched upon the circumstances of her murder and could well have gone on to explain them, but a brain tumour killed him before he had the opportunity.

There were other questions, too. If McGuire was innocent, then who did kill Fossey? And why? And, if someone else killed her, then why was McGuire framed?

I'd read about Rwanda too, about the slaughter of the master tribe, the aristocratic, slender, Nilotic Tutsi by their servants, the Bantu Hutu. I'd read how Stanley first set eyes on the country called Rwanda in the late nineteenth century when he was making yet another of his epic attempts to source the Nile. Stanley described the place as a "land of dwarfs and giants ruled over by a tall, pale-skinned Empress". This woman, according to Stanley's informant, a venerable Arab trader called Hamid Ibrahim, ruled with the lustre of her eyes, the softness of her voice, and the sharpness of poison. She kept out the Arabs, the slavers and ivory caravans, and was feared not only inside the country but out. She ruled remorselessly. Her weapons were her sexuality and her willingness to use witchcraft, or *sumu*, against her enemies and those who thought they were her friends.

I spoke to men in London, academics at the School of African and Oriental Studies, about *sumu*, expecting them to sneer, but they didn't. "It works," they told me, "because people believe. Do you know that *sumu* evolves as the country evolves?"

I didn't. There are men in Rwanda, sophisticated men, who sincerely believe this, I was told. I asked for an example.

"It was night in Kigali, Rwanda's capital," said one Rwanda hand in the SOAS library. "I was walking home before the curfew. Everyone was in a hurry to get home so I was amazed to see two or three men standing, idly, in the street, staring up at the sky. They were talking and pointing up at the sky, and I could hear and see they were really quite excited. I stopped to ask them what they were looking at.

"One said, '*Sumu*.'

"I said, 'What?'

"He said again, 'Up there, *sumu*,' and he pointed.

"All I could see was the glint of a satellite tracking across to the north of Kigali. So I said, 'That's a satellite.'

"But they shook their heads, all of them, and said; 'It may be a satellite, but it's still *sumu*.'

"I didn't understand what they meant, until, a few months later, I was talking to a Rwandan historian here in the library and he told me that this was the way that *sumu* worked. Just as the satellite orbited the world, so the *sumu* circles your enemy's house, so there is no way out. He is trapped once the circle has been completed. He will die, as surely as that satellite completes its circle of the globe. That's *sumu*, and that's the way they think out there."

I asked him about Fossey, and he smiled and said, "*Pangas*. They don't kill with *pangas* in Rwanda."

"So how do they kill?" I asked him.

"With poison," he said, "or *sumu*."

Dear Abdul,
Sorry, I haven't been able to procure you a passport yet. Suggest you write to my former employer at the *Daily Mail*, Sir David English. Or change sex, and call yourself Zola Budd. Have lost job, so like you am available for work in Rwanda. I am deeply interested in the Fossey murder. Please ask your people around Nairobi what they know.

Regards,
Nick

Next day I flew to Washington DC.

Washington DC: April 1992

THE CRIGLERS live in a clapboard white house a few miles outside the District of Columbia boundary in Virginia. Frank, tall and friendly, without any of the stuffiness of his UK counterparts, is now retired from the diplomatic service. He had served as US Ambassador in Rwanda from 1976 to 1979 and he and his wife Betty knew Dian well. He knew Africa and Africans also. He had been posted to Gabon in the sixties, Zaire from 1966 to 1969, and had finished his career in Somalia. He had known Fossey since 1966.

"I first met her when I was the consul in Bukavu, a town in the east of Zaire which borders on to Rwanda. I remember the meeting with her vividly. There was a hell of a lot of shooting going on. Colonel Jean Schramme, the Belgian mercenary, had taken over the town and was holding it to a kind of ransom. He wanted to set up an independent state in that part of the Congo. There had been a lot of killing and people were frightened. We were worried about US nationals and we knew that there was this woman working for Louis Leakey up in the mountains. She was right in the line of fire. There was concern from Washington for her safety, but I never saw her during the trouble. I heard in a roundabout sort of way that she was okay. Anyway a few months later, I was on the Rwandan side of the border at an airstrip when this tall statue of a woman, wearing white, completely in white, carrying an enormous amount of luggage, stepped out of a small aircraft. The whole airstrip was in uproar. There she was, striding towards me, towering over the natives, directing all her boxes into another small plane to take her to her new base.

"She was an extraordinarily dominant woman. It kind of embarrassed me. This wasn't the sort of scene you should be viewing in the sixties. I was busily trying to fade into the woodwork and here in front of me was this neo-colonialist throwback of a woman."

"Did you like her?" I ask.

"Yes, we both did," says Betty Crigler without hesitation. "She did not fit into any category easily. She was the sort of person who liked being different."

Frank interrupts his wife, motioning for her to be quiet for a minute. He is elated, I can see, opening up and blowing the dust off Africa, off the past.

"Here's an example," he says. "Next time I met her was in 1976, not long after I took up the post in Kigali. There were rumblings at the embassy that Fossey was going to pay me a visit. She was coming to call to size me up. Just before I left for Kigali I had broken my wrist falling off a horse and I came to Kigali wearing a cast and a sling. When she walked into my office, she expressed great concern and wanted to examine my wrist. She aked me about the physiotherapy treatment I was undergoing – she had been a physio with handicapped kids, you know – and we hit it off ever so well. It was a joke, I suppose, her coming the medic with me, a kind of pretext, but it worked. It was a charming ploy.

"She was keen for me and Betty and the kids to come to visit her at Karisoke. I guess at first she wanted to see if we could handle the physical challenge of climbing up to 12,000 feet to stay with her in the volcanoes. We went up there with the children at Christmas and she adored it when we came."

Betty interrupts. "Yes, she was such a great home-maker. Whenever we stayed, there were always clean sheets on the beds and fresh flowers picked from the meadows in our room. It was her home, that hut up there in the mountains, and she was the hostess. We were her guests and she never forgot that. And Frank, tell Nick how she adored the kids, especially Jeremy."

Frank smiles at the memory. This didn't sound at all like the Fossey of the books. Fresh flowers in rooms, clean sheets, a sense of humour?

I asked what her biggest problems were.

"Getting a visa," says Frank. "No question about it. That was my biggest problem too. It was my most important function where she was concerned. Dian was never any good at cultivating the bureaucrats even at the highest level. They were suspicious of her. They didn't understand all this work she was doing with gorillas and they had heard about her conflicts with the locals."

"What conflicts?"

"Fights over gorillas and poaching. Rwanda, you've got to understand, is one of the most overpopulated countries on earth. It is a tiny piece of land and every inch of it that is accessible is under cultivation. For the Rwandans the Virungas, the volcanoes where Dian worked with the gorillas, was not a haven for these animals but a valuable piece of land that could be farmed. Anyway, the government people obviously knew her history; they had heard she was aggressive and abusive towards the Batwa . . ."

"The who?"

"The pygmies," Betty explains. "The people who live around the Virungas, in the mountains, the tribes who killed the gorillas."

"Why did they, do they, kill the gorillas?"

"Because they are frightened of them, for revenge, or because they wanted her off the mountain so they could claim it for themselves."

"Revenge for what?"

"Dian would often take the law into her own hands if she believed she had caught poachers. She'd been known to whip people, pistol-whip them, I mean, and she used *sumu* on them."

"*Sumu?*"

"Yes, *sumu*. Witchcraft," interrupts Betty.

"So why would they risk killing a witch if they believed she possessed the powers of *sumu*?" I ask.

The Criglers say nothing.

"Going back to the visa problem," says Frank, "the Rwandans, the government and the security men, had heard about her antics up in the mountains and were suspicious. One way to keep tabs on her was to keep her on a short lead. So she was never ever, to my knowledge, given a visa of more than three to six months."

"Was that unusual for an expat, such a short visa for a person who was obviously on a long-term project?"

"Yes, it was. Lots of people I knew were granted two-year visas."

"How well did you know her? Socially, I mean . . ."

Betty Crigler shakes her white hair and smiles. She leans towards me and smiles again. "She'd often come and stay with us at the embassy. She'd come down off the mountain and change into a pair of white cords with a white silk blouse. She always wore good clothes. She loved lacy lingerie. She had the nicest nightgowns and expensive dresses. Her taste was impeccable. She was my size, maybe five foot eleven tall, slender with narrow shoulders, willowy. And her eyes. They were piercing eyes. Brown eyes. She used her eyes to convey her language, to express her happiness or her displeasure. She'd stare down at Africans, a sharp, angry look. But when she showed approval she'd smile with her eyes and she'd be physical. She'd hug you, but she was only a hugger when she cared for you. She'd flirt too. She was coquettish. She'd hold an arm, or your hair or she'd slap you . . ."

"Like a gorilla?"

"Yes," says Betty, clapping her hands together. "Just like a gorilla. If she had a notion to flirt with you, then she'd give you all the attention she could muster. And there was a great deal of Dian to give. She could be very witty, and she was a very attractive woman when she was made up. Men found her attractive, I guess not only because she was attractive, but because she was famous and she was powerful; there were a lot of things about her that men found appealing but whether she could ever have had an extended relationship with one man, I find doubtful.

"But," she continues, "if she didn't know you, then she could be very formal. And with Rwandans she could be a different person from the Dian I knew. She called them wogs. She couldn't really communicate with the Rwandans. Her French was abominable. Her Swahili was fractured. They'd all cringe at it, and her Kinyaswahili was just awful. So more often than not she'd rely on her body language to communicate. She would gesture, or slap or smile, or point, and make noises."

I can hear someone whistling in another room. It sounds like a version of "Colonel Bogey".

"You're right," says Betty. "It is 'Colonel Bogey'." She gets up from the armchair in the sitting room and motions me to follow her, but quietly. We go into the kitchen. I look for the whistler and see, instead, a parrot. "His name is Kanyoni. It was Dian's parrot. She taught it to whistle 'Colonel Bogey'. She'd stand there in the embassy in front of it and say 'De, De, dededeedee'. She loved that bird. She was such a good musician. She'd play for me at the embassy. Classical music on the piano.

"You know she'd arrive at the embassy always in the late afternoon. She'd look terrible. Dishevelled and as if she'd come down from hell, which I suppose she had. Only it was up, not down.

"You know, she was afraid of heights. Living up as high as she did. She was terrified of the road down and the road from Ruhengeri to Kigali, that was one that scared her. It has a tremendous number of switchbacks with huge gorges and precipices either side of the track.

"She'd have a long soaky bath. She'd do her hair and her nails, make up. She wanted to look attractive; she wanted to be more than the average woman. She took so much care with her appearance. She always looked after her hands and she dyed her hair. She kept it tinted even up that mountain."

"What was her natural colouring?"

Betty doesn't have to think. "Auburn. And she darkened it with tinting. But the weather up there in the mountains, I suppose it was all that rain and wind, hadn't done much for her complexion. It was blotchy.

"She'd come out of that bath and downstairs looking a million dollars. She was a great talker once she had overcome a kind of decompression period. It was difficult finding points of contact with her. I mean, America meant absolutely nothing to Dian, America then, I mean. She could talk about her childhood, about Kentucky, but California where her stepfather lived was a painful subject. She detested him, the stepfather. He was greedy, selfish and possessive. You know, Nick, right after her death, that man, Price, he wanted everything from her. He wanted to be sole beneficiary of the estate."

I ask about the day Dian died.

Frank sighs. "I picked up the phone at 7.00 a.m. It was December 28. The State Department were on. What was Dian's father's phone number? She'd been discovered dead. They didn't know the parents' names even. I called Richard Price, her stepfather. They were talking about bringing the body back. I told them that it would be a terrible mistake. I knew she always wanted to stay in Karisoke. With her gorillas."

"You know it never occurred to me that she had been killed," says Betty.

"It did to me," says Frank. "Even though Rwandans are not murderers."

"What about all the thousands, hundreds of thousands of Tutsi who were killed by the Hutu? That wasn't so long ago."

"That was tribal, the result of centuries of friction. That was revolution. This was different."

"How?"

"Well," explains Frank, "how do you kill a queen in her own palace? That's exactly what happened. Karisoke was, is, a difficult place to penetrate. And I can recall only one foreigner, a Frenchman I believe, who was killed by a Rwandan. They just don't do these things."

"So who did?" I ask.

"I don't believe McGuire was the murderer," says Frank. "It's all too pat. And I don't believe it was an African, I mean one of her trackers. An African wouldn't have removed the panel of the hut the way it was. To me, if an African was out to murder Dian, they would have gotten her out in the woods where they had the advantage, taken her by surprise. Jumped out of a tree or something and slashed her to death there and then. The way it did happen, or was supposed to have happened with her killed in her hut, up there on the mountain, with her body lying on the floor by the bed and the section of the wall taken out for the killers to get in, well, it's just not African, and it's certainly not Rwandan."

"Then there was the weapon," says Betty. "The *panga*."

"What about it?"

"The killer left the *panga* in the room. Why do that?"

"Maybe the killer was in a hurry. Maybe someone had heard her screaming?"

"No. Nothing was heard that night. Her body was discovered at about 6.00 a.m. and her time of death was some hours earlier. And if it had been an African, there's another weird thing."

"What?"

"Well, nothing was stolen. No money, and there were plenty of dollars there. No weapons and there were three guns in the hut. And ammunition. No notes were taken."

"And," says Betty, "there was the night."

I ask her what she means by "the night"?

"Well, Africans are scared by the night. And they were also scared to death of Dian. The combination of darkness and Dian was resistible to most of them."

"What about the way the investigation was handled?" I ask.

Frank pauses and looks at me for a second and then back to Betty and then to me.

I try again. "Just say you had been there at the time of her death, it's a hypothetical question, but just say?"

"The whole investigation would have been handled differently," he says. "In fact, it wasn't handled at all. The ambassador was away. It should have been handled differently."

"Why wasn't an autopsy performed?" I ask.

Frank shrugs.

"I mean, an autopsy could have told a lot," I persist.

But he suggests I put it to Kathleen Austin, the woman who represented the US Embassy at the time, the woman who saw the body, who was first on the scene.

"Do you know where she is now?"

"No, but I'm sure you'll find her."

That night in my hotel overlooking the Watergate Centre, I began to try to analyse the doubts the Criglers had set up in my mind.

First, there was Dian herself. Their portrait of her was not at all conventional. They remembered a different Dian, a softer Dian, a Dian who loved her looks, enjoyed the sensuous side of life, fine lingerie, long baths, a Dian who looked after her hands and dyed her hair. They had even furnished an explanation for her racism: their Dian was a throwback to another, less complex world, where whites ruled and blacks were wogs and everyone knew their place. And they doubted that McGuire had murdered her. They even doubted that a Rwandan, a tracker, had killed her. They were critical of the investigation.

But there was something else they told me, something which had kept me from sleeping that night.

"Someone must know who did it," Betty had said. "There isn't anything in Africa that goes on that someone doesn't either see, or soon hears about. And in Rwanda, no one can keep a secret. No one. Somebody knows. Is there a murder ever committed that somebody doesn't know who did it? It'll be a monumental search, but, who knows, maybe you'll nail him."

I realised, too, that if I were to discover the truth, then the answer would lie, not in Washington, but in Africa. America was going to be good for background to this investigation, but I doubted whether I was going to get straight answers there.

It was another remark by Betty that planted the seed in my mind.

"Dian," she had said as we left the house, "Dian suffered not one death but two."

I stood on the doorstep, and turned towards her. "What do you mean by that?"

"She was killed by a *panga*. But she was assassinated by words and deeds. And this was happening when she was alive."

She wouldn't be pressed on her statement, but that night in my king-size Four Seasons special I knew who she was talking about. The people who had worked closely with her. Not the Rwandans who had been rounded up and taken to the jail in Ruhengeri at the bottom of the mountain, but the researchers, the ecologists, the primatologists, the paper-makers, the guys in search of reputations. These were the people who had provided much of the material for the books written about Fossey's life. It was obvious that they had dusted up as black a dirt cloud as they could when they talked about her life. I wondered how much light they could shed on her death.

These were the same people who when she died were holding up their hands in shock and sorrow, yet while she was alive spent their time criticising her vehemently. I realised then that there were many truths about Dian. She was many things to many people. She would be nice when she had to be nice, usually when she wanted something out of somebody, and she'd act the bitch when she didn't need them.

But was that reason enough to kill a woman? Because she was a bitch?

Sacramento and Seattle: April 1992

SCIENTISTS search for the truth. They are men and women driven by a compulsion to find out why we are the way we are, why we behave the way we do. They are naturally curious. They question, they probe, they observe, they study, they scrutinise. They are fastidious people, these scientists, critical, often difficult, but always meticulous. But most of all, they are honest. They have to be. Their battlefield is the laboratory or the field. Their watchwords: probity, objectivity, dispassion, broadmindedness if you like.

The scientists, the ones I met in the Fossey case, could not be so neatly defined. Yes, they were dedicated. I am certain they were honest. And methodical and analytical and precise, just as they had been trained to be. But it seemed to me one quality was lacking: morality.

There was an irony here. I was searching for the truth and so were they. But *different* sorts of truth. Whenever I asked about the Fossey murder, I was told that I might as well pack my notebooks away, because the murderer would never be found. None of them believed McGuire had killed Dian, yet they were unwilling to put forward any theory other than that the crime was committed by poachers. I was warned not to pursue the case by some.

Why ever not? I asked innocently.

Because you might foul up the whole of the work that has gone on in Rwanda for the last twenty years.

Do you mean I could endanger the lives of the gorillas?

Exactly.

It's hard to believe that scientists so meticulously trained, such exact people, such objective people could say this, but they did.

Sandy Harcourt is professor of primatology at Davis University in California. For many years he was Dian's right-hand man at Karisoke. He is urbane, handsome, a golden child, the sort of professor that gives academia a good name. He was born in Kenya, educated at Cambridge and came to Rwanda in his early twenties. It was at Karisoke that he met and fell in love with his wife Kelly, a researcher and daughter of actor James Stewart. Sandy didn't want to talk to me about Dian. He felt that enough had been said and his fingers had been burnt already by what had been published.

"What if the victim had been your wife and not Dian?" I asked him. "Surely you would have done everything within your power to pursue the killers?"

There was a long pause from Harcourt. It was lunch-time at Davis and he was toying with a plastic box of salad. Behind him was a sticker warning those able to read it that something in the room was radioactive. I wondered what it was. Maybe it was just a sticker.

"Does it matter what really happened?"

"Why do you say that, Professor?"

"Well, once somebody's dead, do the causes really matter?"

I couldn't believe what I was hearing. "Well," I said, "I think it does matter. I think you could argue from a moral point of view that if a life's been taken, then you should actually try to do your best to find out why that life was taken and who took it, and then make a judgment."

Sandy, I believe, wasn't listening. He picked at his lunch in his little office and said, "It was surprising that it hadn't happened before. Dian made a huge number of minor enemies. People also talked about major enemies. I personally don't believe any stories about government officials being involved . . ."

"What officials?" This was the first time I had heard of government people being linked to the murder.

"She made enemies of officials, but she wasn't an annoying enough person for any government official in Rwanda to murder her. I mean it's just too extreme a reaction. If you want to get rid of someone you don't like in Rwanda, an expatriate I mean, and you are in the government, you just make sure the visa is not renewed."

"But surely this is what was happening to her all the time, only men like Frank Crigler spent their entire careers in the diplomatic service renewing it for her?"

Sandy was not to be convinced. He was plodding along explaining why this killer of Dian had to be a minor player. "If, therefore," he continued in lecturing mode now, "it was a revenge killing, it was one of her minor enemies in the sense that this person wasn't a government official. The way she went about protecting the park was very tough. She certainly made lots of local enemies – it could have been one of those, and in that sense, she was living on borrowed time. I personally," he said, "don't believe it was a revenge killing. I think it was a robbery that went wrong. Robberies were always happening around Christmas. People wanted money for Christmas and New Year."

"But nothing was taken."

He nodded. "Nothing was taken. No. But if you panic after you've killed someone – it happens often that robberies go wrong and people run off with nothing."

"But there was no need to panic in this case," I said. "Her body was not discovered by the men until some hours after she had been killed. The murderers had ample time to rob her."

Sandy pushed his flip-flops through my aside. "I think the people that did it didn't know that the house was occupied, ransacked the house looking for free cash or perhaps things to sell and came across Dian, got into a fight and killed her and fled."

There it was, a neat theory. But logical? I knew for a fact that the house had not been systematically ransacked, that nothing had been taken, and nothing had been heard. This didn't match Sandy Harcourt's account.

"What about entering by breaking down the side of the house?"

"Oh, that's easy. These houses are built of thin corrugated iron. If doors are locked, one of the easiest ways to enter is just to cut into the side panels. They had done it before."

"Who?"

"Thieves. It happened in 1980."

"Five years before the murder?"

"Yes. People cut into the house by the side panels – apparently in exactly the same place."

"And who was in the house?"

"Nobody. The house had been empty for a long time."

"And they stole things?"

"Yeah."

"Tell me about Dian. What sort of scientist was she?"

"She was a pioneer. She did things her own way. She had immense dedication, immense self-assurance, but like many pioneers she didn't have the attributes that were necessary to continue the job. Perhaps the best thing Dian could have done was to have gone away and set up another project. She didn't have the scientific background. She wasn't trained scientifically, she didn't have the background necessary to run a research centre, nor the personal characteristics. She was a loner really.

"She was never trained as a conservationist either. You have to remember the whole idea of conservation has changed in the years since Dian first started. When she started the way to conserve was to build a fence and shoot anybody who came inside it. Dian came to Africa thinking that. Now that has completely changed."

"Do you think she felt inadequate because of this lack of training?"

"Sure. We came, me and the others, fully trained as scientists with all the latest methodology for doing field research. But Dian wasn't confident enough to realise that even as we knew more quantitatively about gorillas than she did, we were building on *her* work, on what she had set up for us.

"She began to feel that we, the students, were working, not for her, but against her."

"When did you first recognise this?"

"I was first in Karisoke in 1971 for three months and then went back to do a PhD in 1972, so probably I began to realise this was so about the second year of my PhD."

"It didn't take you long?"

"No, but remember we were not on campus. This was in the forest. Stuck on our own. There's nothing to dilute anything that goes on. You haven't got friends that you can go to, you haven't got the TV or movies, there's no one to unwind with."

I left Harcourt digging his salad and his convictions out of the depths of his lunch box. But as I walked across the campus that lunch-hour, back to the car park, and watched the golfing majors chip a hundred balls on to a temporary green, I wondered what he had meant when he said that he did not believe that any government official was involved in the murder.

Jim Foster is a vet. A scientist, but an altogether different, warmer, more homespun type than the Golden Wonderboy at Davis. Jim lives in a timber chalet overlooking the Seattle Sound. It nestles in a corner amongst the firs. There is a wooden walkway around the house; this could be Switzerland.

Inside, there is a smell of pine and on the walls, in the bookcases, on the floor, there is the spoor of the Man Who Has Been To Africa – wooden carvings, totems, twisted forks, pictures. On the wall of Jim's study is a framed cartoon from the Far Side of a wolf.

Jim saw me looking at it. "You know, Nick, Larson lives nearby. He's mad on wolves. Heard I'd spent time in Alaska studying them and sent me this."

Maybe Larson will send him another cartoon. Of Jim sharing Dian's bed with a gorilla. It didn't quite happen that way, of course, but Foster was the first person to spend a night in her house, in her bed, after the murder. He had been sent to Karisoke by the Digit Fund, the organisation set up by Dian after the killing of her favourite gorilla Digit to monitor the health of the gorilla groups.

"I got to Karisoke," he said, "in August 1986. Eight months after the murder. The cabin was still sealed. There were guards there. You couldn't take pictures. It was still a murder scene and there was still a cloud over the place. Everyone was very subdued. Wayne McGuire had been charged with the murder but had gone home to America.

"I wanted to find out as much as I could about the murder. Hell, Nick, I thought maybe if someone killed Dian, then I could be next."

"So why did you sleep in her bed?"

"There's an old movie called *Laura*. I saw it when I was very young and I hadn't thought of it for years. I lay in her bed, the place where she was killed, and I found that I had this deep affection for her.

"When you go into a situation like this, you don't know what the motivation of the murderer was so from the time I arrived, I decided I would have been insane if I had not tried to figure out who to be afraid of if the time came.''

''Time came? Time for what?''

''For someone to make another hit. Maybe,'' he said, lighting a cigarette, ''there are two conspiracies to look at here. First, a conspiracy to murder, and then a second conspiracy to cover it up. And I do believe there was a conspiracy to cover it up. And I think the motivation for this could likely have been for the benefit of the gorillas.''

Two days in America, and it had to happen. Forty-eight hours, three cities and a conspiracy theory. But this one was different. A cover-up organised on behalf of gorillas! Dian would laugh in her grave. And maybe, I thought, glancing at the cartoon on the wall, Gary Larson, too.

Foster glanced across at me, caught the smile in my eyes, and explained: ''There would have been a stigma attached to gorilla research had someone been executed, someone who was connected with gorilla research, maybe an international incident. It wouldn't have done the image of gorillas any good.''

''But murder is murder, Jim. And the irony about that theory of yours is that if science is about objectivism and truth, then the very people who are involved in finding the truth are involved in trying to sew together a mesh of lies.''

Jim sat back in his chair and drew on his cigarette. He told me that people, those who knew Dian well, felt that she would have liked to have murdered herself for the gorilla cause. This was to be her final statement – to give her life and what could be more dramatic than to be killed in this way?

I couldn't believe what he was saying. How could anyone, even someone as determined, maybe as insane as Dian Fossey, plan to be killed by an enemy? How could anyone want to end up the way she did, with her head hanging off her neck?

''What about this conspiracy idea of yours?''

''Well, take the way we were treated by our embassy over there. It was dreadful. I have so little confidence in the State Department. There was a fellow there who had a German name. He was the Chargé d'Affaires when I was there, but he was totally inaccessible. On my arrival in Kigali, I went to see him to check what was going on in Karisoke. It was for my own safety. I found there was a fellow, a Rwandan, who worked at the embassy who had more compassion and more interest in the Americans who worked up at Karisoke than any of the white individuals in the embassy. I got the impression that the American staff were getting away to summer camp, living the African scene, doing nothing for the American who was there, and wanted to work.

"There was another person there, Kathleen Austin . . ."

"She was the embassy woman in charge at the time of the murder. Frank Crigler mentioned her to me."

"Yes, that's her. I met Kathleen at an Italian friend's home. She had a problem with her parrot and I fixed it for her. A few months later I heard Kathleen was leaving and she was selling her furniture. I needed to furnish the lab I was equipping. I went to see her and I found her the rudest, coldest woman I had met in a long while. I thought that there would be pleasantries, that she'd mention the parrot. But there was nothing. You should speak to her. I think she knows a lot more than she lets on."

North Carolina: April 1992

WAKE FOREST University is founded on Methodism. Southern values abound here. Politeness, generosity, respect, cordiality. It is a silent campus, tucked away off the freeway, near Winston Salem, home of cigarettes and, I suspect, soon to become a magnet for the anti-smoking litigationists. Well, on campus, at Wake Forest, there was not a cigarette in sight. And hardly a student, either. Where were they all? In lectures? On the playing fields? Maybe this was a campus where human beings were not welcome. It wasn't the holidays, but I couldn't even sense the ghost of a cheer, or a laugh or even despair as I walked towards the Rare Books department that rainy morning in April.

This, too, was in hibernation. I was their only visitor. They were expecting me and had the white cardboard boxes all ready for me, stacked up on a polished mahogany table. The light in the reading room was soft, pleasing, almost sleep-inducing. I guess I was tired after flying in from Seattle that morning, and around the walls were pictures, framed letters, telegrams, all featuring the man whose archives I had come to see.

This was a room dedicated to the work of the American journalist Harold Hayes, one-time editor of *Esquire, Life* magazine writer and author of *The Dark Romance of Dian Fossey*. He was also a graduate of Wake Forest and his widow Judy had allowed all her husband's papers to be lodged at the university. Would a British university honour one of Grub Street's finest in this way? Maybe the wisdom and enlightenment of Kelvin MacKenzie would one day slither into Oxford.

I opened the first box. It was full. I groaned. Eleven more to go. I was trying to find out how much Hayes knew about the killing before illness forced him to end the book prematurely. I had spoken to his widow, Judy, who had told me that she thought he had maybe twice as much to write about Fossey, but then the illness took hold of him and he was unable to complete the book. Hayes had applied, under the Freedom of Information Act, for the release of State Department cables between Washington and the embassy in Kigali and I wanted to know what these had to say about the murder.

The third box contained a series of cables. Innocuous stuff, asking for information about the murder, how the investigation was progressing. But many of the cables were blacked out, not just the names of personnel, which would be standard, but whole passages. Many were stamped CLASSIFIED. Why?

On one cable, sent in March 1986 by Secretary of State Shultz, requesting "an update on progress of the official investigation of the case", someone had added a note scrawled in black Biro. It read: "K.H. – a brief note on your latest visit to the secret police." It was dated 3/18. March 18, 1986, three months after the murder. Who was KH? I looked through more cables. It had to be Karl Hoffman, Chargé d'Affaires at the Kigali embassy at the time of the murder and the man who had advised Wayne McGuire before his escape from the country, the man whom Jim Foster had thought so unhelpful.

So why would Karl Hoffman be asked to make contact with the Rwandan secret police in March 1986, if at that time the Rwandans were quite sure that they knew who the murderers were? It didn't make sense.

In another box there was a sheaf of correspondence between Hayes and Senator Alan Cranston. Hayes was clearly having difficulty getting further documents released from the State Department. He had appealed to the State Department's Review Panel for the declassification and release of fourteen documents that had been denied in part to him and a further nineteen denied in full.

With the senator behind him, Hayes, I could see, had won a partial victory. There is another letter, dated June 13, 1988, fully two and half years after the murder, which allows him access to two of the documents. I was to find these later.

As for the others? The letter continued: "The withheld portions of the documents released with excisions continue to meet the classification requirements of Section 1.3 (a) (5) and (a) (9) of Executive Order 12356 despite the passage of time. They contain information on the foreign relations or activities of the United States and information on confidential sources, the disclosure of which could reasonably be expected to cause damage to US national security."

So the Fossey murder was a state secret? What was the State Department trying to conceal? And why?

The two documents that were released to Hayes concerned the question of the hair. When Fossey's body was found, according to Hayes, hair samples were found in Fossey's left and right hands. He wrote in his book that these hair samples were collected and sent both to Paris and Washington to be analysed. The results of the Paris analysis, performed by Professor Ceccaldi at the police laboratory in the Quai de l'Horloge, were published in a Rwandan newspaper shortly before Wayne McGuire fled the country. Ceccaldi's opinion was a damning blow to McGuire. The hair in one of Fossey's hands was Caucasian. It did not belong to Fossey. The inference was clear. The only Caucasian present at the murder scene was McGuire.

Another sample was sent to the FBI laboratory in Washington DC. In a memo dated January 23, 1986, less than a month after the murder, Pam Holliday, Department of State, wrote to Jerry Tucker, FBI Liaison for the Office of the Director of the FBI. The subject of the memo is "Hair samples taken from deceased American in Kigali, Rwanda". It goes on to say:

> Attached are hair samples taken from the remains of Dr Dian Fossey, who was found dead in Kigali, Rwanda. Dr Fossey was

believed to have been murdered. [Even this is inaccurate. Fossey was found dead in Karisoke, over 150 kilometres from Kigali.]

One hair sample was found grasped in her right hand. The other hair sample was taken from the hair on her head.

I would appreciate it very much if you would arrange to have a comparison made of these hair samples to determine if they are the same. Also, can the sample found in Dr Fossey's hand be analysed to determine what type of hair it is (i.e., European or African), as these samples may have been extracted from the perpetrator. Please advise us of the results of your analysis.

The hair was analysed at the FBI laboratory. The director sent a report, dated February 14, 1986, to Pam Holliday. It says:

re: Unknown Subject; Dr Dian Fossey – victim; Homicide.
[The Lab number on the report is 60129020 S UJ WM.]

Specimens personally delivered by [and here the name is blanked out] on January 29, 1986:
Q1 HAIRS
Q2 HAIRS
K1 Head hair sample from victim.
Result of examination:
The reddish-brown head hairs comprising the Q1 and Q2 specimens exhibit the same microscopic characteristics as hairs found in the KI specimen and, accordingly, could have originated from DR DIAN FOSSEY, the identified source of the KI hairs. It is pointed out that hair comparisons do not constitute a basis for absolute personal identification.

I realised after reading this that all I could conclude was that the hair sample found in Fossey's hand did not belong to an African. But why did this report differ from the Paris report? Could it be because different samples of hair were sent to Paris and Washington? Could the reason for the discrepancy be as simple as this?

I remembered that I had read, that Hayes had written, that hair samples from both hands, the left and the right, were sent to Paris, while it was clear from Pam Holliday's memo to Jerry Tucker of the FBI that she was sending him only hair from the right hand. So why didn't she send hair from both hands to the FBI? Was it to protect Wayne McGuire? And could this be the reason why the

US State Department was loath to release those nineteen documents? Hardly, I reflected. Why would it release two documents relating to the hair if it wanted to keep the case under wraps? No, there had to be something else, something far more important, that it wanted to keep a secret.

The boxes, each of them packed full of Hayes's meticulously filed notes, transcripts of interviews, memos to himself, were to yield two other pieces of gold. I found them in a file which contained letters Fossey had written to friends and colleagues.

The first was a letter dated December 21, 1985, written just five days before she was murdered. "Dear Rane," Fossey begins (Rane Randolph was her accountant in the United States), "Enclosed are the November Digit Fund monthly summaries . . ." She goes on to give him news – the Price family (her stepfather and mother) are about to come to visit her and her houseboy is sick. But after the social chit-chat, she drops a hand-grenade.

> Oh, concerning the visa. The Head of the Sécurité (Secret Police) [these are her brackets, and her spelling] has stomped on the Park Director and ordered the Emigration Dept to issue me a resident's visa which is good for a minimum of two years, a maximum of life! This type of visa is truly difficult to get, so you can imagine how thrilled I was to arrive in Kigali and find this big man had set the whole thing in order for me. I had to pay $400 for it (standard procedure), but it costs $400 to go to Kigali every two months (hotels, taxis, porters, food) to get the other type. This time the Director was as obsequious and grovelling as he could be. It was disgusting; I think I prefer him supercilious. In this country as in most of Africa nowadays, one doesn't mess around with the Sécurité or those whom they support. See, it pays to keep your nose clean – achoo!

First, I noted the irony of her phrase "visa which is good for a minimum of two years, a maximum of life". It was to last her, this two-year visa, only ten days before her life was cut short by those blows from the *panga*.

Then I remembered what Frank Crigler had told me in Washington a few days before. He had stressed that Dian had never been issued with a visa that lasted longer than three months. And this had been done quite deliberately so that the security people could keep tabs on her. So why, all of a sudden, ten days before she died, did the head of the secret service issue her with a visa, not for three months, not for six months, but for two years? And why did Dian go to see the head of the secret service? She had spent eighteen years in Rwanda, and she had never thought to go and see him before. What made her approach him now?

I picked up the phone on the table and called up Frank Crigler in Washington. He listened to what I had to say and asked me to read out the letter.

Dian, he told me, "was always one to deal with people. She was always bargaining, trading."

"In what way?" I asked.

"She was a manipulator. If she thought you had something she wanted, she would do her best to get it from you. She would trade."

"So you think she traded something for this two-year visa?"

A long pause. "Could be, but God knows what!"

"Well, Frank, what would be tradable if you were the head of the Sûreté?"

"Information. It has to be information."

"What information?"

A laugh comes across the line from Washington. "You're asking me?"

"Yes."

"Well, I wouldn't know."

"Did you know this guy, this boss of the Sûreté? She describes him in the letter as 'this big man'. Do you think she meant 'big' meaning important or 'big' meaning size?"

"Both, I'd say. She's talking about Augustin. I forget his second name. Anyway, even if I were to have remembered it, I wouldn't be able to pronounce it."

"What was he like, this Augustin?"

"Nasty. Big. Tending to fat. But very nasty."

So Frank Crigler thought Dian had, in the last month of her life, dealt with the devil to obtain what was possibly the most precious commodity she could have ever wished for: a visa for two years. This would ease all her problems. At the time, it was clear from reading the other papers in the Hayes archive that there had been a concerted effort from both the conservationists and the Rwandan Parks authorities to kick her out of the country. Her friends, too, had backed them up. They were saying how frail she was, and how working at the altitude she had to live at was damaging her health. She would be far better off going to America, where she could receive medical treatment and rest and eat food with a proper, balanced diet.

But this two-year visa! That was the answer to all the people who wanted her out of the country. It was Dian's insurance. It was her trump card. It was her way of telling them all to stop interfering, to leave her alone. Dian was clearly euphoric about the visa. It represented a lifeline for her, but did it also carry a sting? Was it her death warrant? Was this granting of the visa, this most unexpected bonus, the very piece of paper that killed her?

Could it be, I thought, that here in front of me was the motive for her murder? Killing her now because she was guaranteed two more years in the country made a lot more sense to me than killing her because the murderer wanted to steal her notes, notes which she was, Hayes writes, far too ill to compile. If I was right, then why would Wayne McGuire want to kill Dian? If he was that set against her, he could always pack his belongings, come down from the mountain, and quit Rwanda. So what, I considered, could the information have been that she might have traded with the big man, the Sûreté boss?

I began searching for other letters written about this time, December or late November 1985.

I'd spent hours in that Rare Books room that day. My bottom was stiff, my eyes ached, I was desperate for a cigarette. They manufactured them by the million just down the road from the campus and there wasn't a haven in this ghetto for the politically correct where I could smoke. The girls in the department kept ferrying me more boxes. Sharon and Megan, good, strong Southern girls with a penchant for lifting and heaving.

It was dated November 24, 1985 and was addressed to Ian. It was a carbon copy, written on foolscap. I guessed Ian was Ian Redmond, the British scientist who had come to Karisoke to study worms and had stayed with Dian to become one of her most loyal and trusted friends. It was Redmond who was asked by Fossey's stepfather, Richard Price, to fly to Rwanda shortly after the murder and make an inventory of her personal effects. While he was there, in January of 1986, he investigated the murder and concluded that

Dian had been killed by poachers, and not McGuire or Rwelekana. The motive, Redmond said, was *sumu*. *Sumu* is black magic. Africans call it ju-ju. Rwandans call it *sumu*. It is powerful stuff, which Dian was perfectly aware of. She had used *sumu*, she had pretended to be a witch, she had commandeered the forces of Africa, especially the forces of the night, and directed them at her enemies, and this had worked for her.

This letter, written to him, was the same letter he had found in her cabin when he made his inventory of her belongings. Hayes, too, had a copy. When I spoke to Redmond about this in London, he told me that what was curious about the letter was the fact that it had never reached him. He had only ever seen the carbon which he retrieved from Dian's papers in her cabin. So what happened to the original? Wayne McGuire would have had no reason to intercept it. There is nothing in the letter that incriminates him. Someone must have taken it, or maybe it was lost in the mail.

I read the letter carefully, noting the passages which referred to the confiscation of the *sumu*, but there was something else here which Redmond and Hayes seemed to have overlooked. As I read the paragraph I started thinking of Abdul and the convoy and the talk around the fire that night all those months ago, the night we were drinking coffee, tuning gorillas and talking to the Somali drivers on the road to Ayod.

Gold. Smuggling gold. Smuggling gold from Walikale. This is what Dian was writing about in the letter which Redmond, curiously, never received.

The reference that had set my mind on a track that led directly back to the Sudan bush came at the top of the second page of the letter.

> The 4th poacher, captured on November 11, right near the Susa group, on his trap line and skinning a beautiful female bushbuck was bloody kali. He is one of the last of the "oldtimers". I, hopefully, doubt that he will survive the Ruhenghiri prison. He is also a smuggler (gold) between Zaire and Rwanda, thus little Nemeye reckons that he will be quickly released; so far, no. [Nemeye was Dian's most faithful tracker.]
>
> I *gently* examined his clothing to find a letter between him and his dealer in Walikale setting up appointment places for gold

> deliveries and then found three packets of *sumu* – bits of skin and vegetation all looking like vacuum cleaner debris. I still have them. Nasty lady. It was like taking a nipple from a baby – he just deflated after I took them. I was very tempted to explore his anus for bits of gold, but the appointment dates were off.

There it was, in black and white. Gold. A letter. Appointments with dealers. A reference to Walikale, the same town the Somalis had talked about that night on the road to Ayod. And Nemeye's comment, the matter of the smuggler, this "oldtimer" going to jail, but not for long. Why would he be released so swiftly? Was it because there were people in Ruhengeri, at the bottom of the mountain, who would make sure of his release? If that was true, then they had to be powerful people in the area.

It wasn't the confiscation of the *sumu*, as Dian thought, that had so concerned this smuggler. It was her confiscation of the letter, the letter that gave away the names and the places of the gold smuggling chain. Perhaps this was the information that Dian had traded to obtain her visa. *If* she had traded. But would this information be worth anything to the head of the Sûreté? I didn't know.

There was one other comment in the letter that intrigued me. A few paragraphs down, Dian writes: "A two-year-old male gorilla was confiscated at the Gyanika border (border between Uganda and Rwanda) two weeks ago; it died shortly thereafter . . . The Rwandese Sécurité killed one Rwandese poacher, severely injured another, and imprisoned four, all according to my best sources of info . . . no one knows from where the infant comes."

Gold and gorillas – could there be a link? It was plausible. After all it takes a chain of corruption to set up a viable network that can traffick illegally in commodities. My knowledge of the illegal ivory trade in Tanzania had taught me this. There the chain spread from the man who provided the Kalashnikov for the poacher to kill the elephants, through to the man who collected the ivory, the man who moved it, the man who provided a safe house en route, the police or the army who controlled the roadblocks en route, to the customs officials in the port of exit. And as the chain grew more distant from the source, the hunting ground, so the cost of corruption mounted with it. And always behind every big ivory killing was the Bwana Mwkuba – the big man – the financier of the whole operation. The Bwana Mwkuba made sure that no one, throughout the entire length of the network, no one in that chain, was left unhappy. But he also looked after other people who were involved, the sleeping partners, the politicians. It was necessary to keep them sweet, to stop them raising questions in parliament, to counter accusations from the conservationist lobbies that the killing of the elephants was out of control.

This was how the chain worked in Tanzania, across the border from Rwanda. It was a polished system that relied on spreading corruption as tightly and as directly as was thought necessary. Everyone involved was rewarded. The more elephants that were slaughtered, the more ivory was trafficked, and the more the traffic, the more the pay-outs became. In fact, ivory was not the only commodity that was illegally moved. Precious stones, currency and weapons were also part of the Bwana Mwkuba's game in Tanzania. After all, if you have the means to move ivory illegally, then why not other commodities that could serve to increase not only your efficiency but also your turnover? It made sense. And if it operated like this in Tanzania, then why shouldn't it operate, in a similar fashion, in Rwanda?

Hadn't the Somali truck drivers told Abdul that night by the cooking fire that they had moved tea and coffee and returned with cigarettes, and what was in the tea and coffee, but gold? So was there a connection between trafficking in gorillas and trafficking in gold? And who was the Bwana Mwkuba in Ruhengeri?

Brussels: May 1992

I SUPPOSE it is fitting that a parish hall such as this one, tucked away off a cobbled street in the Arab quarter of Brussels, should have as its focal point, an altarpiece. Yet there is hardly any religious significance about the way it has been decorated. On the table at the head of the hall is a red, yellow and green tricoloured flag emblazoned in the middle with a large capital letter – R.

R for Rwanda. The effect is somewhat muted because a blank television screen is obscuring the lower part of the letter, and I must crane my neck to make it out. Other flags in the hall compete for attention. They are red and black – a dicolour. The yellow and green have been displaced. Red and black: rebel colours. And the rebels are behind me, drinking Cokes and holding the hands of their children. There are women here too, doing what women always do in parish halls, serving trays of soft drinks and offering out crisps.

No one is toting a Kalashnikov. There's not a landmine or a grenade in sight. Rebel uniform, urban rebel uniform, dictates that guerrilla fatigues, camouflage and military epaulettes, must be left in the bush. This army is dressed not to kill but to persuade, dressed in blazers and ties, striped, spotted, some with university shields. There are men in corduroy trousers and polo necks, men with briefcases, the sort without handles, the ones that rest on hips and hang easily in a black man's grasp. Most are members of the MDR, the opposition party.

There is colour, too, on the grey Formica-topped tables – more red, yellow and green. These are the napkins, assiduously folded by some rebel wife, and lodged with deliberation into empty glasses stamped Schweppes. A child in pigtails ambles by. More beers and Cokes are brought out of the parish hall kitchen.

I can't decide if the meeting has started. There is none of that clearing of throats or scraping of chairs that alarm people into quiet in an English village. No one is about to make a grand entrance. Maybe it has started. Maybe all this shaking of hands up there, in front of the television set, is an introductory stage, maybe all those murmurings of "*enchanté*" are signalling the onset of business.

A photograph of the President of Rwanda, not the current President, but the first President of the nation, the father of Rwanda, succumbs to the heat inside the room. It flops down from the wall. Someone, some rebel, has not applied enough Blu-tack. Some say he was murdered by the present incumbent of the presidential palace in Kigali, others are not sure, but all that matters at the moment is whether this martyr, this hero of independence, can survive the indignity of flopping down on to the floor. As the heat and humidity in the room increase, his chances seem to be getting remoter. No one is coming to the rescue. Maybe there is no more Blu-tack, but then it's not really the sort of weapon that rebel armies are equipped with.

Now music is booming through the hall; everyone stands, except the picture President, for the national anthem. Sheets of words have been passed around and the voices trill and lilt and roar, and then someone arrives with Sellotape, not Blu-tack, and restores the President to right-angular appropriateness. The smile beams at the rebel choir. It is hard to believe that within a year of that smile being captured on film and processed into a million 15 x 12 portraits, this father of the nation, in his grey suit and holding a Bible, would vanish, leaving his subjects only a memory.

Here in Brussels, with the rebels from Rwanda, it is Africa. A different Africa, an Africa without mosquitoes or the noise of the bush, or the sounds of the night. There is no night. Outside Europe plays with itself. Inside the mood is now serious. These rebels are for the most part students from Rwanda, students at Belgian universities. They have travelled from Louvain and Antwerp and Bruges, and there is not a blue jean or open collar in sight. No Doc Martens, no sandals. This is a mature gathering.

An hour into the meeting and not a word of formality has been uttered. Now everyone is sitting at the tables, hands on the formica, waiting. Some sip their Stellas, others pour from suspiciously mineralish-looking bottles, and I'm idly talking to a Hutu intellectual. He tells me he is thirty-one and married. Is that your wife, I ask, pointing to a plump ugly woman in a pea-green ensemble at the end of the row of tables?

A bearded Belgian in a striped short-sleeved shirt has inserted his index finger inside his right nostril. He prospects, inspects, and wipes the result underneath the table. Something for the caretaker to find in the morning.

Finally a man called Alexis, the master of ceremonies, I believe, strides with a measured degree of resolution to the front of the hall, and takes up position to the right of the TV altarpiece. He begins to fiddle with the television set. There is a man with a video camera by him, and I begin to wonder if Beadle will now turn up; perhaps he is already here. A plate of crisps, cheese and onion flavour, is produced for me by a Belgian dwarf. Two bottles are clattered together. No rhythm. A collective shhh exhales through the room. The meeting begins.

We stand. The national anthem is sung again. Alexis hogs the mike for a second and then a black man in a navy blue suit, red shirt and blue tie takes it. He tweaks the instrument, blows into it, and begins to speak. Now here is a politician. He is a master of silence, this speaker. He uses the pause like a marksman aiming at a target, squeezing the silence until he is sure of his aim. He is using the right words, shovelling the stress on to democracy, republic, ethnic, intolerance, independence, tyranny, constitution, reconstruction, ideals, renaissance. He's building a wall of soundbites, the way a priest constructs the mass. *Valeur*. Applause.

Now for the video. The screen flickers and we see the President, the present President, Juvenal Habyarimana, the target of this speech, receiving a VIP white visitor at the airport in Kigali. There is much oompahing as the military band overtures the President's guest, much shaking of white-gloved hands, a snatch of what every African city has erected, a shoddy, spurious stab at pride, a triumphal arch that announces you are now in Kenya, Tanzania, Sudan, Ethiopia. The Rwandan version does not look to be grand, rather stop-gap in fact, white and decked with the colours of the flag and the country's coat of arms.

Now, as the video pictures switch from airport to stadium, the rebels pay more attention. The room hushes as they stare at pictures of a whistling mob demonstrating against the government. There is anger in front of us, on screen, anger in close-up. The mob look to be out of control, almost wishing themselves into this room. And then, suddenly, the mood changes, the mood inside the hall, I mean. Two little girls in polka-dot dresses are limbo-ing in front of the screen. They are shooed out of the way. The mob regains command of the hall. The army arrive now. The images jolt as puffs of smoke blister silently in the background. I can see a roadblock. Men and women are running out of the picture.

But this video is no soap. The audience have had a glimpse of home, trouble in Kigali, and they really are not that impressed. Some are, after all, the Rwandese Patriotic Front – the FPR – and they wouldn't be here, in Belgium, in this hall, if they didn't know how brutal and repressive their government back home really is.

The video breaks down. I think that most of us here are rather relieved. Now the speeches, the formalities are over, the rebels can chat to each other, gossip a summer evening to bed. I can't. I have to meet a man, a leading anti-government politician, a source, someone who I am told knows something about the Fossey murder. I wonder who he is. Alexis, perhaps, or the man with the video. I am tapped on the shoulder by a drainpipe of a man and summoned to the back of the room. I shake hands with the man in the navy blue suit and bright red shirt, the orator. He is the contact. I am told to follow him out of the hall and into a side room, crammed with surplus kitchen equipment, saucepans vast enough to fry dolphins, a Hoover, a floor-polishing machine, three chairs standing on a table. There is nowhere to sit and no floor space on which to put the chairs. We stand, the man in the navy blue suit and me.

I tell him who I am, and that I want to find Fossey's killer.

He is shaking my hand, quite firmly. "It will be difficult. There is danger for you too. Already many opponents of the regime have disappeared."

"How?"

"Car accidents. Poison. Some are in prison. Some have been forced to flee the country."

"All because of Dian Fossey's murder?"

"Not entirely."

He is carrying a glass with him and sips from it. I try to work out what he is drinking. It is either gin and tonic or Seven-Up. He looks a Seven-Up man to me.

He continues: "We believe the murder of Dian Fossey is connected to many other crimes that have been committed in Rwanda over the last six or seven years."

"Directly connected?"

"Yes. Directly connected. But I cannot talk to you here. It is too crowded."

Was he being euphemistic or was he in a hurry?

"You must meet me in another place. You will be told where."

Not much of a talker, the man in the navy blue suit and red shirt, was he? Perhaps a one-to-one was not his style. Maybe his lips needed crowds in front of them. He had spoken no more than three sentences, fewer than one hundred words, but what he had said was dynamite.

Unless . . . unless this was a set-up. After all, who were these people, the FPR? Dissidents, every one of them dedicated to the overthrow of the regime. They would tell me Fossey's murder was connected with other crimes, now wouldn't they? The man who was my initial contact, a French journalist working out of Brussels, an expert on Francophone Africa, had warned me before the meeting. "They hate the regime. They have catalogued its excesses. Much of what they say is true, I believe, but it is difficult to prove, and even more dangerous to write."

There was one indicator, though, which made me think that I was being pointed in the direction of truth. The terseness of the man's statement. If he had wanted to fill me with lies, then he would have done exactly that. I have met dissidents before and they are pitiless in their exposition of the hidden state of affairs of their country. They are hardened, obdurate souls, opportunists as ruthless as the men who have forced them to flee their country. This man was no exception. Of course he could have kept me captive, pinned my back against the Hoover, and retailed all sorts of gruesome stories about brutality, sudden death, corruption, and human rights violations, but he hadn't. He had tipped me off, and gone away.

Now I had to find him again.

And that, I can assure you, was not easy.

Outside Brussels, and housed in a white, tottering château, is the Musée d'Afrique Centrale. It houses the bric-à-brac of the continent brought back or filched by explorers, the artefacts of the past that fed Belgium and made it rich. There are living relics there too. One such relic is Professor Marcel d'Hertefelt, the world's leading expert on Rwandan history. I had come to ask him about Hamid Ibrahim.

I had come across Hamid Ibrahim as I was reading Stanley's account of his exploration of Central Africa. The grizzled explorer, still in search of the source of the Nile, had reached the borders of Rwanda and, seeing the mountains in the distance, had stopped to ask an old Arab what this land to the north was like.

Hamid Ibrahim was an Arab slaver, whom, I reckon, time and lack of money had stranded deep in the interior of the continent. He wasn't successful enough to make a triumphant return to the coast, and he wasn't poor enough to be that worried about it. He entertained Stanley's caravan and proceeded to tell him about the Rwandans. He said that it was a strange country, one that no Arab had ever invaded. It was ruled by a pale-skinned, tall queen who was as ruthless and as cruel as her eyes. The Rwandans, he added, were not to be trusted.

I wondered how accurate a picture old Hamid had drawn. Or was he trying to deter Stanley from going into Rwanda? The Arab's description of the queen also intrigued me. A tall, pale woman, who ruled from a mountain stronghold, a woman who used magic, a woman who was feared by her subjects and her enemies alike. Had I stumbled across an extraordinary parallel? Dian Fossey, tall, pale-skinned, ruthless, alone in her mountain fortress – and this queen of distant myth?

The professor was quite certain and quite censorious about Hamid Ibrahim's recollections. He had already prepared for me a handwritten exposition which particularised a succession of Rwandan queens, or queen mothers. He explained that though the country had, for the most part, been ruled by kings, the position of the queen mother was one of severe power.

"An '*éminence grise*'?"

The professor nodded.

"And what about Hamid Ibrahim?"

"I conclude," said the professor, quite magisterially, "that Hamid Ibrahim is not a very trustworthy informant." But then he added, "Have you heard of Kanjongera?"

I shook my head.

"Now she was a woman like your empress, like this pale-skinned creature of Hamid Ibrahim's fertile imagination. She ruled Rwanda – through her son – at the turn of the century. She was an extremely ruthless woman. Do you know what they call the President's wife? Even today?"

"No."

"Kanjongera."

There was no message waiting for me back at the hotel, no rendezvous to make. I felt stranded. I was like a man marching in the desert, a man without water, who sees a mirage, and then realises the awful truth. I had, for the first time, been told that there was a link between the Fossey murder and other crimes in Rwanda. That indicated that I had been right to pursue the story; that Wayne McGuire might not have killed Dian. But what was the significance, if any, of gold smuggling? And the visa? And why was the President's wife called after a woman who had schemed, brewed, and eventually killed to ensure the succession of her bloodline?

Antwerp: May 1992

"YOU ARE investigating a murder in a country where they used to kill members of the royal family in a particularly disgusting way," said Lambert. "Rwanda's a place where killing still has built into it a degree of wit, a cerebral message, if you like, which the European mind finds difficult to comprehend."

Lambert certainly would never have featured in an episode of *The Bill.* Nor even *Inspector Morse.* He had the looks, mind you: a skyscrapingly tall, imposing-looking Tutsi, Lambert was a former Rwandan policeman, now set up, with Belgian wife and family, in the diamond business in Antwerp. I had come to see him in an attempt to discover more about the underground trade in gold. Who were the traffickers, and were gorillas a lucrative commodity to trade? Instead I was at the receiving end of a stream of intellectualist thought. The subject had turned to murder as soon as I mentioned Fossey.

"*Pangas* were used to kill her, you say. I have read that, too, but I do not believe it. If you want to kill someone in Rwanda, you use *sumu.*"

"How does it work?"

"It can work in many ways. A curse. A sorcerer can make up a curse for you, and lay it. Or poison. Mostly poison."

"Even today?"

"Yes, even today. You must remember what sort of society you are talking about. It is highly in-bred, highly meshed. There are clans, and within each clan there is a hierarchy. Clans fight other clans, and clans murder outside the clan. To understand murder in Rwanda, you have to study the people."

Lambert was in full stride now. There was no stopping him.

"Murder is often ritual. Take the royal family. If one of the members of this family was to be murdered, then it had to be done in such a way that blood was not spilt. This would be a dire offence."

"So, how was it done? Strangulation?"

"Yes, or drowning."

"Drowning in the river?"

"No, with milk."

I laughed.

"You won't realise the irony here," said Lambert. "But milk was always regarded as being a provider of goodness, of health, of beauty. If you were born to a rich family, you would have grown up surrounded by cattle. Milk would have been in good supply, and you would drink it, especially if you were a girl, maybe six times a day. You would drink it even in the middle of the night. Your nurse would wake you and force it on you if necessary. So you can imagine that to die from milk is curious when the very same liquid is used to make you grow, to make you into a beauty."

"How was it done?"

"The executioners were always the Twa, the pygmy people. They were cruel, the Twa, they sang songs and told jokes at the royal courts, but they also tortured and killed for the king. They would force gourd upon gourd of milk down the victim's throat until she either choked on her own vomit or her stomach burst."

I was glad I was drinking black coffee.

"Who was Kanjongera, Lambert?"

"Which one?" he asked, laughing. "Do you mean the real Kanjongera, or this new one?"

"Tell me about both."

He sat back in his chair and scratched his long, thin semitic nose. He laughed again. "Kanjongera was the queen mother. She was the most powerful woman in the country at the turn of the century. She ensured the succession of her son, not the king's son."

Lambert embarked on a discussion of the tumultuous events surrounding Kanjongera and how she weaved her way, successfully and bloodily, through a mesh of Byzantine politics, to ultimate power in the land. The king at the time, the last decades of the nineteenth century (and, I noted, at the very time Stanley talked to Hamid Ibrahim), was Rwabugiri. He was, said Lambert, a Napoleon of Africa. He was an impressive soldier, a reformer, a man whose vision was to keep Rwanda independent. His task was difficult for two reasons. First he was reigning at the time that the European powers were expanding inside Africa, and second,

Rwabugiri had to contend with the intrigue and politics that were threatening to weaken and perhaps destroy his standing in his court.

His favourite wife was Kanjongera, a tall, pale woman, whose dynamism, sexual magnetics and fear she inspired by her use of *sumu* were so powerful that she persuaded Rwabugiri to break all convention, ignore the traditions of centuries, and elevate her to the position of queen mother. To do this, Rwabugiri had the woman who was the present queen mother murdered. There was an heir to the throne and Kanjongera became his adoptive mother, even though she was not related in any way to him. This was considered to be a monstrous crime. But Rwabugiri and Kanjongera were strong enough to survive the backlash. So, here she was, Kanjongera, now the most powerful woman in the land, the wife of the king and the mother of the heir.

She had it all, except for one thing. She did not want Rwabugiri's heir, a son by another wife, to succeed. After Rwabugiri's death, she and her brother Kabare plotted to kill the new king, and she installed her own son in the royal palace as the new Mwami. Kanjongera had pulled off a brilliant coup. The succession of her clan was assured. Her genes, Tutsi genes, had triumphed.

It smacked of Messalina and Agrippina, this pale-skinned murderess who used her mind and her loins to manipulate a powerful soldier-king and win for her own stock a kingdom. But her triumph was short-lived. Colonialism, the coming of the Europeans, muted the power of the court. Her son, the Mwami, was the last of his line.

"So why do they call the current President's wife Kanjongera?" I asked Lambert. "Why didn't they call Dian Fossey Kanjongera? She was a witch, they say."

"The President's family, his wife's family, is a very close-knit and powerful clan. You could not insert this paper knife between them," he said, brandishing a brass replica of a pirate's cutlass. "She has brothers who hold very powerful positions in the country. There is one in particular who you should know about. I think that if he were to know you have been asking questions about this Fossey case, he would be very angry. His name is Protais. Protais Zigiranyirazo. Everyone knows him as Zed. Beware of this man. This Zed."

"What does he do?"

"At the moment, I am not sure. Some say he is in Canada on a further education course."

That didn't sound too dangerous, I thought.

"But he could be there for other reasons. He has investments in Canada. A big estate outside Montreal."

Lambert pronounced the city *Monréal*, the French way. It took me a few seconds to recognise the name.

"You should be interested in him, because at the time of the Fossey killing, Zed was the prefect of Ruhengeri."

"Prefect?"

"Top man, the chief, the boss. He would know everything that went on in that area."

"Including all the trafficking?"

"Yes."

I decided I had learnt enough about Rwanda's arcane and bloody past and tried to turn the subject on to Fossey. I asked Lambert, point-blank, what he thought had happened.

He shrugged his wide, thin, Tutsi shoulders, and said, "I don't know. I am only guessing. There is one thing I find strange."

"What? That she wasn't poisoned?"

"No, that's why I think she was not killed by poachers. It would be more natural for them to use poison, and safer."

"But the American," I said, "McGuire. He could have used a *panga*?"

"Yes, of course, but would you think that the natural weapon of a westerner, an academic?"

"Tell me about poison, Lambert."

"Well, first let me warn you." He leant back in the leather armchair that reclined like a club-class seat and yawned. The office we were in, off a narrow, cobbled street near the docks area of Antwerp was stiflingly hot. Lambert unloosened the collar button of his shirt and pulled on his tie. "First, Nick, remember this. When anyone dies suddenly in Rwanda, people always think, say, suspect, that the cause of death is not natural. They blame poison, *sumu*. I don't know why this is so, but it is a truth. Maybe, deep down in our culture, we have this paranoia."

"Or, maybe, they are right. Maybe people are poisoned, Lambert."

"My great-grandfather was a sorcerer. He spent years at the Mwami's court. There were different sorts of sorcerers. There were the *abateteri*, the *abatondwe*, the *abaresuru*, the *abakobga*, the *abapfamu*, and the *imandwa*. Some told the future through insects, like the *abatondwe*; others used seeds and bones like the *abateteri*. The *abapfamu* used the cow or the goat, and the *imandwa*, they became priests when the missionaries came to Rwanda. They all carried with them *insiro*. *Insiro* – a medicine. Made from tree bark and boiling up plants. It would help the Mwami against his enemies. It would win him the victories he desired. My great-grandfather guarded the *igihango*."

"The what?"

As Lambert rattled off this litany of the unpronounceable, I swear his mind had tracked back to his childhood and the stories he had heard in his mother's kitchen. No longer sitting in front of me in a leather armchair was a former policeman. This man had exhumed his past. This man was now full-metal Tutsi, a warrior, a man capable of calling up the shadows. It sounds bizarre, but that office, airless, and foetid, grew cold. An alien and sinister atmosphere was now pervading the room, shutting out the sun, and admitting the other, darker side of the continent, exposing for a moment the forgotten interior that still exists, the territory beyond the reach of strangers.

Lambert read the bemusement written across my face. Maybe he noticed, too, the fear in my eyes. But this didn't stop him from going on.

"The *igihango*. That was a poison my great-grandfather made. Well, my mother told me he did. It was a mixture of woods that were pounded together and it was always carried in a long cowhorn. It was used in court cases and given to witnesses. They would be told to put some of the mixture on their tongue, like this" – and Lambert stuck out his fine, pink tongue and dabbed his finger on the end – "and if they were lying, the witness would die." He paused. "On the spot."

"What if they were telling the truth?"

"They lived, of course."

"So how can a poison differentiate between the truth and lies?"

"Psychology, Nick. Good, old-fashioned African psychology."

"Go on."

"Well, would you lie if you knew you had to dab this stuff on your tongue?"

I shook my head.

"You see, it was we Africans who gave the world the lie-detector."

Lambert was enjoying this, I could see. He plunged on into his private bush.

"They say, Nick, that my great-grandfather could steal another man's soul. But he could save men from death, too. He could bring the rain, and he could make a woman fertile. He could keep a baby safe from the evil eye. Always, he would hang around a baby's neck a collar of vines."

"Was he a popular man?"

Lambert looked at me quizzically.

"I mean, was he, did he have friends?"

Lambert relaxed in his chair. He laughed. "Friends. He didn't need friends. People were so afraid of death that he was needed. When the country was in trouble, for instance if there was a drought, my great-grandfather could have anything he wanted. Cows, women, virgins, food. He used fetishes, figures, things like the collar of vines, but he didn't hold with the new ways."

"What do you mean new ways?"

"Well, before he died, and I'm talking before I was born, there was this new fetish which was said to be very powerful. It was an airplane, you know, the figure of an airplane, carved in wood. If you sent one of these to the house of an enemy, then that man would die. But my great-grandfather laughed at this."

I was going to tell Lambert about the satellites and *sumu*, but I didn't. I had to change the subject, bring Lambert back to the twentieth century, back to Antwerp, back to his business. I asked him about trafficking.

"Of course, it goes on. You name an African country that doesn't traffick."

I told him what I had discovered during my time investigating the ivory trade in Tanzania. About the networks, the chains of corruption, the Bwana Mwkubas.

"There is gold, drugs, hemp, currency, tobacco, tea, coffee. Almost anything that the country has in raw materials and anything that it needs. There is a fortune to be made avoiding payment of customs duties."

"And gorillas?"

"Gorillas, too."

"How does that work?"

"Zoos want them. There's a man called Walter Sensen, a German, who works with his son. He was convicted in Germany of illegal trafficking in gorillas."

"What's the price of a gorilla?"

"Depends on its age, its health, but a good infant could fetch up to $32,000, and then there is also a trade in gorilla parts."

"Parts?" I said, thinking of Abdul and his tuning, and trying to suppress a nervous grin.

"The hands and the feet. And the heads. I know it sounds macabre, but people actually collect them. They make ashtrays of the hands and feet and stick the heads on their walls as trophies."

"Does the trade still go on? The IPPL don't seem to think so." I could see he wasn't following me. "The IPPL, the International Primate Protection League."

"Oh, them! That's just one woman in America and a couple of offices in Europe and the Far East. She means well, but she hasn't got the resources to track all the activity that could be going on."

"So, you mean, there could still be trafficking in gorillas, but no one really knows?"

Lambert nodded.

"But gorillas," I said, "are not like elephants. I mean they are much rarer. There are only 300 or so mountain gorillas in Rwanda and maybe the same in Zaire. It's relatively easy to find and kill elephants. There's a reservoir of elephants. Surely, it cannot be worth while concentrating on capturing gorillas?"

"No, it isn't. But you can traffick in gorillas as a sideline."

"So the same people who are involved in gold trafficking are involved in the gorilla business?"

"Yes."

It was what I had thought in America, in the Rare Books department at Wake Forest. Now I had to discover the Bwana Mwkuba.

"It will," said Lambert, "be difficult and dangerous. The difference between trafficking in Africa and Europe or America is straightforward and simple. In Africa, if you're going to be a successful trafficker, run an efficient network, you have to involve the politicians, the top boys in the country."

"So who's involved in Rwanda?"

"You had better start asking some questions about your Kanjongera's brother," he said.

"Mr Zed."

Tallinn: June 1992

THE WARNINGS began coming that summer. First Lambert called me to say that he believed that everything I had found out was known back in Kigali. The dissident faction in Brussels was riddled with the President's spies. The Rwandan secret service, he was convinced, was active in the city and had almost certainly infiltrated the FPR. Perhaps this was the reason why the man I had met that night at the FPR meeting had rushed away soon after we started talking. I asked Lambert if he thought that the meeting had been spiked.

"It is quite possible. I think you must take it that everything you have said, all the questions you have asked, everything is known back in Rwanda. From now on, you must be careful who you speak to."

I shrugged it off, shovelling his words to the back of my mind, and then a few days later, I was told the same story, but this time by another source. He was a former colleague of Dian's, and almost as unpopular, if you were to believe what his contemporaries had said about him. Jim Foster had advised me to see him, adding that he was "a difficult man to work with".

It wasn't until June that I could arrange it. His name was Alan Goodall, a frustrated primatologist who now worked in the visual arts department of Strathclyde University. I got on well with Goodall. We met in a hotel off the Cromwell Road and ate dinner at an Italian restaurant in South Ken. It had taken a lot of persuasion to convince him that I was worth meeting. He didn't want to talk, and wouldn't give me a reason, apart from the fact that he believed that my reopening of the Fossey case would damage irretrievably the efforts of the conservationists in Rwanda. He added that there were sound reasons for his convictions. And each time I had telephoned him, he had warned me not to go on with the story.

"You don't know what you are getting into," he said. "There is a great deal of risk involved."

At dinner, Goodall opened up. It was clear that he loved Rwanda, and its people. He empathised with the men and women who lived on the Virungas and understood their need to hunt. I allowed him to ramble. In fact, it would have been cruel to have interrupted. He spoke so warmly of his experiences in Rwanda that I felt he was describing the qualities of an old friend. With the coffee, I dropped the name Walikale. He stopped stirring and tapped the spoon against the side of the cup, impatiently.

"What do you know about Walikale?" And then before I had time to answer: "Have you been there?"

I shook my head.

"I have, and I tell you it's about the shittiest place on this planet. How on earth do you know about Walikale?"

I told him about the letter Dian had written in November 1985 and how she had intercepted the gold smuggler's letter.

"So you think she knew about the gold trade?"

I nodded.

"Walikale is the place where the gold comes from. The Zaire army are based there and it's a sort of perk for them to handle the gold that is mined, panned, in the area. They move people out of the villages to do the work, and then they take the gold to Walikale and sell it."

"Who buys it?"

"The dealers who live there. That's all there is in Walikale. Gold dealers and gold smugglers. The dealers sell the gold and it is taken by road or on foot into Rwanda. Maybe your man was coming through Dian's park because he was carrying an urgent message. I've walked from Karisoke to Walikale. It's a long way, maybe five days, but it is possible." Goodall went quiet again.

He looked into his coffee and then up at me and said, "I've got an offer to make. You take me to Rwanda, and I'll write an article on the gorillas, the forest, the way the conservation thing is going, and I'll be able to take you to places, meet people you would have no chance of seeing if you go by yourself. You are going to go, aren't you?"

I said yes, I would go.

"You have no idea how dangerous this is. I think you are walking into a fire and you just can't conceive how great a risk you are taking."

"Well, Alan, I'm going through with it, and I don't think I can afford your fare. Sorry."

*   *   *

There was a warning too awaiting me in Tallinn, where I had traced Kathleen Austin to Estonia. She was working at the US Embassy in the newly independent Baltic state as an administrative officer. She arranged to meet me for breakfast at Tallinn's best hotel, the Palace.

Estonia was desperately trying to acquire a patina of newness. Elections had been slated and a native currency, the kroner, was about to replace the rouble. The aircraft which had hopped over the Baltic from Helsinki was making its first flight for Air Estonia, yet here the pretence was as thin as the paint that had failed to blot out the markings of its former owners, Aeroflot. Inside the cabin, some of the seats had been arranged to accommodate wooden tables so passengers could play cards or rest their newspapers in front of them. Instead of an aircraft, it looked like InterCity, second class. A large hostess waddled down the aisle of the cabin, brushing her ample hips on the elbows of the passengers unfortunate enough not to have bagged window seats. She carried a tray offering three drinks. Coke, cordial, or water. I chose water.

Even the hotel was under new management. The Americans had taken it over and had installed CNN in the bedrooms. I watched the baseball results before dinner, and tried to calculate how many people there were in hotel bedrooms dispersed around the world who were not in the slightest interested in the fortunes of the Toronto Blue Jays or the New York Mets, but who, nevertheless, kept watching, in the dim hope of catching a sound-bite or two about someone or some place they identified with.

America, too, had moved into the restaurant. The waitress told me I was welcome, or rather velkom, and offered me imported beer, Beck's or Miller Lite, despite the fact that Estonia brewed some thirty or more beers itself. There was more velkom awaiting me in the penthouse bar of the Palace. Three young girls, dressed in black sequinned gowns, tottered on the tips of bar stools, toying with cocktails. A bunch of bananas hung down from the bar fittings and one girl reached out, grasped one, twisted it and began savagely to unzip the skin. She turned to me, with a smile as wide as the Baltic Strait I had flown over earlier that evening, and pressed the soft fruit in between her lips. I wandered through the bar to the casino. Men and women were playing blackjack, losing roubles as fast as their hearts were beating. I sat in a corner booth by myself and looked into my beer.

I needed time to work out what I was going to say to Kathleen Austin. I was surprised she had agreed to meet me, but maybe she wanted to know how much I knew. I thought back to what Jim Foster had told me in Seattle: that his friend, an Italian vet, was convinced that Kathleen Austin was working for the CIA. The vet was called Sandra Molle, she was married to an Englishman and was working in Rwanda for an Italian aid project. She knew Dian Fossey well and had been visiting Karisoke a day or two after the arrival of Wayne McGuire. She was convinced, Foster had said, that Austin was working for the CIA, but then he had shrugged and looked at me, as if to say, who isn't?

"Velkom," she said, sitting down in the booth next to me and making sure that her left breast brushed my arm. She was young, wearing a black velvet short dress which was enlivened by a catalogue-quality – gold chain. She crossed her legs as noisily as she could. I could hear, above the Muzak, the leisurely riff of her stockings as her thighs parted and then slipped together. She pulled at one of the dangly rings that were suspended from her lobes and rubbed my hand. I bought her a drink, a white wine, and asked her how old she was.

"Eighteen."

"Do you work?"

"I am a student."

"Are you Russian or Estonian?"

"Estonian." She told me she lived in a block of flats, where else? on the edge of the city, that her parents had gone away for the weekend to stay with friends, that her sister was a secretary, that she wanted to be a secretary, and that she didn't come to bars like this often. Then she asked me for my room number. I left and went back to CNN.

Kathleen Austin was on time. Eight o'clock, she had said. We drank coffee and stared each other out. She was a small, dark, tidy, efficiently dressed woman, just the type you would imagine working in administration. She looked me straight in the eye and said, before I could begin to ask any questions, "We have checked you out and we've come up with nothing. You're a journalist in London. That's all I know about you. So go on, tell me."

So I'm not on the CIA files, I thought. I began to feel unwanted, disappointed; never mind.

"I want you to tell me exactly, as far as you can recall, what happened the day you saw Dian Fossey's body."

"Okay," she said. "Here it is. I got there [to Karisoke] at the end of the afternoon. The house was tin and one piece had been wrenched from the side of the cabin. The panel had been prised loose from the bottom. Like this . . ."

She leans over the table, takes my pen and draws a sketch in my notebook.

"Beyond that, there was matting which was loose and torn. I went into the kitchen, through the living room and stepped down into the bedroom. The drawers of a chest and the closets were open. I suppose you could say there was a slight disorder in the room. Dian's body was lying on the floor. Next to her body was furniture which was slightly out of place. It hadn't been overturned. I reckoned that there had not been a great struggle. The police were there and a doctor. He was, I believe, a Belgian, Dr Bertrand who worked in the hospital at Ruhengeri. By now it was dark. They were examining the body by lamplight, because there was no electricity up at Karisoke."

"What was Dian wearing?"

"Long john bottoms with socks tucked in and a sweatshirt."

"So her clothes had not been interfered with?"

"No."

"Why wasn't an autopsy performed?"

"The doctor didn't think it was necessary."

"Didn't you insist?"

"I couldn't. I was not a close relative and anyway it was obvious how she had been killed."

I didn't think it was obvious. And anyway an autopsy could have answered a number of questions. The time of death, the state of Dian's health. Was she drunk? Had she taken sleeping pills? The cause of death?

Kathleen Austin went on: "Next morning we searched the cabin and found nothing was missing. We found dollars, her passport, Rwandan francs, an amulet."

"What about the hair?"

"We found hair in both her hands."

"Are you sure she had hair in both her hands?"

"Yes."

"What did you do with it?"

"I sent hair samples from both her hands to the FBI in Washington."

"You personally sent it?"

"Yes."

"Who sent the hair to the Paris laboratory?"

"The Rwandan police."

"How long were you up there, at Karisoke?"

"About eighteen hours. I left at noon the next day. This would be," and here she calculated, "she was killed on December 26, so I reached the cabin that afternoon, so I would have left for Kigali on the 27th."

"What were the police doing all this time?"

"They were very interested in the tracks outside the cabin. They were shoe tracks, not boots. Canvas shoes, I would think."

"So there were no prints of bare feet?"

"No."

"That would rule out poachers, maybe," I said.

"Possibly."

"What was Wayne McGuire doing all this time?"

"I talked with him for about an hour. He was in shock. He said he felt totally surprised by what had happened."

"Let's go through it again," I suggested. "When did you first hear about the murder?"

"The call came through to the ORPTN, the Parks Office in Kigali, at around 8.00 a.m. Maybe by 9.00 a.m. They told the embassy almost immediately and I was there that afternoon."

"What state was the body in?"

"The back of her head was a mess. She had taken multiple injuries. There was one deep gash down the side of her face."

"Was there much blood?"

She shook her head.

"Was there blood on the walls, on the ceiling?"

"No. Most of the blood was on the floor, round, underneath her body."

"Were any photos taken by the police?"

"I didn't see them taking photos that day. They were taking pictures the next morning with the first light."

"What about this man, Kathleen, the Rwandan who committed suicide in prison?"

"The man who was found hanged in his cell, you mean?"

"Yes, Rwelekana."

"I don't know what happened there, but I can tell you one thing. Suicide is very rare in Rwanda. And so is violent murder. The fact Dian died so violently is odd, but it is even more curious when another man linked to her murder kills himself. The Rwandan method is poison."

"So why are suicides rare?"

"I never heard of anyone committing suicide. Wait a minute, yes there was one child. She hanged herself. I don't know why, but it blew the community away when the news got around town. Maybe it's the religion – they are strong Catholics – but people in the Third World don't kill themselves. Life's too hard. It's not like the West. You know, I can only think of one murder that I knew of in my time in Rwanda. The ambassador's driver told me that one of the guys at the embassy, a Rwandan, was stealing gas from our pumps. It was true and we fired this guy. He found himself another job, but one night the ambassador's driver – Valentine – was going home on his motorcycle and he was hit from behind by a car. The guy we had sacked was driving it. Rwandans do take revenge, especially if they have been crossed. They are a jealous people. They pull for each other, the family gathers round, and they expect that if someone makes good they will receive a handout. It's then the sniping begins. If they don't get what they expect from a more successful member of the family, there can be trouble."

"Did you know the prefect of Ruhengeri?"

"You mean Ziggi. Zed, or whatever they call him."

"Yes, Zed."

"I rented a house from him. He's a charming man. He's a big man in Rwanda. The President's brother-in-law."

"Was he there the day of the murder?"

"I can't remember. But I saw him as I walked down the mountain after the funeral. He was on his way up."

(Later, I found out Kathleen had got this wrong. Zed was at the funeral. The man who arrived late was the Director of ORPTN, the National Parks Organisation.)

"Let's go back to the hair."

"Okay." She was looking at her watch. I was running out of time.

"Tell me what you did with the hair samples."

"I collected them personally. I took them down the mountain and brought them to the embassy. Then I sent them off to Washington."

"You know that the results of the analyses in Washington and Paris are different?"

"Yes, the FBI report is not conclusive."

"Why do you think that is so?"

She shrugs.

"Did you ever lose sight of the hair?"

"No."

"So who sent the hair to the Paris lab?"

"The Sûreté. The Rwandan secret service."

"Where did they get their sample from?"

"From us. From me."

"How?"

"A couple of days after the murder, they called, I forget who, and asked for a sample. They came round to the embassy and took a sample from my sample."

"So they left with the hair?"

"Yes."

"And you never saw the sample they sent to Paris?"

"No."

"So the samples could have been switched?"

"Yes, I suppose so."

I flew back to Helsinki and, this time, sipped the cordial that was on offer. The plane was full of Americans, enjoying the new East. They had been sightseeing in Moscow and St Petersburg and were competing with each other for who had bought the best presents for the least money. I have never seen so much hand-luggage in my life. I looked down at the disappearing Baltic and thought of Kathleen Austin's testimony and I wondered whether, indeed, those hair samples had been switched.

But it was her parting words to me that were really echoing in my mind.

"You're going to Rwanda?"

I said yes.

"Then be very careful. It is a dangerous place and there are people out there who will not want to answer your questions. Remember," she said, shaking my hand, "families pull together."

I asked her what families.
"Just be careful at the roadblocks. That's all."

Nairobi: July 1992

I WAS HOOKED into going by now. Threats, warnings, signals could not deter me. Yet I left with more than just a sense of foreboding. As I sat watching Swissair's computer-enhanced video map, telling me where I was at that moment – 22.54 hours, 35,003 feet above the earth, travelling at 501 mph, sorry must have hit an air pocket, 500 mph, with 5 hours and 41 minutes to estimated time of landing, plus a little plane arrowed on screen over the tip of Cyprus – I tried to work out exactly what I knew.

But knowing something – and being told it? My task was to perceive the truth, and what on earth was the truth?

These were the facts.

1 Dian Fossey had been murdered.

2 This happened on the night of December 26/December 27, 1985.

3 The murder took place at Karisoke, her research station in the Virunga Mountains, above the town of Ruhengeri.

4 An American, Wayne McGuire, had been convicted of the murder, but had escaped the country and was now studying at an American university.

5 No attempt had been made to extradite him. Nor had the Rwandan government pressed the US State Department for his return.

6 His accomplice, the Rwandan Rwelekana, had been found hanged in his cell in prison.

7 The conviction was based on evidence supplied by the Paris police laboratory. Hair found in Fossey's hands and analysed at the laboratory was Caucasian and did not belong to her. The court drew the appropriate conclusions. Blood, matching Fossey's, was found on Rwelekana's shoes.

That was fact.

Now, the questions.

1 Why did the FBI analysis differ from the Paris analysis?

2 Had the hair samples been switched? If so, why? To frame McGuire? But why? To get someone else off the hook?

3 What was the motive which drove McGuire to kill?

4 The Rwandans said he killed her to steal her notes. This seems ludicrous. Was there an affair going on between Fossey and McGuire? Sounds equally ludicrous. Had she been sexually assaulted? According to Kathleen Austin, her socks were tucked into her trousers. She was clothed for bed. So sex as a motive seems unlikely. But no post-mortem was done.

5 Why did Rwelekana kill himself? Suicides are rare in Rwanda. His death robbed the Rwandans of their chief witness.

6 Was Rwelekana killed by the Rwandans? If so, why? Could it be to shut him up? Or did he know the truth?

7 The visa: why was Dian granted a two-year visa ten days before she died?

8 Why did she go to the head of the Sûreté?

9 Did she trade information for the visa?

10 Did her knowledge of gold trafficking have anything to do with a) her granting of the visa or b) her murder?

11 What part did the trafficking of gorillas play in her murder?

12 Who is the Bwana Mwkuba of Rwanda?

13 Why were so many people trying to put me off this story?

Unlucky 13, I thought, and then realised there were a whole raft of questions I had conveniently forgotten to ask myself.

Had I talked myself into believing a fantasy? Was I actually on the point of finding out, unmasking a killer? What a joke! I must have known the answers all along. I had kept putting off, delaying this journey. My mother had just died, there was a funeral to attend to, so I couldn't go and then there was looking for work, and I guess I was going through the process of mourning my loss of a job as well as the loss of my mother. And I was smoking too much and was worried about emphysema and the effect high altitude would have on my tarred lungs.

I realised that I hadn't actually vegetated. I had been to America, to Brussels, to Antwerp, to Tallinn. I had spoken to embassy officials, to rebels, to an ex-cop. I had combed Harold Hayes's papers. I had established that an extraordinary amount of confusion clung to this case. Now I had to shift it.

And Fossey herself? I had never met her, but I felt that I was beginning to know the woman. She had no friends; she was a loner with a temper as frayed as the crater edges of the volcanoes she lived under. Sure there were people who said they liked her, who said she was a regular girl, a home-maker who filled vases with flowers and changed the linen for visitors, but most who knew her hated her, couldn't stand her company, and even in the loneliness of Karisoke, 12,000 feet high in the Virungas, they preferred fiddling with their notes or themselves rather than endure the long, dark, drip of a night in her company.

Dian Fossey had no friends. All she had were her gorillas, her pets and her Snoopy doll. Her mother didn't care. Her mother spent her whole life telling Dian that she was too big, that she was ugly, that she was awkward, that she was a physical freak. Her father ran away with a bottle of bourbon, and her stepfather was not interested, at least, not until she was dead and there was money from her estate to grasp, money which could save his building concern from bankruptcy. Her only real love had gone and got himself married, her favourite gorilla had been decapitated, and Dian Fossey had ended her short life in pieces, hacked that way, but by whom?

The trouble was, the more I dug into the grave, the more I found that no one really seemed to care. Dian Fossey may have been a loathsome, behemoth of a bitch, she may have been scratchy company at a dinner party – you know the sort, deliberately contentious, arrogant, cavalier, an occupier of the high ground where morality resides, a woman who never listened, a strong woman who knew her mind was superior to those around her, even though her qualifications did not match theirs, a woman who put you down, not with grace, but with a jolt, you've avoided people like her – yet Dian Fossey deserved better of death than this. She had saved the mountain gorilla; she was news. She was Jackie Kennedy-tall with Jackie Kennedy charisma. She'd outFayed Fay Wray; she'd played with a real King Kong. She was accessible. She was proof there still was a dream to dream in America. She was Miss Mid-West, Miss Main Street, the Girl Who Made It Without Qualifications. She was loved by her public; her lectures were sell-out, her book a bestseller. And she was Green, when green was a mere colour.

So, when she was murdered, why was there no real fuss, no

political row? It wasn't as if she was the only victim. The truth had been murdered too.

I pushed up the window slat and stared out at the night. All I could see was the red light on the port wing flashing and fading, flashing and fading. On the screen in front of me, the little plane was millimetring its way down the Nile towards Juba. Two hours to Nairobi. And Abdul.

This wasn't a fantasy any longer.

Abdul handed over a sheaf of documents at Jomo Kenyatta airport and wheeled my baggage trolley through a jostle of touts who didn't waste a second glance on him, and therefore me, and turned their attention back to the latest batch of tourists who had emerged, fresh from processing, into the drizzle of the airport concourse.

"How's the tuning, Abdul?"

"Fuck tuning," he said. "How's the gorillas?"

I told him where I was in the search for the killer and asked him if he knew anything about Zed.

He shook his head. "Maybe that piece of paper I gave you will help. I cannot read French."

"Where did you get it?"

"I spoke to some Rwandan in one of the clubs. He gave it to me. I told him I was interested in gorilla trafficking. Maybe he thinks I am going to capture one."

I would read it later. I put it in my briefcase.

"We fly to Kigali tomorrow," he said. "Eleven in the morning."

"And tonight?"

"Tonight," he said, "we tune. What else?"

African music is like a virus. It is infectious, and like a virus, it can kill. The Florida 2000, Nairobi's "premier nightclub", is a lethal place. The combination of strobe lights, heavy pulsating BongoMan music, alcohol, and predatory girls, with a one hundred per cent record of AIDS, is pernicious. Unlike more enlightened establishments, in Kampala for instance, the management do not hand out to the clientele "issue vouchers" as Abdul called condoms, or even leave them on the tables.

Imagine a cattle truck filled with human beings, and imagine music so loud that you cannot hear it, and imagine the silence as you feel bodies wriggle past you, feeling and groping you, and imagine girls kicking and scratching each other over a man, and imagine two men, one white, one brown, resting at a table in the shudder of the cattle train as it moved through the night, getting nowhere, and imagine the table drowned in thighs and elbows and breasts and lips, and you imagine the Florida 2000. Oh, and there was a floor show that night also. I suppose it gave the Nairobi girls time to rest their voracity for half an hour or so, to cool them down, to allow them to savour their appetites.

They hunted like wild dogs, these Nairobi girls, in fours or fives or sixes, packs of girls, homing in on their prey as efficiently as any laser-guided piece of hi-tech that was slung under the wing of a fighter plane, and their strike rate, I would say, was as formidable. They weren't prostitutes in the sense that Westerners would recognise. For Nairobi girls this was a job, a night-time job. In the day, they worked as secretaries, or nurses, or clerks, or shop girls. The Florida 2000 was a kind of urban game park where the prey were the men who had come to look and admire. These girls, these rapacious, devouring girls were the attraction, and like the game in the bush, they were not to be taken at face value. They wanted shillings, they wanted a meal, they wanted to dance, they wanted a new life, away from Nairobi, away from the Florida, somewhere in Europe or the States. In short they wanted to marry.

They had to contend with fierce opposition, these Nairobi girls, and that was why they were ready to fight for their prey. Women outnumbered men in the city by two to one so competition was as savage as in the bush and maybe the pressure they faced to make a kill outweighed their fear of contracting AIDS.

Abdul I could see was not impressed. He was drinking whisky silently and watching the floor show, a troupe of semi-naked dancers on tour from South Africa. Contempt was glazed across his face.

"What's up?" I shouted, elbowing a Tina Turner lookalike's braids out of my Safari beer.

"These girls," he said, hoovering the dance floor and bar with his dark eyes, "are *verry* ugly."

He rolled each r, layering on the disdain that he felt.

"I am looking for an Isuzu girl. And there are none here."

Abdul, raised in Isiolo, liked Somali girls. They were, he said, the colour of Isuzu jeeps, beige and cream, not black like the girls in the Florida that night.

"Well, I doubt if you'll see an Isuzu girl in Kigali, Abdul."

"No," he said, and began to tune the breasts of the girl squeezed in next to him. Tuning was an art with Abdul. First he raised his hands so they were level with each breast. Then he tensed the fingers and grasped each breast, and then he squeezed, gently, until the girl giggled and moved away, and pushed her breasts back into his hands.

"But we will see a gorilla, and then I shall make unnatural history."

Rwanda: July 1992

I READ the document that Abdul had given me at Jomo Kenyatta as I sat scrunched in beside him on the airbus that was now flying west, over Lake Victoria, into the heart of Africa. It was a newspaper cutting, by the look of it several years old, headlined: THE DEATH OF THE AMERICAN DIAN FOSSEY IN RWANDA.

"The murderer of the American Dian Fossey is a certain Rwelekana." Nothing new here. I read on. "But the real partners in the crime will be the brother-in-law of the Rwandan President, the ex-prefect, Zigiranyirazo and Colonel Rwangasore, the chief of the Ruhengeri garrison." Zed. The man behind the killing. But why?

The article explained the reason. "The motive for the murder will be attached to the commercialisation of gorillas."

There was also, in the article, an explanation of the death of Rwelekana. "Rwelekana was receiving money during his incarceration in Ruhengeri jail, and frequent visits from Colonel Rwangasore and Zigiranyirazo. However he talked to other prisoners and told them the reason for killing Fossey and who was behind it. His death was arranged to silence him. His body was brought to Kigali and it was said that he had committed suicide to calm the worries of the Americans."

The article had been published in a Rwandan paper, *Tribun du*

Peuple, which Abdul said he believed had gone underground following the story's circulation. Certainly, he said, the author, a journalist called Jean-Pierre Mugabe, had been forced to flee the country. "You see, Nick, I have been sleuthing for you in Nairobi, not just tuning."

Abdul's moustache stretched under his nose as he made his pleasure apparent, but how did I prove all this? That was going to be the problem.

French paras were guarding Kigali airport. French paras were patrolling the city. Roadblocks between the airport and the city centre held us up. The streets bristled with shaved heads topped with purple berets. And then there was the Rwandan army, too, less chic, more ragamuffin Rambos, dressed as they were in hand-me-down uniforms that I am sure had seen service in a score of bush wars before they had surfaced in Kigali.

A pygmy wearing a green bell-boy's suit edged in gold braid had met us at the airport. His name was Zo-Zo and he was the general factotum at the city's prestige hotel, Les Milles Collines and, as he drove us to the hotel, he wasted no time in telling us our requirements.

"Change," he said. "You want change. Then ask Zo-Zo. A woman you want. Zo-Zo will fix."

Abdul was more interested in the rate of exchange. "How much for a dollar, Zo-Zo?"

"One sixty."

Abdul shook his head, making sure the pygmy could see him in the driving mirror. It was a feature of Abdul's character that never allowed him to agree to any deal, whether it was simply hiring a taxi, or something more complicated like booking into a hotel, or paying off a girl after a night's entertainment, without first entering into long and complicated negotiations. This was no exception.

"One eighty," fired back Abdul.

Zo-Zo shook his head. There was a tightening of the lips and his little, stubby hands gripped the steering wheel even tighter. I remembered what I had been told about the Twa, the pygmy tribes who lived in the north of the country, and the role they had played in the ancient Rwanda. Torturers and comedians; which was Zo-Zo?

The courtesy coach drew up outside the hotel and still a price had not been agreed. Zo-Zo struggled in with our luggage. I walked across the bar and down to the terrace which adjoined the swimming pool. No one was splashing in it. The water was Hockney-calm, a vast reservoir waiting for the French and American tourists who this year had failed to come to Rwanda because of the war. Now, only swallows and house martins were taking advantage of the waters, swooping down even more graciously than the tourists would ever contrive to do. Sitting around the pool were two men. As I walked towards them, the taller of the two flashed a half smile, and I realised that he was the man I had met in Brussels at the FPR meeting – the man from the back room of the parish hall.

"So we meet again," he said, shaking my hand and pulling up a chair. "Join us. I heard you were coming here. Primus?"

"Who told you?" I asked, staring at him to see if it really was the man in the navy blue suit and red shirt, the orator. I sipped the beer slowly and couldn't believe my luck. Or was this luck? Maybe it was something more.

"Your colleague in Antwerp, Lambert." It was true I had told Lambert I was flying to Kigali and where I would be staying.

His name was Karamila Froduald. He was a businessman, involved in import-export, and, curiously, a leading member of the resistance. I say curious because here was a man whose ideals seemed not to be driven solely by the establishment of democracy and multi-party government. Freedom for Karamila was the opportunity to be able to conduct business without having to cut in government ministers; freedom for Karamila was a bribe-free Rwanda.

He explained that the country was being strangled by the President and his family, by Agathe, his wife, the Kanjongera of the nineties, and Zed, her brother. "We call it here the Akazu. It means in Kinyarwandan the hut. It is the President's power base, the Akazu."

"You mean like the Mafia?"

"Exactly."

I opened my briefcase and pulled out the now even more tattered copy of the *Tribun du Peuple* article. "What about this, Karamila? Is this part of the Akazu?"

"Oh, so you have seen this famous report! I am pleased you have read it."

"But it is all hearsay. How can I prove it?"

"I have passed the word that you are staying here. You will be contacted. What is your room number?"

"Two one four."

He made a note of it, and then grasped my arm. "You see that man there?" He nudged me, his eyes flicking a signpost over my shoulder.

I sneaked a glance. A tall man, fine-featured, with heavy-rimmed glasses, wearing a Kaunda suit, a light blue short-sleeved shirt and matching trousers, was drinking beer at a table with another man. I nodded.

"That is Colonel Rwangasore."

Rwangasore? The man who had plotted with Zed to kill Fossey, the officer who was i/c Ruhengeri, the killer of Rwelekana.

I sauntered towards the table as casually as I could, and held out my hand to the colonel. He stood up, taking my hand and bowing at the same time. Then he invited me to join him. Good manners for a murderer.

I introduced myself, told him I was from London, was writing a book about the country, a book about conservation, and naturally gorillas, and I understood he had known Dian Fossey.

"How do you know me?" he asked.

"You are famous," I lied, hoping blatant bullshit would charm him into conversation. He seemed to take the bait.

"Yes, I knew her. She was always to be seen in Ruhengeri."

"Did you talk to her? Were you friends, Colonel?"

"We passed the time of day when we met. She was friendly, but we were not friends."

"What about her death?"

"Yes?"

The colonel was masking himself in confusion.

"You were in Ruhengeri at the time of the murder?"

The colonel nodded.

"Then you must be able to tell me something about it."

He folded his arms across his chest. I could see the short-sleeved shirt had turn-ups on the edges of the sleeves. He pushed the glass of beer towards me and smiled. It was a slow, considered smile, edging from knowledge to bafflement. "I cannot talk here. We must arrange a programme, I shall meet you tomorrow. You can come to Kigali Nights. Eleven o'clock."

"Morning?"

As I rose and pushed my chair away from the table, he was shaking his head and smiling.

In room 214, Abdul had unpacked our bags, folded his clothes away neatly and ingeniously erected my mosquito net with a tortuous system of strings and knots around the room that made it difficult to walk past the bed to the balcony.

"There are no mosquitoes here, are there, Abdul? We're up at 5,000 feet here. It's too high."

"Look, Nick, I know you, and tonight, just when I am sleeping and dreaming Isuzu girls, you will wake me and tell me to kill a mosquito, so there's the net. Now use it."

I told him about Rwangasore. The meeting downstairs, the arrangements for the next night.

He looked at me as if I had seen a ghost. "Colonel Rwangasore is dead. He was murdered last year," said Abdul.

"How do you know?"

"The Rwandan contact in Nairobi. He told me to tell you. I forgot. He said that you should read the paper and then he said not to forget to tell you that this colonel was dead."

"So who was I just talking to?"

Abdul shrugged.

"And why didn't Karamila know about the colonel?"

There was a knock on the door. Abdul sprang from his bed and jumped over the web of string which held up my net.

It was Zo-Zo.

"Okay?" he said, holding out both hands and smiling.

"Okay," said Abdul.

"You still need change?"

"Yes. But not at your rates. We will go to the men outside the hotel."

"Okay," said Zo-Zo, knowing that he had lost a battle and that Abdul was a worthy adversary. "One seventy-five."

We never went to the bank in Rwanda. Money was being changed all around the capital, by men like Zo-Zo, who clutched dirty wads of dollars or fished for currency inside trouser pockets the size of bank vaults, as they lurked and lounged on city corners, or by roadblocks, or traffic lights. Wherever you happened to stop, they would appear. They'd approach you in restaurants and clubs, whether you were sitting down for dinner or dancing with a Kigali

Nights girl. The banks of Kigali were as vast and as empty and as useful as the schools of England in the summer holidays, and the exchange rate, a mere 130 Rwandan francs to the dollar was as well received as the headmaster's annual report.

I didn't have to wait long for a phone call. It was a man's voice asking for me.

"Do you know a man in Antwerp?" the voice enquired.

"Yes."

"His name?"

I thought. "Lambert."

"Okay. Come to the Kigali cement works. Tomorrow morning. Eight o'clock. Ask for Jacques."

The phone hung up. Events were moving faster than ever I had imagined.

The Cement Works, Kigali: July 1992

THE CEMENT WORKS is in the centre of town, set off the street in its own compound. Jacques grips my hand warmly and asks me how I had left Lambert.

"Well," I say. "You two worked together?"

"Not quite," he says, motioning me into his office, tucked away at the back of the works. "We liaised. He was a policeman. I was in intelligence. National intelligence."

An old man has knocked on the door and now he enters the office. Jacques hands him some banknotes. It is Saturday, pay day I suppose. As he is being paid, I look out of the barred windows in the little room. Opposite, beyond the compound fence, stand the offices of Air France. A large sign tells the city in blue and red capital letters that cement and building blocks are stocked inside.

Jacques is now ready for me. He leans across his desk, both elbows planted firmly in the heart of it. He is a short and angular man, with close-cropped black hair and a friendly smile. He tells me that he worked in intelligence for a number of years and that his job was to analyse secret files.

"Who was your boss?" I ask.

"Augustin Nduwayezu. Now he has left the service. He is no longer the head of the Sûreté."

"What's he doing?"

"He runs OVIBAR. It's a government-owned concern. Banana wine, beer. It's his reward."

"Reward for what?"

"Keeping his mouth shut. Doing the President a favour."

"Augustine was the man who gave Dian Fossey the two-year visa?"

"Yes."

"I'll have to see him. What do you think?"

"I wouldn't. He's a bad man. If you see him, he'll tip off Zed that you have been asking questions. He'll do it immediately."

He straightens his back in the chair and looks at me for a moment and then he says, "I have seen the Fossey file. The secret file. When I first saw it, it was this fat" – he holds his fingers apart a couple of inches – "but it has got thinner and thinner over the years. It has been stripped. It is kept in the offices of the Sûreté in a large-format envelope. I was a specialist in the analysis and exploitation of intelligence and I have never been allowed to work on this file. I pressed but then Augustin told his secretary that it should be withdrawn and not be subject to analysis. All the declarations I am about to make I have read in this file."

He pauses to allow me to take this down in my notebook. He will not allow me to tape him, and I have promised not to reveal his name.

"Rwelekana was murdered. He was tortured in Ruhengeri prison, transferred to the Gikondo prison in Kigali, and was hanged with his shirt. I have seen the cell where he was found hanging. There is a beam maybe eight foot from the floor. This he could have reached I suppose, despite the poor shape he was in. Remember he had been beaten and tortured in the prison. But I find it impossible to believe that he could have had the strength and agility to jump up, grasp the beam, take off his shirt, and knot it around his neck.

"Wayne McGuire did not kill Dian Fossey. He was on the scene at the time she was killed. He witnessed her murder. He was threatened with death if he said a word. He would have been lynched, he was told."

As he talks, the phone keeps ringing and while Jacques deals with the interruptions I try to take in the office, square, like a cell, yet lit well by the sunshine. The walls are bare save for a calendar showing a scene that could be Switzerland. A tiny bird, a finch, sits at the open window, rubbing its beak against the bars.

"We can see him," says Jacques, "but he cannot see us." I wonder if this bird is blind, how Jacques knows, but he laughs at me and explains that the windows are one-way view.

"Who threatened to lynch McGuire?"

"The prefect, Zed."

"Why?"

"To shut him up. Zed needed to remove Dian Fossey because he wanted to exploit the gorilla market. There was a market for gorillas, their heads and their hands. Dian knew who killed the gorillas and she knew who protected the poachers."

"So why did it take eighteen years to kill her?"

"Because it took her some time to find out who really was the big man and, remember, for many of those years, practically all of them, she was on the point of being thrown out of the country practically all the time.

"She had written her findings about the gorilla trade and Zed's involvement and this is why she was killed. If she had published these findings, the attention of the world would have focused on Zed. The President's brother-in-law, the prefect of Ruhengeri, the man who was legally responsible for everything that went on in this area. So he led a conspiracy to kill Dian and this was despite her fame, despite the fact she was American. You can see how important Zed thought she was. He had to destroy her before she could destroy him."

"How then did Zed know that she knew about him?"

"There was a spy at Karisoke. A spy for Zed. He knew what she was writing. He was called Magayani."

"Was?"

"Yes, was. Magayani was killed four days after the murder of Dian. He too was hanged in the Gikondo prison."

"Like Rwelekana?"

"Yes, just like Rwelekana."

"Could he read, this spy?"

"No, but Dian had talked about what she was going to do."

"But she didn't talk in any of her letters to people at home."

"Maybe she was careful that way."

I remember the letter to her accountant, the one where she had been overjoyed after getting the visa. It was, I thought, a controlled letter; maybe Jacques is right. She did not trust her secrets, the sensitive ones anyway, to the post.

"Zed had realised by December 1985," Jacques continues, "that Fossey was aware of the trafficking. There had been a number of incidents about that time – an infant gorilla had been kidnapped and Dian wanted it. She threatened Zed. She said that she would go to the President, and blow the whole thing, make it public in America and Europe. She wanted the gorilla back. If you like, Zed had no choice. He couldn't trust her, and probably he couldn't recover the gorilla."

"So my theory about Augustin granting her a visa in exchange for information about gold is wrong?"

Jacques looks at me quizzically. I explain.

"Not entirely," he says when he has taken in what I tell him. "Zed is involved in gold trafficking. He owns a mine up in that area and that was germane, but you see, Augustin was under instructions to keep her happy. They tried to seduce her, to make her feel that they were on her side. But, of course, it didn't work. It was a kind of bribe, this two-year visa."

"Why then did it take just another ten days to have her killed?"

"Because Zed knew that she had kept a journal, or at least suspected that she had and he had to have it. The file says he wanted the document and the fact she was killed was not what he intended. The men who were sent to Karisoke were under orders to break in and steal the document. But it all went wrong. She woke. She screamed 'Richard', McGuire's middle name. He came rushing to her. He saw the attack. He could not do anything, so he ran and hid. He was terrified. Some of the killers came in through the roof, others through the panel afterwards. The panel was forced afterwards. The men were on the roof and not all of them could come in that way. They were too fat maybe. They took the documents."

"Could they read English?"

"No problem. There are many anglophones in this country."

"Why the roof?"

"It is the normal way of burglary in Africa. You maybe undo six nails and you lift off the roof section, and you're in. That roof was never repaired. I have seen the pictures."

"So why were Rwelekana and Magayani killed?"

"Because they knew the truth. One knew the motive and the other had seen what had happened. All the men in the camp were arrested and taken to Ruhengeri jail. They were all interrogated. It is a common practice in Africa to question people in order to find out what they don't know. If they know too much, they are expendable."

I ask him again about Augustin: how close was this former chief of the Sûreté to Zed?

"I'll tell you about Augustin's rise. It's an extraordinary story. He was ambassador in Kampala in the early eighties. In 1981, Colonel Kanyarengwe, who is now head of the FPR, the rebels, and then Minister of the Interior, defected. He took refuge in Kampala. He had been implicated in the Lizinde plot – Lizinde was head of security. Are you following me?"

I nod. What this has to do with Fossey I can't tell. But I let him go on.

"Lizinde was jailed and the colonel fled with a man called Biseruka. Augustin brought this man back to Kigali in a box." He pauses. "It had holes in it for him to breathe. It was a large chest. Augustin knew that Biseruka had a mistress in Kampala and Augustin got friendly with her and bribed her to drug him. She gave him something to sleep and then Augustin called a doctor. The man was injected, put into the chest, taken to a car which took the chest and its cargo across the border. It was a diplomatic bag. Anyway Augustin brought the car to the presidential palace up there on the hill and unloaded the chest and when the man woke up, he was staring at the President. He was asked who he was and how he had come to Rwanda. The President does have a sense of humour!"

"What's the link?"

"Augustin became the President's darling. He was rewarded with the Sûreté. He joined the Akazu, and Zed was a leading member of the Akazu. So they are very close. By blood and deed."

"By blood? Are they related?"

Jacques laughs. "Oh, no. I mean blood in the sense that they have spilt it. And that's how Augustin came to know the deepest secrets of the family."

"Was a Colonel Rwangasore implicated in the Fossey murder?"

"You know he's dead? He was murdered last year."

I tell Jacques about the ghost I had seen yesterday. He laughs.

Outside the window a French para, a black soldier, stands guard. Is he waiting for me to emerge from this room? Is he coming to take me away? The para turns and stares at our window.

"The colonel was killed because he knew too much. He was a member of the commission of enquiry into the deaths of the politicians who formed the first government of Rwanda in 1973. In 1985, before the murder of Dian, he was head of the Ruhengeri military sector, so he certainly knew a lot about her death. He was the eye-witness to many crimes. Last year, just before multi-party politics was allowed, people began to speak about the holding of a national conference. He apparently told his family and friends that if such a conference took place, then he would be able to tell a lot of things about the President's family."

I ask what the colonel could have revealed.

"He knew three things," says Jacques. "First, he knew about the deaths of the politicians in the seventies. He knew about the murder of another top-ranking colonel, and he knew about the murder of Dian Fossey. And so he was liquidated."

"How?"

"He had a girlfriend, a 'darling'. He went to her home, with some friends of lower army rank. He drank a glass of beer. Primus. It was poisoned. Two days later he died, but before he died, he spoke to his wife."

Poison. Again. I ask Jacques why Dian hadn't been poisoned.

"Oh, she could have been," he says, smiling. "It would have been quite easy. But she wasn't because Zed didn't intend her to be killed."

Outside, the para is still kicking gravel in the compound. And I have now not one, but four murders to think about: Fossey, Rwelekana, Magayani, and the colonel.

But this isn't the only thing that strikes me as curious. I'd been here less than twenty-four hours and already I had been put in touch with a man who had worked in intelligence, a man with access to secrets. Not only that, I had met Froduald again, more or less as soon as I had stepped on to Rwandan soil. I begin to wonder if the information is coming rather too easily. Am I being set up? Why? To discredit Zed? But he was discredited enough already. I decide I am lucky. I'd done my groundwork. It is paying off. I go back to the Milles Collines to find Abdul.

Kigali Nights: July 1992

THE CLUB was perched on the edge of one of the escarpments that wander aimlessly down from the Great Rift to peter out and converge around the Kagera River and form the bowl in which Kigali is built. It stood alone, set into a hollow that had been chiselled out of the rock face, advertising its presence and lure in decibels that made Nairobi's Florida 2000 sound like a graveyard.

Inside the cauldron, Kigali Nights was revelling in one of its below-the-waist nights. Zaireois rock is designed to draw the lower half of dancers together. To move to Zaireois rock, all that you need is to be capable of standing upright, eye to eye with your partner and grind pelvis against pelvis. The feet move a fraction, the head hardly at all. It is hips work. Abdul couldn't wait to get on to the floor and was deliberating which girl to "select". Girls were swarming on the floor. They were like mosquitoes, only appearing at night, whining around you for a few seconds before they settled on your skin and proceeded to bite. If only they made a girl-spray called Doom. I stared across the smoke and through the strobes, trying to ignore the girls. It was difficult to see right through the room. But I had to find the colonel, the man who was not Rwangasore.

At the back of the disco there was a quieter area with some bench seats fixed on the wall below a serving hatch. The bar. A couple of girls with dreadlocks and red short dresses sat disconsolately on the wooden seats. Instead of clinging on to men, they were grasping litre bottles of Primus by the neck. Here, by the bar, was the AIDS area, I thought, the place where girls beyond dancing bottled out the night.

The colonel was leaning through the hatch, talking to the bartender and nursing a glass of Scotch. He smiled at me and shook my hand. "I have brought you here," he said, "because we will not be overheard. It is far too difficult to trace a conversation."

Despite the noise coming from the disco floor, he had to raise his voice for me to hear, but I supposed that if anyone were attempting to bug our conversation, most of what was said would have been drowned by BongoMan's latest hit.

"Look," I began, "Colonel . . ."

"Charles. Call me Charles."

He smiled. He was still wearing the K-suit I had first seen him in. It smelt clean. I reckoned he had had a number made at a city tailor's.

"Look, Charles, I must apologise. I mistook you yesterday in the hotel."

"Don't worry. I can tell you something about the Fossey case." He sipped his drink and said that I had, at least, got one detail right. He was a colonel. But now, he was "on holiday".

"Holiday?"

He smiled, and touched the nose-piece of his glasses, pushing the frames tight back against his eyes. "Yes, holiday."

"A holiday of your own choice?"

"No."

So this Colonel Charles was in trouble.

"What happened?" Abdul asked in Swahili. For a moment he had shelved his selection, and was sitting next to us now on the bench, sipping a double Scotch.

"I was the commandant of the Ruhengeri sector last year when the rebels took the town. We were overwhelmed and I could not defend it. The rebels were about to break into the prison and free the inmates and I received a phone call in the name of the President. He told me to defend the prison. If I had done so, then many prisoners would have been killed. I asked him for a confirmation by telegram. I never got it. So I surrendered. It was," he said, "a hopeless position to defend."

"And that's why you're on holiday."

Charles nodded. Abdul was at the bar now, fixing more whiskies.

"I have been in prison and now I'm fighting my case. It is going to appeal, so I am waiting for the hearing. That's why I am in Kigali."

I asked him how long he had been at Ruhengeri.

"I was there when Dian was killed. I wasn't the commander then. I was in charge of the military cadet school. The day she was killed, I went to Karisoke to see the body."

"Why?"

"Curiosity, I suppose. I told you that I had met Dian. I wasn't her friend, but I would greet her if I saw her in the town."

"So you went up to see the body?"

"Yes. I went with the prefect."

"Zed."

"Yes. And Colonel Rwangasore."

"What did you see?"

"It's what I didn't see that made me begin to have doubts."

"Doubts?"

"About the official version of her murder, that she had been killed by *panga* blows."

"Go on."

"Well, I have often killed a cow with a *panga*, and I tell you the blood goes everywhere – it spurts out many feet. When I went to Karisoke that day, there was no blood on the walls, and no blood on the ceiling."

"Are you sure?"

"I am certain. The blood was concentrated on the floor around the place her body lay. I remarked about it at the time."

"So, Charles, how do you think she was killed?"

"I think," he said, "that she was killed by strangulation."

"Did you see any bruising around her neck?"

"No. I could not get that close to the body. This is my opinion only. You see, the prefect and the police and the colonel were huddled around the body. I looked from some feet away, and I made sure I looked at the walls and the ceiling, and there were, I repeat, no bloodstains on either." He sipped his drink.

"So, you think she was strangled. Why would she be strangled?"

"Someone broke in, strangled her and then they hit her with a *panga* after she was dead. This would explain the blood being on the floor."

"And the wall? The panel?"

"That was broken down after her death. It would take, I reckon, a good time to remove a panel. And it would make a lot of noise. If the killer had broken down the wall and entered through the panel, then Fossey would have had ample time to get her gun, but the gun was on the floor by her body. She didn't have the time even to load it."

It made sense, what Charles was saying. I knew Fossey normally kept her gun under her pillow. She would have had to have been heavily comatose not to have heard the wall being broken down.

"And," he continued, "there was no disorder in the room. It had not been ransacked. This was not a robbery." Charles drained his whisky and rose from the bench. He was a tall, thin, fit-looking man. As he walked back through the disco, he turned and shouted, "I'm staying in Morahoru Hotel. You can find me there."

"Come on," said Abdul. "I have selected a good girl for you."

I stared at the specimen who was by now sitting astride Abdul's knees, rubbing her bottom into his crotch. She was pale-skinned, not quite Isuzu, and her upper lip was large and generous. Abdul was concentrating on tuning her.

I asked him about the *panga* and killing cattle and he said, "It is true. The blood would have flown out of her body. I have seen it myself. Here, Nick," and he tugged my hand away from the glass of Primus it was resting around, "tune these. They are magnificent."

It was true. They were.

Kigali: July 1992

NEXT MORNING there was a journalist waiting for me in the foyer of the Milles Collines.

I was attracting information like flypaper now. Kigali may have been a capital city, but it revelled in its village identity, and, I suppose, I was a curiosity, a novelty. British journalists just didn't base themselves in this town. If they came to Rwanda, Kigali was an overnighter, a stopping-off place on the road to the Virungas, a telex machine from where to send back to London impassioned despatches on the plight of the mountain gorillas.

This journalist, like so many of his colleagues, I discovered, had served his apprenticeship not only on a news desk, but also in the Gikondo, the city's notorious maximum-security jail, nicknamed by its inmates, "The Amigo", after the prison in Brussels. He was another thin man, very black, wearing a white shirt and dark green trousers and sandals with socks peeking through the straps. He peered at me through steel-framed glasses. Altogether he was a placid character, not at all someone you would automatically tag as a danger to the state. His name, he said, was Theo. He had served six months in the prison for writing stories in the newspapers that had incurred the wrath of the government. "But I am not alone. Many of us have been thrown into prison. There is said to be a free press here, but it is not so," he told me.

I asked him about the prison and he described an urban gulag, with dormitories, maybe three times the size of a single room in this hotel we were talking in, housing up to 200 prisoners. The prison itself was a temporary home for 3,000 men. He said that the beds in the dormitories were tiered, three at a time, with men sleeping under the beds and squeezed in the narrow space between them if they could not find a bed. He talked of "*la frappe*", the beatings, and the "*massue*", the truncheon, with which punishment was handed out. He talked of "*l'électricité*", the shocks that prisoners were subjected to. He talked about men being beaten on the soles of their feet so they could no longer bear the weight of their own wasted bodies. He talked of the place where the tortures were executed, the building which housed the SCR, the Central Service of Intelligence; he talked of the prison exercise yard where, early in the mornings, just after dawn, men were stripped naked and hosed down and made to stand all day until the water froze on their bodies. And he told me about the murder of Dian Fossey.

He had, he said, a good source for the story he was about to tell me. He was a friend of a former President of the Court of Appeals of Ruhengeri, a lawyer who would not see me, Theo said, because, even though he knew the whole Fossey business stank, he felt he had too much to lose by going public, especially with a foreign journalist. Theo had come in his place.

Theo told me there were two versions of the Fossey death. The first report, the official version, was the work of Theo's friend, the lawyer from Ruhengeri. He had been charged with investigating the murder and producing a report. This report, said Theo, maintained that Fossey was killed by blows to the head, delivered by a *panga*; that she had hairs in her hand, and that some of these hairs were Caucasian and did not belong to Dian; that she had been killed by McGuire and the Rwandan Rwelekana whose shoes were spotted with blood belonging to the same group as Fossey; and that the motive for her murder was academic jealousy, i.e. McGuire wanted her notes.

Later on, however, events were to persuade the investigator, so

Theo told me that morning in the Milles Collines, to change his mind. Two days after the murder, the enquiry team discovered that some belongings of Dian's were missing. A rifle had vanished. Her notes had also gone.

I asked how they knew this – that some of Dian's belongings had gone.

"Because," said Theo, "the rifle and the notes were noticed on the day the body was examined."

He continued: "On the same day a man was arrested here in Kigali. He was fleeing from the Ruhengeri area. He was a watchman and he was brought to the Gikondo and was found dead in his cell, hanging from a beam. His own shirt had been knotted around his neck."

More or less the same story that I had heard the day before from Jacques, except for the detail about the missing rifle and notes and that he was on the run.

Theo said that when he was in the Gikondo himself, he had spoken to prisoners who were there at the time this fugitive had been brought in. "They told me," Theo said, "that fighting occurred around the cell the man had been put into and that men were entering every five minutes or so. The prisoner was frequently taken out of the cell and brought back."

"What for, Theo?"

"Interrogation, I would think. He was in a cell by himself, and when his corpse was discovered, the door of his cell was open. Why leave a suspect, a man possibly connected with a murder, in an open cell?"

"I thought," I said to Theo, "that you told me that when a prisoner was interrogated, he was taken out of the Gikondo and questioned at the headquarters of the Central Intelligence Service."

"Yes, but not in this case. This man was never fully, or officially integrated into the prison. There are two sorts of cells there, communal cells and individual cells. If you go to the communal cells you are taken out to the CSI building to be interrogated. As I explained, this man was in the prison for an extremely short time. He was slammed into a solitary cell, taken out of it to be interrogated, and brought back into it to die. There was no time even to charge him with any offence."

"Was this ever officially investigated?"

"No. And that is strange, because the official investigation was in the hands of the Ruhengeri court and they should have been informed about any connections with the case in other parts of the country. They were not informed. Also, look at what is wrong with the first version. McGuire was incapable of plotting. He did not speak the language. Two, Rwelekana had nothing to gain from the attack. Three, why did he not clean his shoes if there was blood on them? Why would he walk around with such tell-tale evidence? And, if the case was clear-cut, why was he interrogated for so long and then taken to Gikondo and killed there? And why was the watchman also killed at the Gikondo if he was guilty? They could have had the crime solved within forty-eight hours if that man had lived, and everyone would have been pleased."

Theo's analysis was as sharp and perceptive as the edges of his spectacles. I couldn't argue with it.

"Did gorillas or gold ever come up when the murder was discussed?" I asked him.

"I was living at Ruhengeri at the time. I knew full well that there was a lot of trafficking going on and she wanted it stopped. At the time of her murder, there had been talk of baby gorillas being taken from the area and the name of the prefect was constantly being linked with the trade."

"Publicly?"

"No, it was not as if you'd mention it in the streets of Ruhengeri, but if you were with someone you could trust, then yes."

"Why the secrecy, Theo?"

Theo smiled and took off his glasses and wiped them with his tie. "I take it you have never met the prefect, the former prefect?"

"No."

"He is the most feared man in this country. You have heard of the Akazu?"

"Yes."

"He is the leading member. He is not the sort of man about whom you voice your opinions." He paused and put back on his glasses. "Publicly."

Karisoke: July 1992

ABDUL WAS standing outside the hotel, hands on his hips, looking as if he had lost two fat rolls of lino. He was bargaining with a clutch of taxi drivers. We had decided to leave Kigali and make for Karisoke, see the scene of the crime, talk to those men who were present at the time of the murder, maybe look at a gorilla. For the moment I was tired of solving a murder, my mind was too full of theories, and I needed the space of the bush to clear it. And besides, we needed to escape from the scrutiny of soldiers who manned the roadblocks, the wet, greasy aftertaste of chicken and chips that we had eaten every day, and the nightly importuning of those voracious Kigali Nights girls.

He had fixed a driver to take us to the base of the mountain, drop us there, pick us up the next day and bring us back to Kigali for 16,000 Rwandan francs. He was pleased with the deal. I saw the car that was to convey us, and wondered. It looked as if it had taken part in the Iraqi army's retreat from Kuwait. The window winders were not working, nor would the back door open from the inside. The tyres were Kojaked and the driver had difficulty starting the motor. I pointed out these shortcomings to Abdul. "What do you expect for this money?" he said. "An army escort provided by the paras?"

Journeys never start on time in Africa. Why on earth should they when time does not really matter? Drivers, the men in control, seldom want to leave for a destination. All their efforts are expended in making sure their vehicle is carrying more passengers than it should, so many, in fact, that too often the vehicle is so overloaded that it has no chance of arriving. Journeys in Africa are never straightforward, either. This idea that you sit in a car or a lorry or a *matatu* and a few hours later you exit, satisfied that you have had a comfortable drive with no breakdowns, no near misses, no burst tyres, and you feel as fresh as the moment you began, is alien to the African. In Africa, you can be sure that if there is anything that can possibly go wrong, then it will go wrong.

Our journey to Karisoke did not, of course, break this rule. True, there was enough room in the car to spread out. We were not sharing it with any strangers, and sure enough for the first five minutes everything went smoothly. Except we were not heading for Ruhengeri, but circling the city, and, seemingly, coming closer to the centre.

The driver's name was Thierry, and I asked him why he was not pointing the car in the direction of Ruhengeri.

"Ah, first," he said, jerking the car across the road as he turned first his shoulder and then his head and then the steering wheel, "it is very cold where we are going. I must fetch my jacket. So I will go home. Then there is the petrol. I must fill the car."

It was an hour before we hit the first roadblock, and that was positioned just a mile outside the city limits, a couple of hundred metres before the road split north to Ruhengeri and south for Butare and the Burundi border.

The car queued for the inspection while little boys walked past into the city, wheeling home-made barrows, built from tree branches. They were carrying sugar cane. Soldiers peered into the car, gazing at Abdul and me. We passed over our papers into the grasp of a brown hand. Above it the eyes screwed over the words written in the passports. A grunt and then a dialogue with Thierry. He pushed his foot down on to the accelerator and eased the car as much as it could be eased away from the soldiers. Beyond the block, there were more soldiers raising their arms at us, trying to hitch a ride. Thierry ignored them, and as he approached the right turn that would take us on to the road north, the road to Ruhengeri, he jammed his foot down and lurched the car off the highway. Abdul crashed into me.

Thierry straightened the car and apologised. "I had to do that. I am very, very sorry, but I told those guys at the roadblock we were heading south for Butare. You see, they would maybe not have let us go north. This is the way to the war."

The car began the long, slow winding climb north between the mountains that laboured to Ruhengeri, a climb that squeezed us through narrow passes carved through the rock by Chinese engineers. Six of them remained, counting from their graves the wretched lorries that exhaust themselves as they toil towards the tops of these mountains every day, trailing behind them a dense and noxious cloud of burnt oil and carbon monoxide. Nature is being overwhelmed here on this road, not only by the trucks that use it but by the men who farm the mountainsides. Abdul looked at each hill, and there were thousands of them, erupting from the valleys, and grazing the undersides of the clouds that rested on their tops and said, "Once this country was forest. Now look at it." Man had terraced every inch of hillside and planted banana groves, sweet potatoes and rice.

A bus with soldiers leaning out of the glassless windows, slapping and banging the thin metal sides with their fists, and drowning with their chant the roar of the engine, swept past us on the way to Kigali.

"They are on leave," observed Thierry. "The war is over for them. Well, at least for a few weeks. Now they will go back to Kigali and tonight they will be fucking."

"What about you?" I asked.

Thierry shook his head. "In Ruhengeri, no. There is a curfew there. I will have to be in my hotel and stay there at eight o'clock."

"That's time enough," said Abdul.

"No, I do not like the girls in Ruhengeri. They have AIDS."

"Don't the girls in Kigali?" Abdul said.

"In Kigali," laughed Thierry, "the girls are either bottle neck or basin."

"What do you mean?" I asked.

"It depends which way you want them."

I still didn't understand, but from the smile that had hijacked Abdul's lips and was now about to develop into a case of full-blown laughter, I knew he had copped on.

"Explain, Thierry," I said.

"Well, there are girls with basins for putting it in and girls with bottle necks."

Abdul poked me in the ribs. "Nick, I have heard the same in Mombasa. If you want to stick it in their backsides, you ask for a bottle neck. Me, I'm a basin man."

It wasn't until after we had negotiated the third roadblock that the tyre burst. The car slewed to the side of the road, its rear offside rubber tube flapping miserably and uselessly around the wheel. The spare tyre looked in need of intensive care. Some men approached and offered to help change the tyre, but Thierry shooed them away, anxious to impress Abdul with his pit-stop technique. Or maybe he just didn't want to part with any more francs.

By the time we arrived in Ruhengeri it was already three o'clock, and we still had to reach the foot of the mountains. Thierry went to change the tyre at a garage on the edge of this one-street, frontier town that contained every cliché in a John Ford film, even down to the twenty-three large-calibre bullet holes that I counted on the steel doors at the entrance to the town's prison. This was the town Colonel Charles had surrendered only twelve months before, the decision that cost him his career and his freedom.

The car was a Renault which Thierry had bought in Belgium and had shipped out to Mombasa. It was a 1983 model and still carried the name of the Antwerp garage which had first sold it. On the bonnet Thierry had fixed a Peugeot insignia, perhaps to give the car more originality than it deserved. It had ferried us to Ruhengeri reasonably quickly despite the tyre burst, but between Ruhengeri and the mountain, this Renault-Peugeot shuddered to a halt every five minutes. Dust from the unmade road was blocking the carburettor, explained Thierry, as he switched off the engine and opened the bonnet and then hammered the carb until he was satisfied it was free of dirt.

Now it was four thirty. The purple peaks of the twin volcanoes, Visoke and Karisimbi, had vanished as the late afternoon mist settled around them and swallowed them up for the day. Thierry advised us to return to Ruhengeri for the night, but I was tired of the delays and reckoned the sickness that had gripped his car engine might be terminal. Rather the mountain than the Renault-Peugeot.

We were surrounded by porters who, hearing the car, had emerged from the huddle of mud and tin dwellings called Kinigi. Abdul chose three to guide us and carry our bags to Karisoke. After about half a kilometre, a park ranger with a .303 slung over his shoulder joined us. The way to the mountain led through fields of tobacco and sweet potatoes and thick hedges of bamboo. By the time we had reached the trail that led to the mountain top, Abdul was exhausted. He could, he said, go no further. But he rested and gasped his way upwards, through the zigzag that had been cut by the wind and rains and the tramp of men and buffaloes and *duiker*, shaving his legs against the brittle touch of nettles and occasionally demanding to rest so he could swig from my last bottle of Safeway's mineral water.

It was dark now, and the drizzle was closing in. I was sweating. I could hear the call of chimps on the mountainside and the echoing insistent call of a blue jay, probably making its ultimate cry before nature's curfew silenced it. There were buffalo, *mbogo*, on this path too. Sandy Harcourt had almost been killed by one. The ranger with the gun bent down and sniffed the dung and pointed to the damage in the undergrowth where the buffalo had blundered across just minutes before. He moved to the front of our procession, cocking the gun and his ear for the deep bellow that would tell him where to aim.

It was just before we saw the lights of lanterns swinging furiously across the mountain and making sense of the wild shapes that were darting about to our front and sides that Abdul planted his walking stick into the soft earth by the side of the path and refused to climb another inch.

"I would rather get AIDS in Kigali Nights than climb this gorilla hill," he gasped. "Fuck gorillas!" And then he saw the lights ahead and straightened up. The men from Karisoke had come to meet us.

I didn't notice how cold it had been on the mountain until I was sitting at a wooden table in the hut the Karisoke people call the "restaurant". Three whites and a Rwandan sat around the table. They were eating and invited us to join them. Most of the table space was taken up with large aluminium pots which contained a kind of meat and cabbage stew. We helped ourselves and then I handed over the food we had brought. A couple of tins of corned beef, pilchards and a six-pack of Heineken.

"We only heard you were coming two hours ago," said Peter Clay, a tall, thin American whose hacking cough and sunken cheekbones made me wonder if he really should be at Karisoke. At the gate to the park, there was a large notice which no one could fail to miss, stating that anyone displaying symptoms of colds or flu should not risk the climb. This was not a precaution aimed at protecting the health of visitors but designed to ensure that the gorillas on the mountain did not come into contact with any human disease.

"Never mind," said Dwight Nelson, another American, whose grey hair tied in a spotted red headband made me think of Willie Nelson. "Have a beer." Dwight's job was to rebuild Dian's house. He had already pulled it down and promised to show me around the building site in the morning.

"So what do you want to do here?" asked Peter Clay.

"Talk to the men."

"About?"

"The murder."

"Oh, that. Well, I'll approach them and see what they have to say. You are in luck. Nemeye is here and so are some of the others who were here at the time. But I warn you they may not want to talk about it."

"Don't you ever discuss it?" I asked.

"No, not really. It's over now. It's history."

I could see Clay wanted to rest. The sweat was rolling down his forehead. He rose from the table and showed Abdul and me to our hut. Even though it was only about fifty or sixty metres from the restaurant, I was shivering uncontrollably by the time I stepped inside. There was a charcoal fire glowing in a room that was bare except for three beds and a table. Clay left with us an electric battery lamp. It wasn't even eight o'clock.

"Bloody Siberia," I said. "But at least we have this stove."

"You want to be careful of those charcoal fires," said Abdul. "They can gas you. If you feel dizzy in the night, wake me."

He was already in his sleeping-bag, fully dressed down to the boots. Abdul always, whenever he was in the bush, slept with his boots on. He explained it by saying he never knew what would happen in the night. At least it was too cold for pythons.

Nothing did happen. The Karisoke rats rattled and probed and scratched in the room. Night became day as lightning lit a flare in the sky. The hut rocked with an ovation of thunder so sharp and accurate that I woke, thinking the rebels had attacked. The mountain moved in the storm and then the rain slapped down.

Next morning, by seven, the men had been assembled by Clay. They were waiting outside their quarters. Clay took me inside and said, "They want to be paid. They have talked to journalists in the past and they have been promised money, but it was never paid to them."

I called Abdul into the hut. We agreed to pay.

First in was Nemeye, the man who had been Dian's most loyal lieutenant at Karisoke. He was forty years old, Alphonse Nemeye, and he had first met Dian in 1969.

"I was here on the day of the murder," he said. "I was told

about it at ten minutes past five in the morning. Rukera found the body. He told me. I saw the body lying on the floor. She was lying alongside her bed. There was blood on her head, her hands, and in her mouth."

I asked him if there was blood on the walls.

He looked at Abdul who was interpreting, and then towards me and said, "No, there was no blood on the walls. I think," he said, "that she was killed by a hammer. Her brain was shattered."

"Not a *panga*?"

"No, a hammer."

"Were there any other injuries?"

"Her mouth had been slit."

"How?"

"Like this," he said and put his little fingers into the sides of his mouth and stretched his lips sideways across his face.

Abdul looked across at me and said, "Like the Mafia do. To people who talk too much."

"Or the Akazu," I said. "What happened then?"

"The prefect came here. Between two and three in the afternoon."

"And then?"

"I was taken to the police station in Ruhengeri. Colonel Rwangasore interrogated me. I was then taken to Chanak, a place on the border between Rwanda and Uganda."

"Why?"

"It is an electricity power station. They wired up my feet and hands and the side of my head. They hit me with a stick. They asked me if I knew who had killed Dian. They asked me if there were any Europeans involved in the murder, any white men. I asked them if they were interested in trafficking, but they said no. I told them I knew about the poachers but they said they weren't interested in that. They only wanted to know about the involvement of any white men."

I asked him about the letter Dian wrote, the one where she mentions the gold smuggler, the "oldtimer" that he and Dian had arrested in the November before she was murdered.

"Yes, I remember that day. The man was called Sebahutu. I remember he was carrying a letter about gold smuggling."

"You told Dian that he would not be in jail for long. Why did you say that?"

"Because," said Nemeye, "he was well known to the big shots. He had already been caught that March and he was put in prison, but he got out soon afterwards. But I do know he was in prison when Dian was killed."

I asked him if he had ever heard of a man called Magayani.

"No. Who is he?"

"A watchman who worked here at the time of the murder."

"No. Never heard of him. The watchman was called Sehegari. He was a cook also and he was sacked. He had cheated Dian. He stole her Rwandan francs, and she got rid of him. He came back to the camp the next day and begged for his job back. He said his wife was pregnant."

"When was this?" Abdul asked.

"Back in 1969. But he was one of the men who was questioned after the murder."

"In Ruhengeri?"

"No, not in Ruhengeri."

"How do you know he was questioned?"

"Because I heard he had been released. He lives in Bissati now."

Next in was Sekaryongo. He is the head of anti-poaching, and was trying to work out his age. He counted on his fingers for a few moments and transferred the calculation to his brain.

"Forty-two. Next Easter." Sekaryongo smiled at me.

He didn't add much. Maybe the effort of working out his age had finished him for the day. He told me that he was on patrol at the time of the murder and arrived back at Karisoke at the same time as the prefect and Colonel Rwangasore. He told me that he never liked Wayne McGuire, that the American was always cross and never listened to him. I asked him if he knew Rwelekana.

"Yes, he was my friend. He was off duty at the time. He was called for duty by Dian, but he did not come. It was Christmas and he wanted to stay with his wife."

"Where was his house?"

"About three hours away from here."

Rukera followed. He was the man whom Nemeye said found the body. He was forty-two years old and had been at Karisoke for seventeen years.

"My task was to chop firewood and fetch the water."

"You discovered the body?"

"No."

"Nemeye says you told him."

"Yes, I told him, but Kanyarayana discovered her. He told me."

I sighed. "Where is Kinya . . ." I gave up on the name. "Where is he?"

"He was sacked. For thieving."

"When?"

"About six months after the murder."

"What happened when he told you about Dian?"

"I heard him scream and I went to wake up McGuire. He was sleeping. His house was a long way from Dian's. There was no one sleeping within a hundred metres of her."

I recalled the noises of the wind and rain and thunder and lightning that had kept me awake the night before. "What sort of night was it? Like last night?"

"No. It was a quiet night. Only the wild animals were making noises."

"Don't you think it strange that no one, none of you in the camp, heard a thing?"

He had no opinion on this.

"I was arrested," he said, "and I spent five months in Ruhengeri jail. Rwelekana was in prison with me. I know he was taken out of the prison two times to see his wife."

"That was nice of them. Did you see your wife?"

He shook his head, quite violently. "No, they did not do this as a favour. They brought his wife to him and they beat her in front of him. I was beaten too and given electricity."

As I pushed my body away and up from the table where, amid the debris of last night's dinner, more cabbage, I had been taking notes, I noticed the photos on the wall of the hut. There were pictures of Fossey in this hut where I'd questioned the men. A kind of family album, snaps of her smiling, dwarfing the surrounding men, snaps of her next to Nemeye who was tortured after her death and Vitari who that morning was on patrol and I couldn't see, shots of her with her gorillas. They are old pictures now; these men and Fossey were young when the photos were taken, and it was difficult to make out the detail, not just because the image on film had faded, but because the men had attempted to preserve their memories of her, keep them safe and whole from the wind and the rain and the damp that seeped into every corner of this hut, and the only weapon with which they could combat time and nature was the one pitiful sheet of stained plastic someone had pinned over their past.

Outside, it was still raining. It was cold too, and not ten in the morning. I wandered through the camp, past the restaurant and across the stream which when we arrived last night was a trickle, but now was a torrent, drowning out every other sound on the mountainside. We couldn't even hear the generator which was powering the drills and saws that Dwight was using to reconstruct Dian Fossey's house. He saw us eventually and called us over. It was a huge house, twice, maybe three times the size of the Siberian hut that was last night's bedroom. It would not have looked out of place in a Swiss valley with its gabled ends and large windows.

Dwight patted a plank of eucalyptus. "Brought this up the mountain. Every piece of it. See that generator?" He pointed to the throbbing machine on the grass and mud on the edge of the building site. "Took eight men to drag that up here." He said it proudly.

"Do you think Dian would have liked what you are doing here?" I asked.

Dwight shook his head. "I ain't sure about pulling down this house. It holds a lot of history. I photographed every damn piece of it. She was a part of every piece to me."

"Was the roof ever interfered with, Dwight?"

"Nope. I took off the panels and they were as good as the day they were put on. I could tell you if they had been pulled out of the timbers. The nails holding them in were clean."

So Jacques's report had got that detail wrong.

"What about the side panels?"

"No way they could have entered that way either."

"Why?"

"It was a hell of a job pulling them down, too. I guess it would have taken those men twenty minutes to move that side panel. And they would have woken the devil doing it in the middle of the night. They would have needed the right tools. You just can't do that sort of thing and expect to get in in five minutes."

"So how did they get in?" I asked.

"Through the door."

Beyond the house is the graveyard where Dian and her gorillas are buried. There are sixteen graves there in all, hers and those of

Frito, Wageni, Lee, Quince, Imanzi, Tiger, Mbarga, Poppy's newborn, Kurudi, Kazi, Nunkie, Mwelu, Uncle Bert, Marchessa, and Digit, her favourite. Each of the gorilla graves is marked by a simple wooden cross inscribed with a name. Hers is a grander affair, a marble black tombstone. It carries her name, her dates and her Rwandan name.

I pointed out the word, Nyirmachabelli, to Abdul. It was curious. Dian was tall, so why should she have been given a nickname that did not describe her accurately?

(It was in London where I found the answer to that question. I also found out that the name had been spelt wrongly, too. The original Nyirmachabelli, or as it should be, Nyaramicibili, was Aliette de Monck, Dian's first friend in the area, a Belgian expat who had taken her to the rainforest and encouraged her to settle in Karisoke. Aliette was a small woman who did move on foot with the speed of a *duik-duik*. She was given the name by her head porter Guammogazi, who later worked for Dian. It was probably this man who transferred the name, but how he corrupted the meaning, I never did find out.)

So the name on the grave was wrong. I read the rest of the inscription, and some of the wording struck me as being wholly out of place. "Rest in peace, dear friend," it said.

They don't bury gorillas at Karisoke any more. I wondered how long they would go on burying the truth.

Butare: July 1992

I WAS running out of money now and that meant time. Before me, a mass of contradictions were competing with each other. Dian was *panga*-ed, Dian was beaten with a hammer, Dian was strangled. The killers entered through the roof, the side panel, the front door. Dian knew too much. Dian knew who was trafficking in gorillas. Dian knew who was trafficking in gold. And then there was Rwelekana. Had he been murdered? And who was this mysterious Magayani? Why had men like Nemeye been tortured? And his tormentor, Colonel Rwangasore. Had he been poisoned because he knew too much? And the Akazu, the shadowy, all-embracing conspiracy that was controlling the crime in this country – what part had they played? And why had the State Department refused to declassify so many documents relating to the murder? Why had Wayne McGuire been allowed to flee the country?

It was a jigsaw. I had found many of the pieces, but I wasn't yet sure what shape they were, so it was going to be even more difficult to complete the picture.

There was, however, one name that was a constant. Whoever I saw, wherever I went, that name emerged: Zed. I had to find him, build up a portrait of this man, and to find Zed, I realised I would have to gamble on seeing Augustin, and hope that he didn't tip off the former prefect.

Abdul had advised me to stay put, sit it out, but when I revealed the state of our finances, and that we were down to few more chicken and chips and Primuses, he blenched and declared he would forgo lunch that day.

"And Kigali Nights?"

"And Kigali Nights. Anyway, I'm eating at Ontee's tonight."

"Where?"

"Ontee's."

"What's Ontee's?"

"You mean who."

I didn't know what he was talking about. Was Ontee's a new restaurant? A nightclub? No, with Abdul, Ontee had to be female.

"Yes, Nick, Ontee is taking us to Butare. Theo just called to tell me. Ontee is his auntie, only Theo says Ontee." Here Abdul pursed his lips and then spat out the second half of the word. "I hope Ontee is a beautiful woman. Then I will be happy to eat with her tonight."

"But you told me you were eating with her, so what does it matter?"

"She hasn't invited me yet, Nick."

"And what if she is not beautiful, Abdul?"

"Then you can take her out."

Ontee was waiting for us outside the Milles Collines in her cream Peugeot 405. She was, to put it conservatively, a large woman, size 16-plus, or OS as they say in the rag trade. She wore Edna Everage spectacles and Diana Ross hair. Abdul smiled quite sweetly at her, and shook her hand. We both sat in the back seats.

She didn't talk much on the journey to Butare, the old capital of Rwanda, just fifteen kilometres from the Burundi border. Instead Ontee played her cassettes, the Rwandais equivalent of Various Artists Volume 22 with, of course, the back speakers on. I could tell Abdul liked this music the way his hips were dancing on the seat. He was also pretending to like Ontee, tapping me in the ribs and tuning her behind her back. Ontee was no slouch at looking in the mirror and I was certain she had spotted his strange hand movements, though whether she interpreted them correctly, I could not tell.

"You know she poisoned her husband," Abdul whispered.

"Go on."

"Yes. One of the taxi drivers told me as we were getting into the car."

"You don't believe it, do you?"

Abdul took a look at her in the mirror, caught her stare, and said, "Yes."

The Ibis Hotel is the hub of Butare social life. At least it was that lunch-time. We sat in the sun on the hotel terrace, sipping Primus, and talking to two girls who had joined our table. Ontee had gone off to find the contact. She had said she would be about an hour and she would bring him back to meet me.

An hour went by; no Ontee. I was practising my French and had learnt the girls were sisters; the elder one, who wore a gold chain with a "G" suspended from it, was called Grace, and was coming to Kigali to see me the next day.

Ontee returned, by herself. The meeting was off?

"No," smiled Ontee, motioning me towards the Peugeot, with a degree of unconcealed impatience that frogmarched her late and unfortunate husband into the front of my mind.

We drove, Ontee and me, down Butare's main street, turned right, and pulled in at La Perle Hotel, a small establishment on the edge of the main town. Ontee parked the Peugeot and strode into the hotel, through the dining room, and halted outside a door marked "Privat". She waved me onwards, and turned on her size nines and marched off as quickly as her bulk could manage.

I push open the door. Inside, sitting at the head of an oval polished pine table, is an army officer. He has a Trevor McDonald moustache and is an instructor in the military school at Butare.

He tells me that he wants to be paid for the information he is about to divulge. I have no choice. I hand over 3,000 francs. He wants more. I say he can have the rest, another 3,000, after he has finished. He agrees.

He recalls the time in 1986 when he worked for the chief of staff in Kigali. There was talk there had been a plot to kill Dian Fossey. She was believed to have known who was behind the trafficking of gorillas. The plotters implicated the prefect. He certainly knew who had committed the murder. I ask the officer if he knows the names of the plotters. His lips start to catch flies. I ask who named the prefect. More flies are being caught. Some are being masticated. One hand has vanished into his armpit.

Two *brochettes* arrive, metal skewers the length of an arm, spearing tough gob-sized chews of lamb. "Trevor" takes his skewer in both hands and plays it as if it were a harmonica.

What does he know about the prefect, about Zed?

"*Chomp, chomp, slipp* . . . not much. I know that *chomp* a judge in Kigali *chomp* who wanted to be an MP *chomp* owes his job to Zed."

"How?"

"Zed wanted his wife in return for his influence." He has finished the *brochette*. The skewer has been picked as clean as any starved vulture could have managed. Now "Trevor"'s finger is probing inside his mouth. Bits of lamb are being retrieved from inside and smeared on to the table top. I pass him a toothpick.

"What was this judge's name?"

"Fidel Ntuyenabo."

At least that was something, perhaps the only fact that "Trevor" had come up with. The rest would have to be checked as much as it could be.

I leave the room, but at the door "Trevor" asks for the rest of the money. I shake my head. I tell him that he can have the balance, and more, when he comes up with hard fact.

Ontee is waiting in the Peugeot. She drives out of La Perle, turns right, away from the Hotel Ibis, and takes the road that leads out of town. After a kilometre, she reaches the perimeter of town. I can see soldiers. This is the way to the barracks. She's going to the barracks! But she pulls up a couple of hundred metres from the gate and drops "Trevor". Ontee waves to him, slews the car around, and heads back to the Ibis. So much for secrecy.

* * *

That evening I went to see the Minister of Justice. I had fixed an appointment with him through a contact I had made in Brussels, and I had called the minister as soon as I had arrived in Kigali.

It was a big square office sitting at the top of four flights of stairs in a south London-style high-rise block that had been built near the airport. The lifts were not working. The minister, John Smith cast in ebony, rose from his aircraft-carrier desk to greet me. He was wearing an immaculate grey-blue pinstripe, with a brown spotted tie and matching handkerchief that had been stuffed, with a certain amount of deliberation, into the breast pocket. His button-down shirt was white with a double pale blue stripe. The polished black slip-ons had silver buckles. It might not be Gucci, but the ensemble was certainly Brussels.

The minister was not, I had been told, a government man, a presidential appointment. Now that multi-party democracy had been initiated in the country and because the war had been going badly for the President, efforts had been made to find a settlement with the rebels. The President had given ground and allowed the opposition into the cabinet. The Minister of Justice was in the opposition party. He might be frank.

He smiled when he saw that I was out of breath. He murmured something about the elevator and then sat in the World of Leather armchair that faced away from his desk. He pointed me into its big sister sofa. I was marooned under the dim lighting in soft leather. Outside it was raining and dark and a solitary mosquito floated around the room.

I asked him if he was entirely satisfied with the case.

"It is," he said, taking off his glasses, "very difficult for me to make a judgment because I am new in this job. The case was finished years ago."

I told him that I had learnt that certain of the suspects had been tortured and that there was a lot of talk that threw doubt upon the verdict.

"I am not aware of people being tortured," he said. "I heard about the death of someone in prison. Whether or not he was assassinated, I do not know. But," he said, "if there was evidence of irregularities occurring in the investigation of the case, then, certainly, I would reopen the case."

"Is it possible to reopen the case politically?"

The minister was circumspect. He paused, rearranged his glasses, and said, "Politically, that remains to be seen."

I told him that I had heard a lot of stories linking the murder to prominent people, especially to one man.

The minister did not smile. If he knew anything, he was not surrendering it. Eventually, he said, "I learnt that she had problems with poachers and gorilla traffickers."

I said nothing.

"There is," he said, "a second story."

"About?"

"About gold smuggling in the Virungas. I heard about the gold story back in 1985 and 1986. I was told that Miss Fossey intercepted one or two gold smugglers who were carrying details of the trade between Zaire and Rwanda. These smugglers were said to be working for big men in her area. She was said to be threatening to expose those men and their trade."

So the minister had heard the story at least six years before I stumbled across it and pieced it together. Now we were getting somewhere.

"Who told you?"

"An army officer. I will try and remember his name."

"Could you put me in touch with him?"

"I'll try."

"What about the visa?" I began to tell the minister how Dian was granted a two-year visa after being limited to a three-month one for so many years.

He leaned towards me. "Legally," he said, "I do not see why she was given so short a time when everyone here knew she was working for the interests of Rwanda for so many years."

"Has this, the two-year visa, anything to do with the murder?"

"At first sight," said the minister, "no. But in a way the man could have delivered the visa so as not to be suspected of putting any obstacles in her way."

Jacques had said almost the same. They tried to seduce her, he had said. Tried to win her over.

The minister's room was neat, and ordered, like the man who controlled it. The light green walls (I suspected this was a uniform government colour) were bare except for a primitive painting to his right. It was a tapestry showing village children dressed in white going to their first communion. Beneath it, on a shelf, was a fax.

There was a clock, a calendar, a steel grey filing cabinet, a Rwandan flag, and, of course, a picture of the President.

"There was something else I heard. Something we were discussing at the time of the murder, or shortly afterwards," he said. "Miss Fossey had learnt that Zed and Colonel Rwangasore had captured a young ape. She was going to denounce them if they did not return it. She was going to tell what she knew about their involvement in gold smuggling. The officer told me this, the officer I mentioned before. I will try and find him for you."

I hadn't mentioned Zed once during this interview at all. I was nervous about using his name because I didn't know who was trustworthy and who wasn't. Now I badly needed the name of that officer, the minister's source.

Back at the Milles Collines, Grace, the girl with the letter "G" around her neck, the girl I had talked to at the Ibis in Butare, was waiting for me. Abdul had arranged to take Ontee for dinner and said he would return to the hotel at 9.30 to pick me up.

"What for?"

"Oh, you want to spend the night with the lovely Grace?" Abdul pronounced it Grass.

"No."

"Good, then I will eat with Ontee and then she has arranged to take us back to her place."

"What for?"

"A party. At Ontee's."

I took Grace to the fourth-floor bar, the posh one, for a drink. We shared a Primus. This was hard going. She said that she wanted to eat. I asked the waiter for the menu and he said he would fix a table in the next-door restaurant that looked out over Kigali.

"No," said Grace.

"You are not hungry?"

"Yes, but I prefer to eat in your hut," she said, underscoring her intentions with a peck on my cheek.

Nine thirty was a long time coming.

We sat together in my room, on the balcony, beyond the mosquito net and its supporting ropework. She told me that she wanted to leave Rwanda, come to Europe. She was twenty-eight, and had been married for two years. Now she was single. I asked why.

"My husband changed the day we were married. He beat me for a year."

"What changed him, Grace?"

"Prison. We are," she said, smiling at me, "now divorced."

I never did learn what crime, if any, this man had committed. Actually my mind was concentrating on the clock and hoping that Abdul would not be delayed with Ontee. What if she were to poison him? Maybe, I thought, I should get some *sumu* myself.

While we waited for room service, Grace went to the toilet and then lay on Abdul's bed, adopting what she considered to be a provocative pose. I stayed where I was on the balcony. There was a knock on the door. Poison was no longer necessary; the food had arrived.

Ontee's house was a large bungalow near the football stadium, the place Kigali people call "Little Chile" or "Pinochet's Palace". This was where the opponents of the regime had been herded just before the onset of the war, and kept without food or clothing or water for days while they were being interrogated. Every dictatorial regime needs a soccer stadium.

Inside Ontee's I was surprised to see a picture of the President. He was smiling benignly at us guests. There was Grace, yes, she was still with me, Ontee, a soldier friend of Ontee's, and Theo. And, of course, Abdul. Theo came over to me and asked me to translate the Phil Collins song that was playing. "I have difficulty with his English," he said, but how do you translate into French someone clearing his throat? I shook my head.

Abdul insisted I dance with Ontee. He whispered, as he drank the Johnnie Walker Red Label that she had poured for him, that Ontee was a mover, a queen of disco, despite her weight. "She's like a hippo, man. I should know," he said. "I was runner-up in the All-Kenya Disco Dancing Championship in 1978."

I didn't know this before. Certainly, Abdul was a constantly contradictory man, capable of crudeness and kindness, and having seen him perform on the floor of the Florida 2000 and in Kigali Nights, I would not have judged him as being Travolta-ish. As for his opinion of Ontee as a muse, I have never been that close to a hippo, so I couldn't really compare, but Ontee certainly did a lot of damage in her living room that night. It was when the music changed tempo, from Phil Collins to French West Indian pop that

Ontee lost control. Her arms flailed above her head, almost scraping the plaster off the ceiling, the parquet floor trembled, and I retired hurt.

"Sierra ... Tango ... India ... November ... Kilo ... Yankee ..." said Abdul, quite deliberately.

"Copy." I didn't know whether he or the Red Label was talking. I stared at him.

"Nick! The Sudan," he whispered. "Remember when I was Alpha Papa and you were November Golf."

These were our call signs on the convoy. Alpha for Abdul, Papa for Perera, November for Nick, and so on.

"Copy," I said.

So what was this Sierra Tango thing he was saying?

While I was fuddling through his code, the soldier, Ontee's guest, began to look quite intently at the pair of us. He was fingering, as he lounged in Ontee's large settee, a two-way radio. He didn't look at all happy, despite the copious amounts of Scotch that he had put away.

"You know army code, then?" he said finally.

I hoped he hadn't worked out what I had just worked out, that Abdul was describing Ontee's armpits, or who the call signs were aimed at.

"Yes," said Abdul, casually, "we always talk like this when we have had a few drinks. We worked for the UN and this is their language."

"And mine," said the officer.

It was curfew time, approaching 1.00 a.m., and Ontee was begging us to stay. So, too, was Grace. The army officer friend did not encourage us. He said he would drop us back at the Milles Collines. We left.

Abdul did solve one of life's more enduring mysteries that night. It wasn't the Fossey murder. This enigma had baffled man not for seven years, but for centuries; Abdul discovered where mosquitoes go in the daytime.

Before we had left the hotel for Ontee's he had been busy, bending under the beds and peering in the dark recesses of the cupboards, anywhere inside the room, in fact, where the shadows had won a battle with natural light. This inspection was followed by a blast of Doom, until a cloud of gas had enveloped the room.

I had been doubtful about the efficacy of his plan. It was too simple. Why hadn't man thought of it before?

"No, no," he had said, "you wait and see." Blast, blast. "Oh, yes, Nick, they sleep down there, in the dark. Now they are waking up and they'll be," blast, blast, "hungry." Blast, blast.

I did look under the beds and in the cupboards that night when we returned to the Milles Collines. It was true. The body count amounted to half a dozen.

If only the Fossey case had proved so simple.

Kigali: July 1992

ALPHONSE Nkubito was sitting opposite me at breakfast. He had ordered a plate of scrambled eggs and they had turned up fried. We sent them back. While he waited for the kitchen to get his order right, he discussed the death of Emmanuel Rwelekana. He sipped his coffee and said, "What no one at the time could understand, and remember we were all lawyers together who were talking this case through, was that if Rwelekana had committed the murder, then why on earth didn't he denounce the American, McGuire? It could have been a possible way out for him. And why was he brought to Kigali, to the Gikondo, when the man in charge of the file was the Procureur of Ruhengeri?"

Alphonse was a former Procureur Général of the Kigali Court of Appeal, and as an examining magistrate had valuable experience in investigations. He was a friend of the Minister of Justice, too, and this had swayed his decison about whether or not it would be wise to meet me.

I asked him who had voiced concern about the handling of the case.

"Judges, lawyers, politicians. It was the talk of any intelligent person in Kigali." He paused. "Private talk."

"So who was the man who was killed in the Gikondo, or died in the Gikondo?" I asked Alphonse.

"Rwelekana."

"When did he die?"

"Within two weeks of the murder of Miss Fossey."

Abdul passed him the transcript of the court judgment.

He peered at it. "Yes."

"It says here that Rwelekana committed suicide on August 8 1986, and you're saying he died within two weeks of the murder of Dian, so you're saying he died in January 1986," said Abdul.

Alphonse looked confused. I felt confused. Abdul tried again.

"Have you heard of a man called Magayani?"

"No."

"You see, Alphonse," I said, "I have been told another man, a second man if you like, was arrested within two days of the murder, taken to the Gikondo, interrogated, and was found hanged in his cell."

The waiter had returned. In front of Alphonse, he flourished a saucer, containing two boiled eggs, and set it down on the table.

Abdul went mad. "Don't you know your eggs in this country?" he shouted. "Bring scrambled eggs." He made a beating motion to the waiter, who, I am sure, believed that it was he and not the eggs that were going to be treated so brutally.

"There might be a problem," Alphonse said.

"Not now," said Abdul. "He has the message."

"What problem?" I said to Alphonse, ignoring Abdul.

"The problem of involvement of other people. High-up people."

"The Akazu?"

Alphonse poured himself another cup of coffee. He had ignored my question. "You have to understand the Rwandais," he said, adding milk. "We are not what we seem. When the first President was killed, they erected a statue to him. You can see it at the airport. They honoured him, and these were the same people who had assassinated him."

"So what has that got to do with Dian?"

"Have you heard of the International Gorilla Fair?"

I nodded. It had taken place in Kigali, at the soccer stadium in the summer of 1990 and I knew it had turned out a fiasco. Not only that, the FBI had investigated the financing of the fair after it had been discovered that hundreds of thousands of dollars had gone missing.

"The President and his son were involved in the Gorilla Fair. It was a scandal and people were saying that it had been organised solely to cover up the killing of Fossey. It's like I said, you get killed in this country, and then you are fêted."

I remembered the small book of poems I had seen in the offices of the ORTPN, the Ministry of Tourism and National Parks. It was called *Une Créature Sans Pareille,* a 1,000 line epic poem, paying homage to the mountain gorilla. Its foreword was dedicated to the memory of Dian Fossey. The author of this stirring work? Jean-Clàude Habyarimana, none other than the President's son.

I also recalled the conversation I had had with one of the party of Americans who had been invited to come to the fair. The first Ann Sargent knew of the fair was the day in the summer of 1990 when she received a phone call inviting her to come to Rwanda and see the gorillas. Ann was involved in an animal humane society in Boston, Massachusetts, and thought that her work with the society had brought her to the attention of the Rwandans. Her name, she believed, had been put forward by a friend who was a consular official in Monaco. She didn't have to pay a penny for the trip. She assumed the Rwandan government was footing the bill.

"The journey was a disaster," she told me. "We gathered in Washington to fly out on a Wednesday. This was August 1990, and we found there was no plane for us. There were twenty of us. That's all. I was asked to drum up some more people. I managed to find another thirty. We waited for two days in Washington at the Grand Hotel. Again the bills were paid. We finally left Washington on the Friday evening. Not for Africa, but for New York. From there we flew to Lille where we bussed to Paris. We spent the Saturday night at the Novotel at Charles de Gaulle airport. By now, there were about sixty-five of us. Finally a Belgian charter, a very old plane, a real boneshaker, took us to Kigali. Mind you, that plane served us the best meal I've ever had in the air.

"When we reached Kigali, we stayed at the Meridien, a super hotel. But we found that only four people would be allowed to go to the Virungas to see the gorillas, and no one would be allowed to go to Karisoke. I went to the stadium and I watched ballets and displays of dancing. We had been promised that major black entertainers would be there, Miriam Makeba, for instance, but no one famous turned up. I believe the President came on the Friday night, and the rest of his family were there on the other nights. Around the stadium were lots of booths manned by Rwandan companies that were sponsoring the exhibition. Oil companies, a soap company, there was a booth that sold malachite and one displaying the first children's books to be translated into Kinyarwanda."

The man behind the fair was a certain Monsieur Barry, a West African who had come to the President's wife, Agathe, with the idea of organising the fair. The aim was to put Rwanda on the world map of conservation, exploit its most precious natural resource, show the world that Rwanda cared for its gorillas, promote tourism, and so demonstrate to the world that this was not just another third-rate Third World country, but one with a sense of justice for all, including its animals.

It all sounded so plausible, and then the Akazu stepped in. First Kigali businessmen were approached and requested to sponsor booths at the venue of the fair, the stadium. They were given little choice. One businessman I spoke to had the courage to refuse. His business interests, he told me, suffered consequently.

Then Barry was given the task of rounding up the guests. America was targeted because it was considered that this was the one area where the Fossey killing had had an enduring and deleterious effect on the credibility of Rwanda's conservation efforts – and America was a vast reservoir of tourist dollars. Promises were made to the guests which, of course, could not be kept. The plane was not available; a makeshift charter aircraft was pulled in at the last minute; the visit to Karisoke was never on, and the stars who were scheduled to appear at the fair were never booked.

Why had the Akazu stepped in? First, to use the fair to defuse any of the debris, potentially still explosive, that clung to the murder of Dian, and second, according to the man who organised the fair, to make a killing on the international drugs market.

Barry alleges that his most fervent supporter among the presidential set was the President's wife, Zed's sister Agathe. Once she was behind the idea, there was never a chance that the fair was not going to happen. It was Agathe, too, who introduced Barry to her other brother Seraphin, and it was Seraphin who suggested to Barry that in addition to Barry transporting the guests from America, he should also import, on the same plane, $1 million worth of cocaine. In return, Barry says that Seraphin, representing the Akazu, would pay him $50,000 for every company which agreed to participate in the fair.

If anything, Rwandans can never be described as being naïve, or unworldly. They are an insular, leery, xenophobic people and they were not in the slightest bit nonplussed when the fair turned out to be not the raging success that had been forecast in the President's official newspaper. Nor were they – even those businessmen of Kigali who had been prevailed upon to contribute $4,000 each to sponsor the fair – at all shocked when the man who had organised it, the President's wife's favourite, Monsieur Barry, turned up in the country, in Kigali itself, and booked into the Meridien Hotel. The least of their surprises came a few days later when the same Monsieur Barry left the country a free man.

Barry, however, says that during his days at the Meridien, he was kept a virtual prisoner, and that the correspondence between himself and the President was taken from him forcibly.

That was the sordid little story of the Gorilla Fair. Whether Barry's allegations about it being used as a cover by the Akazu to bring cocaine into the country are true or not, two things are certain. Many Rwandan businessmen lost money in the venture and a large share of the nationwide raffle that had been organised to fund the fair went missing. There is something else too. The very fact the fair was supported and endorsed by the President's family and then hijacked by his inner circle, the Akazu, led by his wife Agathe and her brothers Seraphin and Zed, illustrates the point that these people were willing to cash in on gorillas, something which Dian Fossey, had she been alive, would have opposed vehemently, and possibly violently.

I realised now that Alphonse had raised the story of the fair quite deliberately. I believed that he wanted to lead me to a signpost that would point me from a murder in Karisoke to an immensely powerful group of people in Kigali, a select and secret cabal who were cynical and greedy and manipulative enough to exploit practically any resources the country had to offer. In this case it was gorillas and tourism. And had Dian been alive, it could never have taken place.

Abdul's threat had clearly motivated the waiter. He got the eggs order right at the third attempt, but by then it was too late. Alphonse had another appointment and had already left.

Kigali: August 1992

THERE ARE seven million bananas in Rwanda and Augustin Nduwayezu exploits every single one of them. Not a sip of banana juice, a glass of banana beer, a demi-sec sniff of banana wine or even a spread of banana jam is consumed in this country without Augustin profiting.

Before he became boss of OVIBAR, Augustin knew the intimate habits of many of those Rwandans who every day would use the by-products of *la banane* to neutralise the miseries of their lives; in his previous life, Augustin had run the country's secret service. He was the chief of the Sûreté, and the "big man" who had granted Dian Fossey her one and only two-year visa.

Despite being warned not to go near him, I had decided that I had to talk to him. I had heard that Augustin was a ruthless operator – the man who had, according to Jacques, become the President's darling after bringing back from Uganda an enemy of the state in a packing crate.

"Do not trust Augustin," I had been warned. "He is charming, he is sociable, but he is a cobra."

The OVIBAR HQ is on the edge of town, a sprawl of warehouses, offices and stills. You know you're on the right road for OVIBAR because you can smell fermenting bananas a hundred metres away. The sweet scent of rotting fruit pervades Augustin's office.

He is a powerful-looking man, nearing six foot. He wears glasses and a dense moustache. He is putting on weight. Possibly there is too much banana beer and not enough stress in this new role for Augustin.

"So you are interested in Dian Fossey. I am very happy to learn that you are interested. The death of Dian Fossey has troubled me for years," he tells me in a rush, leaning towards me, as if he was imparting a confidence.

Am I about to receive a confession? I look over the desk at

Augustin. Now he has rearranged himself, taken control again. Hardly the pose of the penitent.

"She sent me a signed copy of her book. I received it three days after she was murdered. And the words she wrote were whole-hearted words. If I had known you were coming, I would have brought the book here for you to see."

If I had known you were coming . . . What would Augustin have given to be still the head of the *Sûreté*?

I ask him when he first met Dian.

Augustine avoids the question. "We will come to that later. Let me tell how I first heard about her. I was at university in Dakar, studying geography. We were forced to study bio-geography – all about plants and why the world is full of them. I chose Central Africa and my teacher included in the reading list several *National Geographic* articles written by Dian Fossey. Then I learnt about the volcano region of this country and I was surprised that a foreigner was engaged in such deep research and that this was going on here in Rwanda. But it wasn't until 1985 that I first met her.

"The President was inaugurating a commune in Kinigi, the village at the foot of the Virungas. I had to be there with him because I was in charge of his personal security. Afterwards, there was a reception in the Muhabura Hotel, in Ruhengeri, and it was here that I met Dian Fossey. I was then head of the secret service and it was my duty to discover who was who in the hotel. By now the President had left for Kigali by helicopter, but I had to remain behind because a number of government ministers were attending the reception."

"When was this, Augustin?"

He can't remember. He says it was not long before she was killed. He is writing figures on the pad of paper in front of him. I crane around to read what he has written. It says: 26:12:85 – The date of the murder of Dian Fossey.

"I went over to greet Miss Fossey," Augustin rambles on. "I said I knew her from her articles in the *National Geographic*. As usual, I asked her if she had discovered new things."

"Why as usual? You had never met before."

Augustin swats away the interruption. He was not used to being interrogated, this one-time super spook turned General Banana. "She said she had difficulties. She said she felt threatened because she had no visa. I told her that if she had problems she should go to the immigration people. I didn't see it was at all inconvenient to extend her a visa for two years. I knew the President was supporting her work in the Virungas. I knew we had a policy to encourage foreigners not just to work here, but to retire here. I knew that this was their real home and that they were not used to living anywhere else. Besides if we encouraged people like her to stay in Rwanda, it would attract younger people. Especially if they knew that they would not be kicked out at the end of their contracts."

"Do you think there was a connection between you granting her the visa for two years and her murder?"

"I know I did the right thing," declares Augustin. "You see, I had a personal motive. She had helped me get my degree, inspired me I should say, and she had spent eighteen years here helping this country, so there was no reason for me to refuse to help her."

Augustin would have performed well sitting next to John Major in the Commons. "Ten days later, she died. I was personally touched. I had had the chance to speak to her and she had sent her book with the dedication."

I ask him again about the visa and the murder.

"I think she had many enemies. I was told that after her death, her radio cassette, her camera, her clothes and three firearms were found in her house. They had not been stolen. Now if a poacher, a black poacher, had killed her, then this man would have taken those things. No black poacher would leave a radio or a camera or a gun. And why would he leave her clothes? All these things are valuable. So I rule out the black poacher theory. I think the man who killed her was well off enough not to want these things of hers."

"If you were so taken with Dian, why didn't you personally take charge of the case?"

Augustin shakes his head, so violently that I think it might fall off his neck. "It was impossible."

"Why? You were head of the Sûreté. You could surely do as you like?"

"True. But I dealt with secret cases. The kind of thing the public did not know about. This was an event. Everyone knew about her murder. This was an 'open case'. And, anyway, if I had interfered, then I might have been accused of putting political pressure on to the investigation."

It didn't ring true. I am certain accusations such as these had not deterred Augustin in the past.

"What about the hair samples, Augustin?"

"I gave the hair samples to the French lab and to the American Embassy."

"Are you sure?"

He nods, but he is lying. Kathleen Austin had told me, categorically, that she had taken the hair samples from Dian, brought them to the embassy and despatched them to the FBI in Washington. She had added that the Sûreté had asked her for the samples and she had given them some hairs to send to Paris.

"But you said that you had nothing to do with the investigation. So why were you involved at this stage with the hair samples?"

Augustin smiles. "You see, I was in Washington for a meeting of Interpol in September 1985. So I knew the Director of the FBI. That's why I sent the samples."

"What about the results?"

"We got them from Paris, but we got nothing back from Washington."

Because he never sent the hair samples to Washington. "Didn't that strike you as odd?"

"What?"

"That the Americans never replied to you, never gave you the results."

Augustin is floundering. He neatly sidesteps the question and says; "There was something that did surprise me. One of the three weapons that was found in the hut belonged to the CIA."

"How do you know that?"

"Because the gun had CIA on it. I have seen the gun. It had 'CIA' written on the butt of the revolver, on the side."

"So, now the CIA writes its name on its weapons before giving them out! I expect the KGB do the same."

"Don't laugh, Mr Gordon. I am serious. When the CIA asked for the return of the gun, I gave it back to them personally."

"Who did you give it to?"

Augustin smiles. "I can't tell you that. Someone at the US Embassy."

"Why don't you try and get this man McGuire back here to serve his sentence?"

"There is an extradition warrant out for him."

"There isn't. I checked with Interpol."

Augustin throws his head back and laughs. "We applied for a warrant and if it hasn't arrived, then it has disappeared. Rwanda has no interest not to get this man back."

And Augustin, I know, has tried-and-tested ways, his own methods, of recovering "lost property".

"Why did you allow McGuire to leave the country?"

"We didn't. Maybe he was put in a diplomatic car and we could not handle the people in it."

"He wasn't," I say, "and, anyway, McGuire had no diplomatic status. It's very curious, but here you have a man you suspect is a killer, and you do not have him under surveillance."

"He was a foreigner. We don't like disturbing foreigners, especially Americans."

"But, Augustin, you just said so yourself, that people in your country had not been helpful to Fossey. You helped her, but you were the exception. And she was foreign and American."

"Would you like a copy of my book?" asks Augustin. Before I have time to accept, he is up out of his chair and has wrenched from a bookshelf on the window-sill one of a half-dozen copies of a light brown paperback. He is signing it for me. "It is," he says, passing it to me, "a history of the troubles between the Hutu and Tutsi. Now, let me take you on a tour of the factory."

"A thousand thank yous for your visit. Your fraternal friend, Augustin," says the inscription.

I pretend my stomach is playing up when we reach the end of the banana production line and it is time to sample the OVIBAR range of products in the laboratory. I have to avoid taking a drink from Augustin. But when I see we are going to share the same bottle and realise that even Augustin would not be so stupid as to attempt to poison me on his home ground, I begin to regret my timidity. The Cuvée Spéciale des Milles Collines, a *demi-sec vin de bananes,* tempts me, as does the Liqueur de Bananes which Augustin is swallowing with an amount of relish and pride in the product. He has gone through the banana card. First the *jus,* then the milky brown Indakamirwa, a sort of beer, and now he is draining another glass of liqueur. There is only the *confiture de bananes* to taste, and I suspect, rightly, the jar containing it will not be opened.

* * *

Back at the Milles Collines a fax is waiting for me. There is a note attached to it. From Augustin. He has sent me the dedication Fossey wrote in that spindly copperplate which only Americans still contrive with their pens. Her message was sincere and concise:

> With deep gratitude and appreciation to you for your kindness in allowing me to continue my work – research and conservation of the Mountain Gorillas of Rwanda. Please know you are always welcomed to Karisoke and the gorillas of Rwanda.
> Sincerely,
> Dian Fossey
> Dec 6, 1985

Overleaf, she had written: "I remain ever so grateful to you Monsieur Nduwayezu." And she signed her name a second time.

Twenty days later, she was dead.

I had survived Augustin. I had nothing to lose now. I would go for Zed.

Kigali: August 1992

KIGALI may be a village, but it wasn't easy finding Zed. People were not reluctant to talk about him, once they were sure of me, but when I asked for hard fact, where he lived, for instance, the conversation, the accusations, the comments on his florid lifestyle, dried up. This was where fear stepped in, where gossip in city restaurants or nightclubs was replaced by caution.

Even so I had managed to piece together a picture of the man I was seeking. Zed has two flaws in his character, two weaknesses, if you like: money and sex.

He is a tall, handsome man, between forty-five and fifty. He is a charmer, polite, well-groomed in his selection of K-suits, a man who makes women feel important. He likes the feel of gold on his body. He wears two large expensive rings. He doesn't drink much and he doesn't frequent the more raucous of the city's nightspots like Kigali Nights and Chez Lando. Zed prefers to entertain in the placid and sophisticated surrounds of the fourth-floor bar and restaurant of the Milles Collines, or in a private suite he rents at another Kigali hotel, the Rugiro. He has been married twice, has one child, a boy, and runs five mistresses, which, of course, costs money. Three of the girls live in the Ruhengeri area where he was raised, and two live in Kigali.

He was born in Gisenye. His parents were business people who sold food – beans, sorghum. His father was reasonably successful. He ran a car. Zed was not a particularly bright pupil. He left high school after four years and did not go on to university. Instead he trained as a teacher, and he might well have stayed in education had his sister, Agathe, not married the man who was to become the President. It was then that Zed emerged from the shadows. He was appointed the prefect of Ruhengeri, despite the fact that he had no practical qualifications for the post other than perhaps the one that was most important: he was related, through his sister's marriage, to the most powerful man in the country. Nepotism had paid off for Zed, and he repaid the President by setting out to make the family into the most powerful in the land. Not the President's family, of course, but his own, Zed's family.

Soon his brothers, Seraphin and Sagatwa, were found jobs in the government which gave them access to the secret world of Rwanda. Being close to power in Africa opens lots of doors and Zed was a man who was never shy of knocking on them. If he found that the door was bolted, then he had the means and strength to make a forced entry.

As prefect, he was not a popular man. He abused his position like a man abuses a stolen cheque-book. To this day a sum approaching twenty million Rwandan francs that went missing from the prefecture fund has not been accounted for, and allegedly he augmented his salary unconventionally. Zed would intervene on behalf of a constituent, so if a man was having trouble with any particular arm of government, he knew that he could always go to Zed and, for a price, Zed would smooth things over. Sometimes money did not change hands; sometimes Zed would exact the payment in flesh; sometimes the price was a beautiful wife.

But all this bribery, or rather, all this interceding on behalf of his constituents, was petty money where Zed was concerned. He was leading an extravagant lifestyle and the women in his life were making extraordinary demands on him. Zed could cope sexually, but he required money, lots of it, to finance his compulsions. He needed a coup. And he realised he was in a position to pull one off. Through his sister Agathe, he had the President's ear; his brother Sagatwa had been placed in an influential role in the intelligence services; and his other brother Seraphin had found a niche in the Central Bank. The *réseau*, the network, now existed. All Zed had to do was exploit it.

Rwanda is a land-locked country. Everything that is exported has to leave the country by road or by air, but mostly by road. Likewise, any commodity coming into Rwanda has to be trucked across the border. Customs duties are exorbitant. So are import taxes. Here was another open cheque-book. Cigarettes, beer, coffee, tea, currency, weapons, drugs, especially *urumogi* or Indian hemp, gold, diamonds and wolfram were the raw materials that Zed dealt in. Trafficking was to make Zed not only a very rich man, but an extraordinarily powerful figure in the country. That was apparent. What was still as misty was his connection with the gorillas and Dian. Where was the evidence?

For sure, something had halted Zed's rise; something had happened after the Fossey killing. For some reason, Zed was no longer the President's favourite; he was punished. The President removed him from the prefecture. He was banished abroad – to Canada, where this up-to-now reluctant pupil suddenly discovered the joys of higher education. He lost his local power base; but not his position of influence in the country – far from it. The Fossey case was a temporary bleep on the graph. Zed knew that he was in a position of strength, despite his current disgrace. Zed knew what the President knew. He was an immovable, albeit less visible, force in Rwanda. He had briefly emerged from the shadows, and now he was about to return to them.

He began to concentrate on business deals in Canada. Zed had established a lucrative business link in the Montreal area where he bought land and built himself a large house set in its own estate, complete with Tutsi caretaker. But as the opposition to the President's regime grew back at home, and with the outbreak of the civil war, the President decided that he needed to utilise Zed's undoubted and proven abilities. He was recalled and given a brief to destabilise the country.

The war had forced this on the President. Now that the FPR had formed a well-equipped and highly undisciplined army capable of taking and looting Ruhengeri, and now that the balance of world politics had shifted away from the Cold War, the President had been forced to make concessions. Multi-party politics were allowed, a semblance of democracy took root in the country, and newspapers, most of them critical of the regime, started to flourish. Opposition politicians were given cabinet portfolios, not the crucial posts like Minister of the Interior or Defence, but even so, it appeared that there was no way that this President was going to be able to stifle the spirit of reform that he had nurtured, much against his will, in Rwanda.

Perhaps Zed could help him regain the balance, defuse this time-bomb primed with the dangerous seeds of democracy. Zed relished the task. There was plenty of material to work on – disaffected soldiers, demobbed after the peace negotiations had been set in motion, were looking for a role. There was an abundance of surplus arms and explosives cached around the country. And there was a target. Kigali began to experience a series of terrorist attacks, bomb blasts, grenade attacks, casual shootings. And who was blamed? The FPR, of course! How could these rebels be serious about peace when they were busy killing innocent people in Kigali?

As Zed's influence inside the presidential palace, nowadays a sealed-off no-go area on the upper-class slopes of the city, grew, so his unpopularity increased on the streets of Kigali. He was being blamed for many of the country's evils. Unemployment, inflation, extortion and murder. And it wasn't as if he hadn't realised how deep the hostility against him ran.

He was changing his address three times a day, using safe houses, sleeping somewhere different each night. He was even using three cars each day. He was a frightened man.

This was what they were saying about Zed in Kigali. And I had to find him.

How was I going to start when a) I didn't know where he lived and b) each of my sources was warning me not even to think about looking for him.

I began with the women. One of Zed's women, Emma, I was told, lived near the soccer stadium, around the corner, in fact, from Ontee's house.

Abdul is waiting for me in a taxi. We drive past Ontee's to the edge of the city. The car leaves the tarmac and splashes through potholes filled up with last night's rain along a bumpy red mud road. The driver stops alongside a concrete grey wall whose top is spiked with barbed wire. All we need now is a Doberman. I bang on the stout red iron gate. No answer. Then a doorman comes. He doesn't open up. He shouts across the wall. I ask for Emma. Try next door. The wrong house. Emma's gate is blue. Iron, but corrugated. I pummel the gate. It opens a fraction. I look through the crack into the courtyard. A plump woman, maybe in her twenties, is standing at the gate, holding the edge. Behind I can see a couple of children. Are they Zed's? I ask the girl if Emma is home. She shakes her head. I decide to leave a note, with my hotel room number. As I turn to go back to the taxi, a girl with braided hair, Kigali Nights-style, a white tee-shirt hanging out over long khaki shorts, immaculately creased, comes to the gate.

"Emma?" It's a guess.

"Who are you?"

"I am looking for Zed."

"He's not here."

If this was night and Kigali Nights, Emma would be all over me, nudging herself on to my body, but it's 3.00 p.m. and Emma is as nervous of me as I am of her.

"Where is Zed?"

"Not here."

"Can I leave him a note?"

She nods. I finish the scrawl I had begun before she walked into my life. So much for finding Zed.

Next, I tried his wife. She worked in an office next to Rwanda Airlines, just opposite the presidential palace. She'd gone home. The office was locked.

Two blanks and already I'd run out of women. The other mistresses could have been anywhere in Kigali or Ruhengeri for that matter. I suggested to Abdul we go back to the hotel, give up for the day.

"Wait a minute, Nick. I've got the phone number of an Indian in Kigali. It's worth a try. He's in business and he might know Zed." He told me he had been given the number when he had booked the air tickets to Kigali and he had forgotten about it until now. I let him phone.

"Well?"

"No more mistresses, but this guy said to go and see a businessman, an Arab, who might know Zed."

We went. Not to the right place, of course, not to the Arab Abdul was talking about. But it didn't matter. It was one of those strokes of good fortune which brought us nearer to our quarry.

Kigali: August 1992

NURILDEEN had just dissolved his business partnership with Zed. Nurildeen was a rich man. His house, perched on one of Kigali's hillsides, beamed down on the poor of the city. We were sitting in the large living room which was furnished wall-to-wall with leather settees, each of them capable of seating an elephant.

"We hate Zed," Nurildeen said simply and quite finally. "He tried to take us over. Now we have had to pay him thousands of francs just to get rid of him."

Nurildeen's business included soft drink distribution in Rwanda plus a great deal of import-export. The little Arab with the Chaplin moustache straightened his jellaba and looked at his watch. It was Thursday evening and he was anxious that he was not late for the mosque.

He explained that the partnership with Zed had gone sour when the company accountant was gunned down while watching TV in his home. Thirteen men who were either military or dressed as soldiers burst into the house. But this was not the only time violent death had touched Nurildeen and the company. Only a few weeks before our meeting, a cousin had been killed in a grenade attack. Two men had broken into his house and while he was raising the alarm, one of the intruders had pulled the pin out of the grenade he was armed with and hurled it at the cousin. He died instantly.

"We rushed to our cousin's house," said Nurildeen's son, Hamoud, "and we were there within five minutes of the attack. But it was too late. By the time we got back to the house, Zed was on the telephone, commiserating about the murder."

"How soon afterwards did he call?"

Hamoud looked at his father, as if seeking confirmation. "Maybe, no more than fifteen minutes."

His father cleared his throat. For a moment I feared he was about to spit on the floor. "It's very strange, this phone call. I mean fifteen minutes. How could he have known about the murder? Not even all the relatives had been told then."

"So how did he know?"

"He said that he had heard it from a friend of his in Burundi. He was speaking on the telephone to this man and the man was listening to the radio and the news came over the Burundi radio."

"Do you believe that?"

The old man shook his head.

"For the radio station in Burundi to have that news, including the name of our cousin, and broadcast it within fifteen minutes of the murder. Think about it. It is impossible," said Hamoud.

The old man, his father, was still shaking his head. "We have relatives in Bujumbura, in Burundi, and they didn't know until we told them," he said. "And that was after Zed's phone call."

"So why do you think Zed called?"

"It was a warning."

"Aren't you frightened?"

"We can look after ourselves. There are plenty of us," said Nurildeen, looking at each of his sons. There was one son to one settee.

"Why was Zed warning you?"

"He wanted to take over my company," said the old man. "We refused. At first, at board meetings, he was charming. He would talk very nicely, but if he didn't agree, if things were not going his way, then he would change almost immediately."

"I've seen him lose his temper the way my father is saying," said Hamoud. "He didn't become violent in his speech or his actions. I mean he wouldn't thump the table or anything. He just went very quiet, and cold, and he'd walk out of the meeting."

"Why," I asked, "did you ever decide to go into business with him? You must have known that he was a dangerous man."

"My father wanted to use him. Use his contacts. But he is a dangerous man. He will eat you and take out your eyes."

"So where is he now?"

"Not in Kigali," said the son.

"In Ruhengeri?"

"No, he's in Canada. In Montreal. We received a fax from him this morning. He's agreed to the deal we put to him. Now he is no longer our partner."

So Zed was in Canada. I didn't know whether to laugh or cry.

I checked out of the Milles Collines the next morning. There was now no point in staying in Rwanda any longer. I had come to find a killer, and the man most likely to have organised that killing was thousands of miles from Kigali. Abdul had agreed that we should go. He had had his fill of Rwanda. He had been entertaining vague ideas of setting up in business here, but what he had heard the night before in Nurildeen's house had made him change his mind.

"Not even one more evening at Ontee's could persuade me to stay," he said, as Zo-Zo stacked our bags into the hotel's combi.

"You are leaving then?" said a voice behind us.

"What are you doing here, Charles?" I asked. "I thought you would be in court this morning."

"No, my appeal has been postponed. My counsel is on holiday."

"Not your sort of holiday?" asked Abdul.

"No. Just holiday this time." Lawyers, it appeared, were as dilatory in Rwanda as they were in the Temple. "I have come to see you, Nick," he said. "The minister suggested it."

"Minister?"

"Yes, he did not know that we had already talked."

I realised now that it was Charles who had given the Minister of Justice the information about gold and gorillas. Sources were now turning in a tight circle.

"You have time to talk?"

"We'll make time," I said, drawing Charles away from the front doors of the hotel and making for the seats by the picture windows that looked down on the empty pool.

"Zed knows all the details of the story, the murder. It is a *magouille*. An organisation."

"The Akazu?"

"Yes, but this *magouille* is inside the Akazu. They call it 'Réseau Zéro'. Network Zero. There are fifteen men inside this country whose sole purpose is to hang on to power. Zed is a leading member. So are his brothers."

"And the President?"

Charles looked around the foyer. "And the President." He paused and took a cigarette from me. He had never accepted one before. "There is a human rights delegation about to come here from Europe. I will be seeing them. They will return to Europe with full details of Réseau Zéro."

"What did you tell the minister about gold and gorillas, Charles?"

"I told him what I knew. I told him that the trade was going on, both trades. Do you know Zed was even trading in sleepers at the time?"

"Sleepers?" Was it drugs he was talking about?

"Railway beams. Sleepers. He was using his agents in Zaire to bring all sorts of stuff into the country. He was working with a man called Colonel Karangwa. Karangwa is now chief of the gendarmerie, but then he was the head of the operational unit at Ruhengeri. He was to the paramilitary what the prefect was to the civil authorities. Zed could do nothing without him. Their roles complemented one another."

"So could Karangwa, or his men, have been involved in trafficking?"

"Certainly."

"And do you recall an infant gorilla being kidnapped from Uganda at this time, and . . ."

"And," said Charles, "there was a shoot-out inside Rwanda and the Rwandan who was picking up the gorilla was killed."

"Exactly."

"The man in charge of the gendarmerie was Karangwa."

"So why did he have the man killed?"

"Maybe this man was double-crossing him, or Zed."

"And you told this to the minister?"

"Yes."

"Why?"

"Because I was there at this time. I could have got involved with these people, but I didn't like what they were doing."

"You know Zed is not in Rwanda?"

"No. I assume that is why you are leaving. Are you coming back?"

"I shall."

"Good, I will find out what I can for you."

We shook hands, Charles and I. I wondered whether I would see him again. If he lost his appeal, he would almost certainly be sent back to the Gikondo.

Kigali: November 1992

"TAXI?"

"Fuck taxi!" said Abdul.

"Change?"

"Fuck change!" said Abdul.

"Girl?"

"Fuck girl!" said Abdul.

We had just emerged into the freshness of the Rwandan morning from the foyer of Les Milles Collines. Last night's downpour had left its marks on the car park. There were brown puddles of water to negotiate besides the toutings of the taxi drivers. Thierry, who had driven us to Karisoke in July, had spotted us first and it was he who was tendering the three services he guessed we might want. What he didn't know was that this time we had come to Rwanda with our own transport. It was a dirty white Peugeot 504 estate, with bald tyres and window winders that creaked on their ratchets. There were no handles on the doors, so getting in and out was rather a slow process. But once you contrived to prise open the doors and close them, and as soon as the engine fired, the car moved. Abdul was delighted. Now he had independence, now he had a project he could work on, now he would restore this car as well as he could, now he could flaunt his superiority over the taxi touts of Kigali.

We had returned to Rwanda to continue the investigation. We had heard that Zed was back in the country and we were here to find him. In the time we had been away, a Belgian human rights group had revealed the existence in Rwanda of a secret organisation called Réseau Zéro. There had been a press conference in Brussels where the methods and the members of the Réseau had been revealed. The Réseau ran the death squads in the country. The Réseau was behind the removal of those who opposed the regime – the Réseau was called Zéro because its prime motivator had a name that began with Z. The Réseau was the creature of Zed.

I had been warned by the human rights people that it would be dangerous, possibly foolish, for me to return to Rwanda once the news of the existence of the Réseau had been made public, but I decided to come because I felt that now the fact that death squads were at work in Rwanda was known and that the man behind them was Zed, perhaps the publicity might force him to defend himself, to emerge from the shadows, to come into the open. Anyway, Réseau or not, I had to follow the Fossey trail, and that trail was leading me inexorably to Zed.

Colonel Charles was still alive. He was waiting for me, dressed in his short-sleeved, pale blue K-suit, in the garden of Chez Lando, a hotel-cum-nightclub which served the best *poulet grillé avec frites* I had eaten in Kigali. As Abdul and I walked in, we could see Charles waiting for us, sitting in the shade of one of the eating booths that edged the garden. He had taken off his glasses and was polishing them on his handkerchief. He saw us, wiped his eyes with the handkerchief and replaced the spectacles.

"You're still here, then," Abdul said.

"Yes."

We sat down and waited for the waitress to take our orders. A bottle of Mutzig beer for Charles, Primus for Abdul and me, and chicken, of course, all round.

"But I am a lucky man."

"What happened?" I asked.

"There have been two attempts on my life. I am not worried about myself. It is my family I care about. If I am killed, I do not know what will happen to them."

The chicken arrived, but unlike us, Charles did not touch his.

"Now people are talking about the next man to be killed. They are saying it will be me."

"Who has been killed then?"

"Haguma."

"Who?"

"Commander Haguma."

"Is it?" said Abdul with concern,

"Who's Haguma?" I asked.

"You remember," said Abdul.

I shook my head.

"Haguma was the guy in charge of the Gikondo Brigade the night Rwelekana was found hanged in his cell," said Abdul. "You know, I think I am getting to be more of a detective than you now."

Charles laughed. "He is right. Haguma was in charge of the prison when Rwelekana was found dead. He died on October 8, three weeks ago."

"How?"

Charles shrugged. "By poison," he said quietly.

"So what happened to you, Charles?" I asked.

"The Réseau sent a commando of twenty men. This was on October 1. I was at home in the morning because I wanted to see my mother. In the afternoon I was planning to attend a political meeting in the commune. I went to the meeting and on the way back to Kigali, we met on the road a gang of men throwing stones and bottles. They broke my glasses and wounded my brother. Someone ran off to the village to fetch the Burgomeister. He came with some men from the President's party. They stepped in and stopped the trouble. The men were rounded up and brought back to the commune. They were interrogated by the gendarmerie and released. There were no arrests. One of these men was someone I recognised . . ."

"Who?"

"He was one of the Presidential Guard. They had put him in with a bunch of thugs and it was his job to kill me. He knew where I would be that day, he knew where my house was, he knew I was seeing my mother – yet the Burgomeister and the prefect let him go. I was very lucky to escape. If it hadn't been for my friend who ran off to the commune and alerted the authorities, I would have been killed by that mob."

"What about the other attempt?"

"That happened at my house. Three men tried to break in at night. They were armed with grenades. I called the French colonel here, Monsieur Bordet. He came around immediately but by the time he arrived they had given up. They couldn't get in and they couldn't throw the grenades because my windows were barred."

"How did you know they were armed with grenades?" asked Abdul.

"I saw them."

"At night?"

"There was a light on outside the window. They were very close."

"What about your case? Has it come to court yet?"

Charles took off his glasses and wiped his eyes again. He smiled at us. "No. Of course not. It has been deferred again."

"So what will you do?" I asked him.

"There is nothing I can do. Only wait."

"Wait to be killed?" said Abdul. "You must be mad."

"There is not much choice. What else can I do? I would like to leave the country to study law, but where can I go, and how can I afford it?"

I asked him when he first felt that his relationship with the President had gone wrong.

"That is not difficult to say. I was enjoying a successful career up to the time the rebels, the FPR, took Ruhengeri, but for me there was a personal enmity with the President that started well before 1990. In 1978, President Giscard came to Rwanda and inspected the military school in Ruhengeri. As you know I was running it at the time. He was very impressed and awarded me the Chevalier de la Légion d'Honneur. He even invited me to come to Paris and be his guest at the Bastille celebrations the following year."

"Did you go?" asked Abdul, who was now finishing off the *poulet* that Charles had left.

"Of course, and many people were jealous of me. Including the President. This was the beginning of the rift, I believe. The following year I was invited to go to the USA to take part in a shooting competition. When I returned I decided that I would start my own shooting team here in Rwanda. We took on the President's team and, unfortunately, we beat them."

"Why do you say unfortunately?"

"Because I was told that I must disband the team. That to train a team of marksmen was an act of treason. The President and his people thought that I was organising an elite, a military elite, who could shoot better and straighter than his men. They accused me of creating an elite who could overthrow him. And then there was the chess. I suppose that was the worst crime."

"Chess a crime?"

Charles laughed quietly. He sipped his Mitsig. "In this country there are many crimes that are not written in the criminal code. I like chess and one day in the officers' mess I was asked by a Belgian lieutenant to play. I beat him, and afterwards he bought me a bottle of sparkling wine, and we were drinking it to celebrate my victory when the President walked in and asked me why I was drinking this wine. I told him that the Belgian had bought me the bottle and the reason for this, and the President said all right, Colonel, now I will play you, and we'll see who is the champion. Of course, I won. I beat him. Quite easily as I recall. The President can't bear to lose. For me it was a game. For the President it was war."

Charles got up to go. He shook hands with both of us.

"I don't play chess any more," he said. "It is far too dangerous. All the people who know something are going to be killed. Slowly they are vanishing. You must see Haguma's people. They can tell you how he died. I would look for Colonel Anselm. He too has been in prison, but I believe you can find him at the Hamid Pharmacy. I think he knows Haguma's people."

As he walked out of the garden of Chez Lando, alone and upright, and with dignity, Abdul shook his head and muttered, "Chess? Crazy people play chess. Bobby Fischer."

"Charles," I said, "is he crazy? Like Fischer?"

"Yes," said Abdul. "He must be. He should have thrown the game."

Kigali: November 1992

THE HAMID Pharmacy was in the Kanombe district of Kigali, tucked away on the dip of a hill from which you could see the glint of the mountainous tail-plane of that night's Air France. Hamid was away on business and his son had never heard of Colonel Anselm, but, he said, we should wait for his father's driver to return. The shop smelt the way chemists' smelt when I was a child, sharp, acrid and vinegary, with shelves tinglingly jammed with deep ocean blue concentric bottles with glass stoppers which would whine as they were eased off, and, on the counter, white corrugated pill boxes, all of them empty, all of them awaiting the dull drop of pills or a capsule and a neatly written label to provide them with a purpose.

Abdul was scanning the shelves intently, from left to right, and over again.

"Looking for issue vouchers?" I asked.

"No. They give them away in this city. There's no need to buy them. Anyway, I have my own supply. Ribbed."

"So what are you looking for?"

"Shit medicine. That chicken. It was too greasy, and I'm diarrhoea-ing. Sorree, Nick, here's another Norman coming."

The driver, Hamid's man, the one we were looking for to take us to the colonel called Anselm, unfortunately for himself, caught the full impact of Abdul's lower intestinal woe, in itself an aptly reversed tribute to the record of Chancellor Norman Lamont, whom he blamed for the recession in the UK, America, the EC and Kenya and for the fact that there was no work in Isiolo.

The driver wrinkled his nose involuntarily for a second and then agreed quite readily to take us to Anselm's house. It was a few steps away from the pharmacy, around the corner in fact, near enough for us to walk, and possibly to the driver's relief, not far enough for him to have to travel for any length of time closeted beside us in the confines of a vehicle whose windows could not be opened, however great the emergency.

Kigali is a city of hills connected by wide rolling avenues, lined with eucalyptus trees and high brick walls. In Knombe, near the airport, there are few people on the streets. They are to be found behind those mud red brick compounds, wasting the day on their verandahs, waiting for their watchdogs to wake their doormen so that the double corrugated-iron gates can be creaked apart, first to scrutinise the person outside, and then, if all is well, to allow them to cross over the threshold from the wide avenues of the city and into the tight suspicions of their own territory.

Colonel Anselm was quite content to massage his misgivings. After all, he had just been released from a spell in the Gikondo prison. Furthermore he was not expecting us. And, anyway, he didn't want to talk, not until I mentioned the name of one of the human rights activists who had blown the news about Réseau Zéro and that I was trying to discover what had happened to Dian and who had killed her.

"Start from the rear," he said.

Abdul looked across at me, trying to see if I was laughing; I decided to ignore him.

Anselm didn't notice. Instead he continued: "With Rwelekana."

I nodded. I asked him what he meant.

"If you can find out what happened to him, then you can find out why Fossey was killed."

"Well, we know what happened to Rwelekana," said Abdul. "He was found hanged, he killed himself, he committed suicide, in the prison here."

"No," said Anselm. "He was murdered."

"Prove it," I challenged. "Can you?"

"No."

I fished in my pocket for cigarettes. This was going to be another package of rumour, of hearsay, of refutable second- or third-hand testimony.

"The man who killed Rwelekana was Haguma. He was the commander in charge of the military prison where Rwelekana was held. He was ordered to kill him."

"Why?"

"Because Rwelekana had witnessed the murder. He knew the truth. You'll find that this happened in August 1986, about eight months after the murder of Dian. By this time the co-accused, the American, McGuire, had fled the country. The authorities were faced with bringing to trial one Rwandan who had denied everything. They did not want him to go on trial, yet they could not let him go free for fear he would talk about what had happened."

"So they killed him."

"What about Haguma? Why would they kill him?"

Anselm stretched his back into his chair. He asked us if we wanted a drink. We said no. I could see Abdul twisting his fingers, not I guessed in anticipation of the next revelation, but because he was fighting to pacify the straggling remnants of the grilled lunch that was at war in his intestines.

"Four reasons," said Anselm.

"And I," said Abdul, before Anselm could begin, "I think maybe I can think of a fifth."

"Haguma was killed first because of Fossey and Rwelekana," said Anselm. "Then during the October war in 1990, he murdered a number of soldiers who were against the war and the regime. Third, he had been told to terrorise people in the Kibuye region.

He had received orders from the President to set people against each other there. Fourth, he refused to do it. He is from that area and this was too much for him. So he was killed."

"And the fifth reason?" I asked Abdul.

"Because of us."

"Why us? We have never met the man."

"Precisely," said Abdul. "And that's the way they wanted it to be. You were on the trail. So who was the next person you would be likely to see? Haguma. It makes sense."

It did. And that was when I began to feel afraid.

Kigali: November 1992

THE LATE Commander Haguma's brother-in-law was expecting us. Anselm had contacted his wife who in turn had passed the message to Cyridion. This was the way news carried in Rwanda, via relatives and through whispers. So by the time I was sitting opposite Cyridion in his large office on the polished ground floor of the United Nations Development Programme's Rwanda HQ in Kigali's *centre ville* I fully expected the message that we had sent down the human line would be adulterated. I expected to hear that Abdul and I had come for a job, that we were consultants for the UN Refugee Programme or that we were interested in setting up an import-export business, but between Anselm and Cyridion there had been no mutation of the message. He knew what we were here for and, unlike many of his countrymen, he wasted no time on formalities or even Francophone cordialities.

"The rumours," he announced, "concerning my brother-in-law's death are not rumours. I spent the last hours with him and I can tell you he was murdered."

Cyridion emphasised the point by leaning across the desk, and then nailing his back into his seat, almost as if he were trying to draw us towards him and over to his side of the table. I could see he would make a compelling witness, this grey-suited academic who was the chief of a United Nations development programme in Rwanda. He talked quietly, detailing the final tortured moments suffered by Haguma, and as the time came near to describe the death of his brother-in-law, as the story climaxed, if you like, Cyridion's voice grew quieter, and more concerned, reflecting, empathising, soothing the agony of Haguma, as if he were gently mopping up the perspiration that was tumbling down the forehead and choking the eyes of the dying man.

"Haguma," said Cyridion, "could speak to the very last minute of his life. He died on Thursday, October 8, at 2.30 p.m. I stood with him in the bedroom of his house from 6.30 that morning until he died. When I saw him that morning he told me he had a lot of pains in his belly."

Cyridion pushed himself back into the depths of his swivel chair and rubbed his stomach with gentle circular movements. "I could see that his belly was swollen. He had diarrhoea. No appetite. At about 10.00 a.m. he wanted to drink. We gave him milk and Fanta."

"Who was with you at this time?" I asked.

"His wife, Agnes. And a friend of the Hagumas."

"What did he tell you?" asked Abdul.

"We said to him that we could see he was suffering. We asked him what had happened. He said that on the Monday, three days before, he went to work at a village near Kibuye where the ethnic troubles had occurred."

"Ethnic troubles? Anyone hurt?" I asked.

"Yes, there were clashes between Tutsi and Hutu and some people were killed. This was a flashpoint area. It is said, though I have no proof of this, that these troubles had been inspired by the government so that they could paint a picture of a country which was being torn apart by internal dissension – a crisis which they could blame on the opposition. At midday, he took a glass of beer with the Burgomeister and the Inspector of Schools in that area. There was also, he said, a fourth man present, a man he could not identify. This man had turned up on a motorbike. Haguma asked me to check who this man was. I called the Burgomeister and I asked him. He was evasive."

"Did he say that this fourth man was there?" I asked.

"That's the strange thing," said Cyridion. "Haguma was not even dead when I rang the Burgomeister, yet he denied that the fourth man had ever been there."

"Maybe he wasn't," said Abdul.

"I checked with Haguma after I had spoken to the Burgomeister, and he insisted the man was there. And that he had taken a beer with him. That same Monday, Haguma said that he went on to Kibuye and the pains started there the following day. He began to vomit. His stomach hurt and there was diarrhoea. He went to the local hospital and then to the commandant's house to rest. He took some medication there, but on Wednesday the symptoms persisted. His driver, a man from his own commune, went to see him and was shocked by his condition. The driver noticed a very peculiar symptom. The extremities of the body, his hands and his feet, were cold. Immediately the driver telephoned Agnes."

He paused.

"Haguma's wife. He got Haguma to telegram the chief of staff here in Kigali, demanding that he be evacuated from Kibuye by helicopter. The helicopter arrived and took him to the military hospital in Knombe, by the airport. But there was no bed available for him there and he was sent to his home. That was Wednesday evening. On Thursday, the relatives came looking for me. I arrived at dawn. As soon as I saw him, and after I had heard what he had to say, I called a doctor."

"What sort of doctor?" asked Abdul.

"An indigenous doctor. He came and within three minutes he made his diagnosis. He said that Haguma would die. There was nothing he could do for him. By this time he could not move his hands and feet. About all he could do was speak. He continued to vomit and he still had diarrhoea. The doctor gave him medicine. At about 1.00 p.m. he had convulsions. His body tightened. We gave him a Fanta bottle to hold but he could not control his movements any more. He was shaking the Fanta all over the bed. The same thing happened when we gave him a piece of pineapple on the end of a fork."

"Was he suffering from malaria?" I asked.

"We treated him for malaria, but he had no fever. We also checked him for meningitis, but he told us he had been vaccinated twelve months before, and I know the immunity lasts for up to three years. There was no fever, no headaches. Only vomiting and diarrhoea. I was convinced he died because of one thing."

"What?"

"I am sure, certain, he was poisoned."

"But isn't everyone who dies suddenly in Rwanda?"

Cyridion looked at me, and shook his head, slowly, to the left and to the right, and then he stopped, and said, "You are right to be dubious, but have you considered why I should even be talking to you about this? It would be far easier for me to keep quiet. I don't know you, and I don't know what you will do with what I tell you. But think, why should I tell you this?"

What was equally true was the fact that this testimony that we were hearing was coming not from the mouth of a peasant, not from an uneducated man, not from someone caught up in the political maelstrom, but from a quietly spoken, intense, and wholly unimaginative intellectual who had been educated in Belgium and who held a responsible position with the UN.

"What about a donation, Nick. Maybe Haguma had a donation?" Abdul was whispering to me. This was his way of saying that the commander had AIDS.

I asked Cyridion.

"No. I am sure he did not have AIDS. He was thirty-six and very *sportif*. He was a good football player. He was strong for his size. I'd guess he was about one metre seventy, and as long as I knew him he never had health problems. He was married in 1986 and he had three children."

"What else makes you convinced this is poisoning?" I said.

"I have known other men who have died in this way. There was, a year ago, a certain colonel . . ."

"Rwangasore?"

"Yes. Colonel Rwangasore. I spoke to his people after Haguma had died and I compared the symptoms of the two men. They were almost identical. When I described to them how Haguma had died, they immediately recognised what I was talking about. There was also another soldier who died in similar circumstances. I went to his widow and she said her husband had suffered in exactly the same way."

"If Haguma was poisoned, then what was the reason behind it?" asked Abdul.

"My brother-in-law was a man who knew a lot of secrets. He had been at the centre of certain events over the years. He knew the truth."

"What truth?"

"He knew about the Fossey case. He was in charge of the Gikondo Brigades at the time that Rwelekana was killed."

"Killed? Why do you say that Rwelekana was killed?"

"Many people say it. After the death, Haguma was interviewed by the prefect and he went to meet the President. There was an enquiry and the conclusion was that it was suicide, but not many are convinced by that."

"Did he say anything to you about Rwelekana?"

"No. Whenever the subject was raised, he always got nervous. After the hanging, he was very quiet, very close, very anxious. I think that his personality changed after Rwelekana's death. He seemed to me to become more cautious. I'd known him for a long time. He taught me when I was in primary school and then he became related to me by marriage. I noticed this change of behaviour, but what caused it, I don't know. I don't draw conclusions. Yet I wonder if some of these events were something to do with his death."

We left the office with another poisoning to consider. I told Abdul that we must find Haguma's widow and talk to a doctor.

Cyridion accompanied us to the steps of the UNDP building. He shook hands and said, "I am prepared to give evidence about this. I am convinced my brother-in-law was murdered."

Abdul wriggled through the passenger window of the Peugeot, muttering about the locks and how he would have to fix them before he too succumbed to a rapid death. When he had opened the door for me, he asked me what I thought about Cyridion's testimony.

"He's telling the truth. That's for sure."

Abdul put the car into gear and it groaned out of the parking lot and into the Kigali traffic. "And he's not an activist either," he said. "He's an agronomist."

Cyridion had told us that Haguma's wife could be found either at a school in the Myrambo district of Kigali, near the green mosque on the edge of town, or in the General Hospital. She held down two jobs: nurse and teacher. We tried the school first. She wasn't there. We had missed her by five minutes. We went to the hospital. She wasn't there either. There was no point in going to her home. She lived behind the barbed-wired walls of the army compound at Knombe. We would have to wait at the school or the hospital. Abdul selected the hospital on the grounds that we would probably be parked outside for the best part of the day and staring at the nurses who were coming on duty or going home would keep us occupied.

We'd been sitting watching the shifts come and go for about forty-five minutes; doorstepping the hospital they'd call it in Fleet Street, only this was the rue de la République or some street with a patriotic tinge, and there wasn't a bar in range of a spit in which to take a Primus.

I was about to suggest we give up for the day because I was tired of looking at fat, well-fed nurses and hobbles of soldiers, fresh from the war in their clean bandages and pressed trouser legs, but Abdul had other ideas. He had left the car and was talking to a woman, thin, bespectacled and not in the least a Kigali Nights girl.

He brought her over to me. "You remember this lady, Nick."

I didn't, but I smiled anyway.

She was holding her hand out to me, returning my smile and doing what all Rwandan women do when they are lost for words. She was mmming. "Mm," she murmured. "Mm."

"We met her in Nairobi at the Rwandan Embassy when we went to get the visas," explained Abdul.

"Mmm."

"So."

"Well, she's a doctor."

"So."

"So she'll know Haguma's widow."

"Oh."

"Well ask her then," he said.

I did.

She didn't.

The doctor ignored the question and asked where were we staying.

"The Milles Collines."

"*Chambre*?"

"Three, three, three."

"Mmm?"

"*Trois, trois, trois.*"

"My mother is coming to stay with me. Do you have 6,000 francs for me?"

"I do not carry money. Ask Abdul." I pointed to him.

She went over to Abdul who was fiddling with the window

winders. He fished in his shirt pocket and gave her a couple of hundred francs. She went off.

We failed to find Haguma's widow that day.

Kigali: November 1992

THE JOURNALIST Theo, the thin man with socks peeking through his sandals and steel-rimmed glasses, the man who had told me back in the summer about his six months in the Gikondo prison, was waiting for me in the lobby of the Milles Collines.

"I heard you were back," he said simply. "Lambert told me. And anyway you were spotted at the airport."

We shared a Primus. Theo told me he was in more trouble. He was facing a court appearance on November 24, in three weeks. "I am charged with insulting the President."

"What did you do?" I asked.

"There was a press conference and I stood up and asked him when he was going."

"And that's offensive?" said Abdul.

"My follow-up question was deemed to be," said Theo. "I told him why he should go."

"What's the maximum?"

"Five years." Theo laughed. "I need to get out of this country," he said. "But so may you."

"Why? We haven't been offensive to the President, have we?" said Abdul.

"*You*'ve been offensive to the German Ambassador," I said. Last night there had been a party in the Milles Collines hosted by the Swiss Ambassador. Abdul and I stood in the lobby at six o'clock watching the dignitaries draw up outside the entrance to the hotel in their black Mercedes limousines, each of them distinguishable only by the flag flying from the nearside wing. The diplomats and their wives choked the hotel. The Americans, French, Belgians, Dutch, Chinese, and then His Excellency, the representative from Berlin, whom Abdul looked in the face, raised his left arm high in the air and said, quite audibly, "*Heil Hitler*."

"No, it wasn't that," said Theo. "It's about the CIA. There is a story going round the city, a story which people believe. They say that two CIA agents are in town. One is British with fifteen passports. The other is Goan with eight passports."

"Goan!" groaned Abdul. "Is it! And why have they given me only eight passports and you fifteen? I'll bet those eight don't include a British passport."

"Who is saying this?"

"The Réseau. They are letting it be known that you are here for two reasons. The first is to destabilise the country, and the second is to gather evidence for the human rights enquiry next month."

"What about the book?"

"That's only your cover. You are not serious."

I told Theo I wasn't too worried about the CIA story. After all, it was just another lie. And if people did think we were working for the CIA, then maybe we would be less likely to be picked off than if we were perceived as mere journalists.

But Theo hadn't finished with the rumours. "There are," he said, "three Sicilian hit men in Kigali. They are said to be linked with an organisation in Kigali called Amici dei Rwanda."

It was all too ludicrous; even so Abdul asked where the information had come from.

"From a man who works in a Kigali cement works. He told someone who told me."

Abdul looked at me. We both knew the source. Abdul's eyes told me to say nothing.

I think Theo was enjoying himself, studying the discomfort written so suddenly across our faces. I decided not to indulge him. Instead I told him that we needed his help. We wanted to see a number of people connected with the Fossey case. Karangwa, the officer in charge of the gendarmerie at Ruhengeri at the time of the murder; Bushishi, the Procureur at Ruhengeri at the time of the murder, the man who investigated it; Ros Carr, Dian's friend; and, of course, Zed, himself.

"Bushishi is easy. He's in Butare. Just go there. And on the way see a Belgian doctor called Quaestiaux. He's been here for years and could be valuable. Ros Carr lives in Gisenye. You can go and see her. I know Karangwa. I'll try and fix a meeting. As for Zed, I think you should go through Seraphim, his brother. He works at La Centrale – that's the name of his company. He's left the bank now and he's running his own private company. Import-export. I'd call him when you are ready."

It was dusk before we checked out of the hotel for Butare, and in the resolute drizzle the gendarmes, in their white helmets and long white raincoats which drifted down to lick the water off the asphalt, materialised out of the gloom like phantoms, waiting for travellers to draw up alongside the scrappy branches and piles of half bricks and stones they had flung across the road.

"These roadblocks," said Abdul as he braked and rolled the Peugeot gently to the side of the road. Panting, his head and shoulder disappeared beneath the dashboard as he wrenched the handbrake up. Outside the silence was broken by the insistent and regular beat of the wiper blades. "You talk all that Froggy at the roadblocks. Talk English. We're English. Listen to me."

A gendarme pushed his head up against the window. In his whites he reminded me of an English lollipop man, only this lollipop was made in Russia and labelled Kalashnikov. "*Où allez-vous?*" loomed the lollipop man.

"Sorree," said Abdul, a grin pinned across the top of his moustache. "English. English. No speak Frenchy." He shot his arm across my body, elbowing me back into my seat, and grasped the hand of the gendarme. He wrenched the limb up and down, forward and back, pulling it into the car.

"*Continuez.*" Only the size and shape of the gendarme's helmet prevented the man beneath it from being propelled into the car. I could have kissed the smile off his face. "*Continuez.*" I sensed the phantom was now getting nervous. Abdul braced himself to release the handbrake, struggled with it, and pushed the car into gear.

"You see. A black man cannot resist a white man's handshake. Now he will tell his friends what good men we are."

As the car passed the block, I nodded to the phantom and said, before I could stop myself, or indeed think of the possible consequences, "*Merci.*"

Abdul scowled. "*Merci*, Nick, to you. Fuck you. You should have played that part in *The Great Escape*," he said. "Remember the scene where the Gestapo officer tricks the British by talking in German and then ending the conversation by saying goodbye in English. He caught them out. You'd have been shot by now."

I made a note to remember not to say *merci* next roadblock. What with Réseau Zéro narrowing its sights on us, and now the gendarmerie wishing to shake our hands, I couldn't afford to rouse more suspicions.

Dr Quaestiaux had lived in central Africa for sixty-eight years. He was, he said, just two years old when his parents came to the Belgian Congo. Now he was semi-retired, living on the Kigali–Butare road, in a small cottage a couple of kilometres outside Gitarama, opposite the Kapguye maternity hospital where he delivered babies every day. He was a neat dresser, a small man, wearing a sports jacket, white shirt and slacks. There was one point of ostentation about him – the hand-tied bow tie he wore.

He was a man who came immediately to the point. No wasting time with Quaestiaux. "Zed did it. He was the man behind the murder," he said to me immediately after I'd told him why I was in Rwanda.

"Do you know him, Zed?" I asked.

"Yes, I know him. He is someone who can assume all the faces imaginable. He is a master at duplicity. His first name is Protais. It's the name of a Greek god. Do you know the power of Protais?"

"The god or this man?"

"Both. They share the same gift."

"What is it, Doctor?"

"Protais was, is, able to change into anything he wants to be. A lover, a seducer, a wild animal, a killer, a charmer. This is your man."

"How do you know he was behind the murder of Fossey?"

"I can't prove it, but there have been so many stories, and so many people, men, involved with the Fossey case have vanished."

"Poisoned?"

"Yes."

I asked the doctor whether he had ever come across any poisonings in his time in Rwanda.

"I know of two cases," he said, sipping his whisky and replacing the glass on the small, wooden plain table that stood on the bare stone floor of the little front room of the cottage. He settled back in his armchair and straightened his bow tie. "One was involving a European. He was a restaurateur in Kigali." He paused and took out of his trouser pocket a handkerchief and proceeded to dab his nose and then blow it at length.

"A homosexual. This man had a lover. He was a very healthy

man, the restaurant fellow. Well one morning I was called to see him at his home. He was suffering from diarrhoea and vomiting. He died the next morning. I refused to sign a death certificate. There was no classical reason for his death. But he had only been dead one hour and there were already twenty Rwandans in his room. They had known what was going to happen. They weren't grieving. They were fighting over his life insurance."

I described to the doctor the symptoms suffered by Haguma.

"Yes, poisoning is possible. No fever, you say."

I nodded.

"And the extremities of the body were cold, you say?"

"Yes."

"A sign that the body was near collapse, near death."

"You said, Doctor, that you refused to sign a death certificate for this homosexual. What happened?"

"Well, it was taken above my head. There is, anyway, no necessity for a death certificate if the patient dies at home. It's the same with birth. If a woman has a baby in hospital, there is a birth certificate, but most children are born in the hills, in the communes, and there is no law saying they must have a birth certficate. The baby will be registered when and if the parents want it to be done."

"So, when the military authorities refused Haguma a bed in the military hospital, do you think this decision was taken because they did not want him to have a death certificate if he died in the hospital?"

"That could be so, but, on the other hand, you must realise there is a war going on and there could genuinely have been no beds available."

"Even in an emergency?"

"It depends who decides what is urgent and what is not."

"What about the other case of poisoning?"

"Oh, that was similar to the first one I told you about. It is such a difficult subject to know anything about. But I can assure you, it goes on."

"How can I believe anything that anyone tells me here?" I asked.

"With difficulty," said the doctor, laughing. "I'll tell you this. All Rwandans are liars; lying is an art form. It is engrained in the genes of the Rwandans, it goes with the feudal system. It's like the court of Louis XIV; a man may be your enemy but he will, with a smile on his lips, tell you he is your friend – you will never know the truth and it has to be this way. If you have a master, then you must always tell that master what he wants to hear, not what the truth is. Parents teach their children here to tell lies. They teach them never to say what they really think or feel. Even if they suffer, they never express their emotions. You come with me to the maternity wards and you will not see a woman scream when she is in labour. You will not hear a sound. But in Zaire, the women there, they scream their heads off when they give birth."

"So you think it will be difficult for me to find the truth?"

"Not necessarily. It will be hard. But not impossible. You must speak to Bushishi. He is an honest man."

I told him what Colonel Charles had told me about the lack of bloodstains on the walls and ceilings and the hair in Fossey's hands.

He poured himself another Scotch and drew his chair closer to me. "It doesn't make sense. If someone hits you with a *panga* there would be lots of blood, and it would spray all over the place, but I doubt if there would be hair in the victim's hands."

"Why?"

"Because your assailant would be at some distance from you. Here, look." The doctor stood up and wielded a newspaper at me as I sat down. He was standing maybe a metre away as the newspaper, rolled up now, smacked my ear. "Try touching me."

I flailed and missed.

"Now stand up and try and touch me. Go on."

I still couldn't reach him.

"You see what I mean? For the victim, for Dian, to be able to reach out and grab someone's hair would mean that she was standing near to her attacker. Within arm's distance."

"So you think she could have been killed in another way?"

"If there was not all this blood around as you say you have been told, then yes, it is quite possible she died in another way."

"Why did you say to me as soon as I arrived that Zed did it?"

"He had every reason to want her dead. She was impinging on his poaching activities. She was a nuisance."

"But I keep saying that there weren't enough gorillas to make poaching worth while and, besides, they were far too well protected."

"You are right, but Zed was involved in all sorts of trafficking. Wolfram, cassiterite, precious stones, coffee. You name it. Tourism."

"Gold?"

The doctor shook his head. "Gold? I am not certain of that one." He looked at his watch. "I must go now. There is a woman who is due any time. Before you go, one word."

I stopped as I was going through his front door. I turned back to him. He held out his hand.

"Be careful of the god Protais. Remember he can be anyone, anything that he wants. He'll charm you. That's for sure. But he is also capable of killing you."

Butare: November 1992

BUSHISHI was busy. I was told to wait. Along the wooden *stoep* which sheltered those who, like me, were waiting, from Butare's morning sun and afternoon rains, a woman was leaning through one of the open windows of the prefecture haggling with the office workers inside. She was attempting to sell them a large, flattened fish which she had smoked. It was very smelly and the bureaucrats were doing all they could to resist her sales technique. At the end of the *stoep*, a group of disconsolate men, each of them dressed in pink trousers and tunics, sat around on tree stumps, watching the comings and goings, and in turn being watched themselves by an armed gendarme. They looked like extras from an Issey Miyake fashion collection in Paris, waiting for leggy half-clad girls to walk by. In fact they were convicts, temporarily released from their cells in the prison across the road from the prefecture, waiting too, I was told, for their cases to be heard, or for the outcome of their appeals. They looked a gentle crowd, but I am certain that this had more to do with the fact that they all looked so pretty in pink. The matching cotton ensemble of short-sleeved tunics and trousers, with not a hint of a black arrow-head, served to deny to the onlooker, should that onlooker be harbouring uncharitable thoughts, that the wearer had ever been a bad man. Crims in pink!

Child molesters, arsonists, perverts, rapists, fiends, murderers. In pink! Never.

At any rate, as Abdul observed, dressing them in pink was a brilliant piece of penal reformative thinking. "Who," he said, "would even consider violence when the consequences of being caught are to end up like that?"

Mattheus Bushishi was a stout, short, grey-haired man wearing steel glasses and a light blue sleeveless pullover. He welcomed us into his small office and called for an extra chair to be brought in for Abdul.

"You know," he said, "you must really see the Fossey dossier. I have one here, but it is not the full account. What do you want to know?"

I saw the pile of papers spilling out of a file on his desk, just to his left. I was tempted to snatch them up and make a run for it. Abdul sensed what I was thinking, I believe, because he reached over and touched my arm.

"You were present at Karisoke and saw the body?"

"Yes, I was in charge of the investigation."

"One eye-witness who was there with you told me that he thought there was not enough blood for her to have been killed by *pangas*? What do you think?"

"I think that this is correct. There was no blood on the walls, nor on the ceiling. That was very curious. I have always believed Dian was strangled."

"And the *panga* attack?"

"That came afterwards. Like the hole in the wall."

"What do you mean afterwards?"

"I mean simply that whoever killed her mutilated the body with *pangas* after she was dead and then they removed the panel in the wall to make us believe this was a burglary."

"But," said Abdul, "that is not in the report."

"Have you seen the report?" smiled Bushishi.

"No."

"So how do you know what is in it and what is not in it?"

Abdul smiled back. He said nothing.

"But is it in the report?" I asked.

"No. That is my opinion, what I have just told you. The report is everything. I am only a prosecutor. I stick to the facts."

"So your assertion that she was strangled and then afterwards she was *panga*-ed, and only then was the panel removed, is an opinion?"

Bushishi looked at me for a few seconds. "I am only the prosecutor," he said finally.

"How did they get in if they removed the panel afterwards?" asked Abdul.

"With a key."

"What was the motive?"

"To find documents."

"What documents?"

"McGuire wanted her research. We found many of her papers in his cabin."

"When?"

Bushishi opened the file on his desk and leafed through some papers, licking his forefinger and thumb as he turned over the pages. "February 3,1986."

"About five weeks after the murder," I said.

"Yes."

"Do you believe that McGuire and Rwelekana were guilty?"

He nodded. "Rwelekana," he said, "had bloodstains on his shirt, the same group as Dian. He had bloodstains on his boots. He was her enemy. He came back to the camp to work as soon as she had died."

"Hardly the action of a guilty man," I said.

"We had a good forensic report. The Paris report."

"What about the FBI report?"

"I never saw it."

"Why not?"

"It never came."

"Didn't you wonder about this?"

"Yes, I did. But the fact is it never came. It is inexplicable."

"Who took the hairs from the body to give to the Paris lab?" asked Abdul.

"I did."

"No, Kathleen Austin told me she took them," I said.

Bushishi smiled again. "I gave the hairs to Kathleen Austin. She took them to the American Embassy. A few days later I went to the US Embassy and took a sample from her and put them in an envelope and handed them to the French Ambassador in Kigali and he sent them on to France."

"That is not what she says. She is convinced she took them from the body."

Bushishi laughed now. "I believe Dian was CIA. There was that gun with CIA marked on it, on the stock."

"What about trafficking?"

"Yes."

"Was there a connection between her death and gorilla trafficking?"

"I don't know." He paused. "It is possible."

"And gold?" said Abdul.

"I don't know."

I decided to push my luck. "And Zed?"

Bushishi said nothing, only stared.

"The prefect," said Abdul.

Bushishi laughed. This time very loudly. "Why do you say this?" he asked.

"Because a lot of people are saying it."

"You had better read the dossier. And go and see Karangwa. He was the gendarme in charge of the investigation."

Abdul sucked in his breath. He could see the dialogue was going around in circles. "So how do we get this dossier?" he snapped at Bushishi.

"You know the Minister of Justice. Ask him."

Kigali: November 1992

ENNO was drunk by the time we reached his house in Kigali that night, leeching on to one of the brick supports that held up his verandah. He was a tall, overweight man and his legs curved around the pillar of brick as if he were trying to reassure himself that it did belong to him, that it was part of his body, a third leg he could depend upon. He certainly needed one. In his right hand a bottle of Johnnie Walker Red Label slopped; the left was waving us in, welcoming the pair of us, and the mouth was working overtime, telling Abdul to eat and use the telephone, and make himself at home. But for me, Enno had different plans.

We were going to meet someone in Kigali that night. Only the two of us. Abdul would have to wait in the house.

Enno was a German journalist, an Africa hand as calloused as Capucinski, though, unlike the Polish scribe, waiting to be discovered. He had spent over twenty years in the continent, mostly in the west, and his belly hung over his knees. He had survived coups, counter-coups, cock-up coups. He had survived bouts of malaria, dysentery and brought up a family, though whether his wife and children could endure him was debatable. Enno's job was to train government journalists. Raise news agency standards, he said. Train them for what? I thought. Staying out of prison? Withstanding interrogation? Drinking? Enno had pushed his card into my hand a few days before at the Milles Collines and as we talked over a line-up of Primus, I realised he knew just about everybody in Kigali. He had seemed genuine enough in his interest in my Fossey story and had offered to help. So when I called him from Butare and told him that the Minister of Justice had given us permission to read the dossier and we would need a translator, Enno had said he'd look out for someone and invited us to stay with him on the way to Ruhengeri.

Of course, it wasn't quite as simple as that. Enno had tried, but he hadn't been able to find a translator. He shook his head quite violently and waved the bottle of Scotch. "Not enough time, not enough notice." He waved our objections away. "Don't need translator," he said. "Give you my photocopier."

By now he had heaved himself into his Mercedes four-wheel drive and was failing to fit the key into the ignition lock. Abdul was standing outside the house, underneath the verandah, wondering whether to let me go alone with him. I joined Enno in the cab of the Mercedes, less concerned about who we were going to meet than whether Enno was capable of reaching the rendezvous.

He charged the Mercedes backwards through his double gates, revved up the engine, and bounced along the track that led down a red mud escarpment into the city. I hung on to the crash bars so thoughtfully provided by Mercedes, as every thrust of acceleration and jolt of the track threatened to throw me through the windscreen.

We crossed the city, careering around *le rond-point*, the big double roundabout near Les Milles Collines, and headed out to Myrambo, past the mosque, past the school where we had looked for Haguma's wife. It was here that Enno's lack of sobriety clashed head-on with the seventy-per-cent-proof injection of confidence that had supercharged into his veins.

A red Fiat with Swiss plates had the temerity to overtake us. Enno saw the tail lights of the Fiat blur into the distance ahead; Enno saw red. The Scotch, still sloshing around in his system, took over, and he put his face forward so that his eyes seemed to lick the windscreen, and his foot down flat on the accelerator pedal.

"That fucker. I'll have him. That bastard." He batter-rammed the gears, up and down, out of fourth, into second, now first, torturing the engine. The Fiat came closer as if it was being pulled back to us on a piece of elastic, and then as quickly it drew away. Enno cheated in the end, overtaking it on the inside, scattering a crowd of urchins who were kicking stones by the side of the road. To emphasise his skill, he whipped the Mercedes around a right-hand junction, forcing the vehicle in between the kerb and a keep right sign and only managing to keep it upright by mounting the traffic island. He was inventing cambers where no cambers existed.

"They know me in Kigali," he said, by way of an excuse. "I've been driving this way for years and they know to keep out of my way."

Perhaps Kigali did know Enno was out that night. Certainly the town was empty, the streets more or less deserted, with only a handful of those with sufficient nerve to form an audience for the crazy Kraut. Or maybe it was nine thirty on a Sunday night and Kigali was grounded. Enno didn't care. The Mercedes ground its wheels into the mud as it went off the road, and finally spun with a shudder and a roll and jerked to a halt on the side of a muddy road where the street lighting was down.

"I think this is the house," he said, "but be careful, there is a large ditch somewhere around here."

There was. A drainage ditch, which fortunately for Enno was not filled with rainwater that night. He found it and, of course, fell in it. I stretched my hand out to him and attempted to pull him out. "You got a winch on the Mercedes?" I asked.

The man we had gone to see had spent seven years in an American university and was fluent in English. This was just as well because as soon as Enno sat down next to me in the man's front room, he dozed off to sleep. Georges said nothing about the German's behaviour. For him, Enno was not an oddity; he worked with him. And his driving? What did Georges think of that?

"Yes, I am going with him to Gisenye tomorrow." He sighed. "You want to know about Fossey?"

I nodded.

"I was working as a journalist here in the seventies and early eighties. I was in the States for seven years from 1982 and I missed the killing of Dian, but most people thought that the American McGuire had killed her."

So what am I doing here? I thought as I sipped the Primus beer and kept the rest of the bottle away from the sleeping Enno's reach.

"But," said Georges, "people have changed their minds."

"Why?"

"Because of the war. The war broke out in 1990 and a lot of information started to circulate. There was freedom of speech for the first time in this country. It was a time when people wanted to air their grievances and settle old scores. And the Fossey case was something that began to be talked out. Piecing together the information, they say that Zed was behind the killing, that Rwelekana was killed by Haguma, that Haguma was killed by the President's people, that Rwangasore was killed because he knew the truth, and now there's been another killing."

"Who?"

"Haguma's Premier Sergeant-Major, that's his closest colleague if you like."

"What happened to him?"

"He was shot down in the Remera district of Kigali on Friday night. Two days ago."

"Shot down?"

"Executed. In the street."

"Why?"

Georges shrugged. "Because he knew who killed Haguma, I suppose. There is also talk that Haguma's chauffeur was killed."

"Don't you know?"

"He's missing."

"What was the motive for killing Fossey?"

"You have to see things this way," said Georges. "Zed is the kingmaker in this country. He makes people and he destroys them. Everything he does is for the benefit of the President and his family, to keep them in power. Fossey was killed because Zed realised there was a great deal of foreign exchange to be accumulated from tourism. Fossey was against tourism. She wanted to keep the park and her gorillas away from the world. But the President and Zed thought otherwise. Why do you think they backed the International Gorilla Fair in 1990?"

I said nothing, and anyway Georges, I could see, was about to answer his own question.

"They backed it because they could see that a great deal of money – dollars – could find a way into their pockets if more tourists came to Rwanda. That's why the President has a couple of hotels. But Fossey wanted nothing to do with this. So they killed her."

"So you are saying that her murder had nothing to do with trafficking? Nothing to do with gorillas? Or gold?"

"He was involved in all sorts of trafficking. Zed, I mean, and yes, this could have been behind the murder, but the primary reason was her opposition to tourism. You see, look at how the ORPTN was put under the control of the President's office. Why do you think that was so? And it explains why he built the Ribero Hotel and opened Kigali Nights. He's got the Tam Tam restaurant in the *centre ville* and the Canard Sauvage in Gisenye. So they became involved in exploiting the tourist market . . ."

"But owning hotels and a nightclub and a restaurant or two, that's legitimate," I said.

"Yes, but if business is bad. Look, people, tourists, don't come to Rwanda to eat at the Tam Tam."

I laughed.

"They come to see gorillas. And Fossey was stopping them."

"So why kill her at this point in 1985? They could have got her out of the country easily enough."

"They couldn't. She had been given the visa for two years. She had to be killed."

"Killed?"

"Yes, or at least frightened enough to leave."

What he was telling me fitted with what Jacques had told me in July. Maybe here was the motive. Maybe trafficking was part of a long-running sore, but tourism was the catalyst that jerked them into action.

"There is a man you should see," said Georges. "He is a former colleague of mine. Jean-Baptiste. He was the state news agency man in Ruhengeri at the time of the murder. He lives near here. Try and talk to him."

Jean-Baptiste's house had no ditch protecting it. Even so we brought into his living room half of Kigali's mud stuck to the soles of our shoes. As I attempted to scrape off the street, Enno allowed himself to be embraced by one of Jean-Baptiste's armchairs and was immediately swallowed by sleep.

"Do you know him?" I asked Jean-Baptiste.

He laughed. "Enno is always coming round unannounced. It is fortunate for him that such a thing as Rwandan hospitality exists. But he does a good job."

"What exactly does he do?"

"He trains Orinfor journalists not to tell lies, not to print rubbish."

"Who are Orinfor?"

"The state news agency. I worked for them when I was in Ruhengeri. Now I edit my own paper."

"Why did you leave Ruhengeri?"

"I had to. I was not very popular with the prefect."

"Zed?"

He laughed. "Yes, Zed. Protais."

"What had you done?"

"I was fed up with having to show him all my copy. Everything I wrote or was going to broadcast on the radio had to be shown to him to get his sanction."

"Everything?"

"Well. Everything relating to the murder of Dian and the investigation."

"Was that unusual?"

"Yes. Though Zed thought that as he was the prefect, he had the ultimate decision on what to publish and what not to publish."

"So he acted as a kind of censor?"

"Yes."

"What happened then?"

"I'll start at the beginning. Then it will make sense. Another Primus?" He leant over the table towards me and refuelled my glass. "I don't think Enno will be wanting one," he said, grinning at the fat German, whose back had now fallen into the seat of the chair so that his legs were splayed across the room, preventing anyone, should they want to, from opening the front door.

"I was the only journalist based in the area, in Ruhengeri, in 1985. Even from the beginning, I found it very difficult to follow the enquiry. The authorities, the Procureur Général, and the prefect, the gendarmerie, too, gave me problems. They refused to allow me to interview people, they never gave me information when they were following a particular clue, they never explained why they were following a certain line of enquiry, and when I waited for information, for a lead from them, it never came."

"But you must be used to working like that. It happens in Germany and Britain, too." Enno had woken up.

"I tried to interview McGuire and when I came back to Ruhengeri I was threatened."

"How?" I asked.

"I was asked why I had stayed up in Karisoke with a monster, a killer, and I was asked whether I was frightened for my life."

"Who said this to you?" asked Enno.

"Captain Karangwa. He is a personal friend of Zed. He was his right-hand man, the gendarme in charge of the police investigation."

"When did he say this?"

"In February."

"Did you interview McGuire?"

"I saw him at Karisoke in February. This was when I was warned about him. He told me the Rwandan gendarmerie, Karangwa's men, were terrorising him. He said he didn't kill Fossey. It was a very difficult interview for me because his French was very bad. I spoke English with him in the end. He said that he believed Fossey had been killed by poachers because she was making their lives very difficult. I wanted to ask him whether these men were poachers who had decided to kill her for themselves or had they been commissioned by someone else."

"Wanted? What do you mean wanted to ask him?"

"I was frightened. You have no idea how it was up there, alone with him. I was sitting with an alleged assassin. I was sharing beer and bread with him. We spent two hours together."

"If you were frightened, then how was McGuire?" asked Enno.

"I don't think he was. In fact he was rather calm. I don't think he did the murder."

"Why?"

"Because, if he had, then he would have hardly stayed in Karisoke for so long. This was February now and the gendarmerie were after him. And another thing, her sexual organs were mutilated. An American would not do this."

"Wait a minute," I said. Here was something new. "How were they mutilated?"

"The clitoris had been cut out. I do not think an American would do this."

"Did you see the body?"

"No."

"So how do you know this?" I didn't believe him.

"I was told by Aloys Mundere. He was the journalist who was in Ruhengeri in December when she was killed."

"I thought you were."

"No. I came after Mundere."

"What happened then, after you interviewed McGuire?"

"I got into trouble with the prefect. I refused to read out a prepared statement about the case. It was to be a news bulletin on the radio and I said no."

"What did it say?"

"That there was enough proof against McGuire and Rwelekana to convict them of the murder, that Rwelekana had hanged himself with his own shirt in the prison."

"What was wrong with reading that out on the radio?" I asked. I looked over to Enno. He was asleep again.

"I was sure that Rwelekana would not kill himself. If he was one of the murderers, then why would he kill himself? I thought it would have been better for him to take his chance at the trial. He could have betrayed McGuire and maybe negotiated lenience. So I refused to read out the letter and I was reprimanded. Afterwards, to save my job, I reported what had been said during the trial."

"Anything else that made you feel suspicious?"

"Yes. If McGuire was the chief suspect, then why was he allowed to leave the country? He was being followed night and day. He was at the airport for over twelve hours. His plane was delayed and he just sat there, waiting for it to arrive. The security people could have had him picked up, arrested, at any time. But they let him go. Why?"

"Why?"

"Because they knew that if he came to trial, he would talk at the trial. He would raise a lot of questions. No, it was far easier to let him go to America, and let everyone believe that he was fleeing the country to escape a trial."

I asked Jean-Baptiste what he knew about trafficking in the Ruhengeri area at the time.

"It was common knowledge."

"What was?"

"That the prefect was engaged in trafficking."

"What sort of trafficking?"

"Gorillas. And Indian hemp."

"Gold?"

"I don't know about gold. No, it was hemp. There was a plantation of it, over 150 hectares, in the Ngungwe Forest. That's beyond Butare, in the south of the country. The man who spread the story about it and who was running it got himself into a lot of trouble over it."

"Who was that?"

"Laurent Habiyareme. He was the director of the ORTPN at the time of the murder."

"A man Dian hated," I said.

"Yes, she did not like him. He did not like her, but he fell out with Zed when he revealed the existence of this drug ring and he was sacked. He's dead now."

"Tell me about Karangwa," I said.

"He is a very powerful man. He is in charge of military intelligence. He is very dangerous. Men like him kill very easily. At the time of the murder, he was in charge of the operational units of the gendarmerie in Ruhengeri."

"Did he form a commando to kill Fossey?"

"I don't know. I think if he was in charge of the killing, then he would have used *braconniers*."

"And what happened to them?"

"They could have been eliminated, but it was not necessary. Some may have come from across the border, Zaire and Uganda, and they could have returned there after the killing."

"And Rwelekana?"

"He was eliminated. In this country it is quite frequent to kill people in prison if they know the truth."

"And Rwangasore?"

"He was my friend. He was the military commander of the area.

He was a bit different from Karangwa. He did not have the same close relationship with the prefect. He was poisoned, I am sure."

"Why?"

"Because he knew about Fossey and he was prepared to speak out about the crimes of the President's family. He made this clear and he paid for it."

"Does he have a widow?"

"Yes, she works in the Post Office here in Kigali."

"Tell me about the sexual mutilation of the body. Why do you think this happened?"

"It could be to do with *sumu*. Whoever did it could have done it to put the blame on to the poachers."

"Maybe the poachers killed her and then mutilated her?"

"But they took nothing. No money, nothing, and the place was in a mess. There were papers all over the place, so why would poachers look for pieces of paper? It's not the work of poachers."

It was time to leave. The curfew was about to come into operation. I got up to go, and shook Enno out of his sleep.

"Who's next?" I asked Jean-Baptiste at the door.

"Next for what?"

"Next to be killed."

"I think it will be Karangwa. The gods here do not like people to survive long after they know their secrets."

Ruhengeri: November 1992

THERE WAS no ink in Enno's photocopier. Nor had he given us any paper. Fortunately, Main Street, Ruhengeri was blessed with a sort of equatorial Rymans where A4 could be bought and copies could be made. Not only that. Lurking inside the photocopying booth, guarding her machine as if it was the altar upon which the Holy Grail sat, was the same sullen woman who has somehow been replicated wherever photocopying booths are situated, whether it be Madison or Kenyatta Avenue.

As Abdul sorted through the files and I selected the items I wanted to copy, a blue card folder with the word "Amafoto" written in blue Biro on the cover slipped out on to the Procureur's desk. I opened it. Inside was a set of pictures, black and white, neatly mounted on to the inside leaves of the folder. The photographs had been taken by the gendarmerie shortly after the murder.

The first was a picture of the outside of the house, taken, I think, to impress the bosses back in Ruhengeri and Kigali. The gendarmerie was guarding the hut in force. I counted nine men with guns standing in front it.

Next to it was a picture of Fossey's body. She was on the floor, lying on her back. Her left arm was lying across her chest. The right arm was under the bed, and the head was hidden under a bedside chest. She was wearing pyjamas, an outfit that looked to be warm and without buttons. The trousers had an elasticated waist. There were bloodstains on the pyjama top. Her midriff was bared and the pyjama bottoms were splattered with blood.

The next photo showed the bed with two mattresses on it. Then there was a picture of the exterior of the house, taken from the front. There was also another picture of the body. In it I could see, under the bed, a pistol and next to it a hot-water bottle. There was one colour picture in the file. This was taken, I would guess, in the headquarters of the gendarmerie. It showed a table on which there was a gun. Someone had written on the photo in Biro the letters "CIA".

There was also a packet of black and white pictures. The first was a close-up of her head. It was completely unrecognisable. Next to the shapeless and blood-encrusted head was a torch and then a large plastic container of Revlon face cleanser, but no amount of make-up could ever have put right the mess that was once an attractive face. There were a couple of pictures of bare footprints in the mud; another of cupboards that had been opened; one of her sitting room which looked remarkably neat, and one of her desk with two drawers open.

Abdul pored over the pictures, describing in detail what he could see and then passed them over to me in case I could spot anything that he had missed.

"It's strange, Nick," he said, "but I cannot see any sign of a hole in the wall of her cabin."

I agreed. "There must be more pictures," I said.

1. Karisoke, Dian's mountain base

© Harvey Mann, FRGS

2. The interior of Dian's hut, the day after the murder

3. The tracker, Rwelekana, 1979

4. Rwelekana's cell door, taken the day his body was found

5. Zed's palace and compound near Gisenye

6. Zed

7. Agathe, the President's wife, at mass

8. Ros Carr in her garden

© Harvery Mann, FRGS

9. Colonel Charles with the author

© François Misser

10. The President

11. Dian's grave, with the tracker Vitari

12. Abdul

Abdul turned to the Procureur who was sitting behind his desk, watching us go through the files.

"There are more pictures, but this is not the complete file. I will send to the office of the Procureur Général for the rest of the file."

While we waited, I leafed through a large red hardback file which the Procureur said had been found in McGuire's cabin. Were these the papers that had contributed so much to the case against McGuire? The papers he had been accused of stealing from Fossey, the papers that Bushishi had found in McGuire's cabin on February 3, five weeks after the murder? Were these the Crown Jewels that McGuire had secretly coveted because he knew that with them he would be able to write an extraordinary thesis that would catapult him, a nobody research student, into the hall of fame of primatology? Were these the same papers on which Fossey was going to base her sequel to her bestselling autobiography *Gorillas in the Mist*? Were these the papers that compelled a man to kill? Were these the papers that compelled a court to sign a death warrant?

The Procureur nodded. "Yes, this is good evidence, what you have in your hands now. This file, everything in it, was found in McGuire's house. As you can see, most of it belonged to the victim."

I could see that, but was this, these papers, this file, the literature of murder? Hardly. The file consisted of a series of reports on mountain gorilla research that dated back to 1979. There were over a dozen of these. In addition, there was a number of already published reports, some papers that McGuire himself had written, the monthly summaries of the Karisoke research centre, detailing where the gorillas were to be found and how they had behaved, and that was about all. And of course, there was no indication of when McGuire had obtained the file, or even if he had been given it by Dian.

"Either way," I told Abdul, "there's nothing in these pages to suggest that McGuire would have killed for them."

"Wait till you see the rest of the file before you make up your mind, Nick," advised Abdul. "Wait till you read the other depositions."

The man who had been despatched to bring the rest of the file had returned. There were, he said, more photographs for us to see. Another file, also with the word "Amafoto" written on it, was first handed to the Procureur and then to us. I opened it. There were eight photographs in it, five on the left-hand page and three opposite. The first showed the exterior rear of the house. There was no sign of a hole in the panelling. The second was an interior of the house. It was out of focus. The third was a complete view of the length of the house.

Abdul took the file from me and pored over the picture. "Look, Nick," he said. "Look at the roof here, over the porch." His finger traced the area he was talking about. "Look at the roof here." He jabbed at the picture. "The roof seems to me to have been interfered with."

It was true. The roof panels looked loose. There was a gap between the leading edge of the roof and the panels.

"Remember what the American told us when we saw him in Karisoke, the man who had taken down her cabin?" said Abdul.

I nodded. I did remember. He had told us that all the panels in the roof had been fixed firmly and that he thought that they had been that way for years. Well, he was wrong. This section of the roof looked as if it had been a casualty of an extraordinarily powerful wind . . . or it had been prised off by human beings. One of the panels was gaping open. Our contact in the cement works in Kigali may have been right. The assassins could well have entered by the roof.

"I wonder," I said to Abdul, "if the report of the magistrate or the gendarmerie will say anything about the state of the roof?"

The next photo showed the body. The head was obscured by the bedside cabinet, so all that was on view was the corpse from the neck down. On the floor next to it was the magazine of a pistol. In the fifth photograph, a *panga* could be seen underneath Fossey's right hand. Lying on the mat were two bottles of medicine and by her left hand there was a cassette. The bed quilt was stained with blood and there were bloodstains on the bottom of the bed. The mattress was numbered 82633 and a pot nestled beneath the bed.

In the sixth photograph, Abdul counted four *pangas* and a sickle lying around the body. There was a torch and the Revlon Dry Skin Relief plastic bottle (150g extra value pack). He pointed out the magazine of the gun, and the gun under the bed. He also found her shoes in the picture and a knitted poncho-shawl with a pendant.

"See this, Nick," he said. "Look, what is it?"

I peered at the photograph. I couldn't see what he was talking about, what he wanted me to identify.

"There. Look."

I saw it. It was a piece of cord or cable.

"Now look at this." Again Abdul had spotted something he thought was peculiar. Now he was looking at the next picture and he was jabbing his finger at the black and white image.

"What's this around her neck?"

It was a cord, and the cord seemed to be biting into the collar of her pyjama top which had a neck that was half-polo. The picture was clear. Could this cord, or string, and not the *pangas*, have been the murder weapon?

The last picture was in colour. It showed two pistols resting on a chair. By the side of the right-hand pistol, someone had written in blue Biro, CIA. Presumably Bushishi.

I squeezed the copied pages of the dossier into my briefcase and asked the Procureur if there was any more to see. He looked at the mess on his desk, and then shrugged and ruffled some more papers which were concealed in a separate file next to the telephone. He opened the file. On the top of the papers was a photograph, black and white, one I hadn't seen before. The Procureur picked it up and held it up to me. It showed a dead man. A black man. His eyes were closed, his tongue was extruding from his mouth. His body, well, the top half, for that was all I could see, was naked, apart from a rag that had been wound around his neck. The head bowed forward. This was no pose for a grateful snapper. This was official. This marked the end of a life, the end of a case, the end of a mystery.

"Rwelekana," I said.

"*Mort dans son cachot,*" murmured the Procureur.

"What?" Abdul was craning his neck in an attempt to see the picture which I was holding. He was crowding me and there was a danger that our enthusiasm for the material that we now possessed was getting out of control. The Procureur too had caught the mood and was edging his body between the two of us to glimpse the photo.

"It's Rwelekana. Here. Look. He's dead. And the photo has been snapped inside his cell. This must have been taken in the Amigo, the Brigade."

"By Haguma?"

"I don't know, Abdul. Probably."

He took the picture from me, turned it in his hands and tried to decipher it. Rwelekana was pictured from the waist up. He was naked, to the waist, as far as we could see. His shirt, a striped long-sleeved shirt, was fixed somehow to the concrete wall. It wasn't a rag I'd seen; one of the sleeves was wound tightly around his neck, the other sleeve attached to the wall. His head was leaning forward, to his left, and resting on his left shoulder. His arms were stretched down to the floor. It was impossible to see if his feet were on the ground, or if he was sitting in a chair.

With the picture was a number of documents. A death certificate, and an autopsy report. The report was signed by a Dr Venuste Rutaganira. I read through the doctor's conclusions. "Death by a broken neck. No visible signs of other traumatisms. Death from hanging."

The end of the case? A man's death gift-wrapped by an official, signed for, stamped, and filed away, in less time than it takes to conduct a post-mortem and type the results on to one sheet of government-issue paper. A few lines, and what appeared to be a hurried explanation.

Perhaps Dr Venuste would elaborate? Maybe the doctor would have something to tell us. If he could be found. If he could talk.

Gisenye: November 1992

"AFTER Ruhengeri, she said drive for fifty-four kilometres and you will see a signpost for the Adventist University. She said it is a big sign. One we can't miss. When we see it, we turn right. Got that, Abdul?"

"Fuck fifty-four kilometres. How can I tell when we've driven fifty-four kilometres?"

He was right, of course. The speedo and kilometre-counter on the Peugeot were broken.

"Well, look out for the sign. That's all we can do. It must be coming up soon."

We were following Ros Carr's directions to her house. Madame Carr, as she was universally known in Rwanda, had been a great friend of Dian's. The two women had known each other for almost twenty years, and it was Madame Carr who had introduced and encouraged Dian to set up her research station in the Virungas.

"She is a sexy woman, this Madame, I think," said Abdul. He rolled his tongue around the word. "Madammme." I looked at him, smiling at the road ahead, and could see on his face, in his eyes, a dark glint of seriousness. He was changing. Up to yesterday, he had been convinced that Wayne McGuire was the killer. Now he had seen the dossier, or at any rate the pictures in it, he was not so sure. That morning, as we drove out of Ruhengeri, past the hospital and prefecture, and nosed the car through the throng of people walking to their work in the town, he had outlined a scenario of Dian's last moments.

"The cord around her neck. Remember it?"

I nodded.

"And remember what Charles said about the lack of blood on the ceiling and walls?"

"Yes."

"Well, I think this is what happened. The assassins enter the house."

"How?"

"You saw the picture of the roof."

"Yes."

"They remove a roof panel, slip inside and start looking for documents."

"What documents?"

"Don't keep interrupting. I don't know what documents but they are looking for documents. She wakes up. She tackles them. One grabs her. There is a struggle. He strangles her. She falls over. They carry on looking for documents. She is not dead. She recovers, enough to grab her gun. She is still on the floor. She tries to load the gun. She can't do it. She has the wrong magazine or the wrong gun in her hand. They see what she is up to. They finish her off with the *pangas*."

"It's plausible."

"It explains why she had the hair in her hand. As that doctor told you, you have to be close to someone to pull out their hair. And it gives them time to remove the door panel afterwards."

"And it fits in with what Charles saw and with what Bushishi told us. He was sure the panel had been removed afterwards and that she had been strangled."

Ahead of us we could see three columns of soldiers, all of them wearing steel helmets, and carrying rifles, jogging along the road towards Gisenye and the border and the war. They were young, conscripts possibly, hoping the Arusha peace talks would intervene before an FPR bullet came their way. A few kilometres ahead, there was another column. This time only the men at the front and rear were armed. The soldiers sandwiched in between were dragging their feet. Some wore trainers instead of boots. They were tired and dirty. They were taller than the men who were escorting them. Abdul thought they must be prisoners of war.

The sign for the Adventist University was, according to Madame, large and unmissable. We realised we had missed it just as we cruised by. Abdul reversed the car for twenty or thirty metres and turned off the road on to a mud- and boulder-strewn track. Madame lived at the end, a thousand bumps from the junction and less than ten kilometres from the border with Uganda. Her cottage, though, could have been in the Cotswolds, with the ivy that blanketed the walls, and the black and white roof beams and the classically designed gardens, planted with rhododendron bushes and lawns that could have been tended by a beautician, and then the illusion was destroyed because wherever you looked, you could see the cones of the three mountains, the volcanoes, each of them playing the part of sentinels, stout, unmovable, and, I suppose, unpredictable, as only humans and volcanoes can be.

Madame opened the wooden front door to us. She was in her seventies, tall and sparse in her black pressed slacks and woolly patterned jumper, with neat white hair which matched the afternoon clouds that were massaging the pale blue crests of the mountains outside her sitting room windows. She invited us in and told us, in her east-coast American accent that we would be having lunch. While we waited, she telephoned a friend, Willard or was he Skip? and enquired about a lawn-mower. I sat in, not on, but in, a wide-bottomed settee, that swallowed up my back and legs. I stroked the fur that covered it.

"It's hyrax, rock hyrax," she said, ringing a brass bell on the dining room table.

While I was calculating how many rock hyraxes it would take to cover the settee, a servant appeared with a tureen of soup. Abdul took a tentative gulp. It wasn't that he wasn't hungry. He was clearly nervous about whether Madame was an aficionado of pork, and I could see he was debating with himself whether to put the question.

"So many journalists have come here asking questions about Dian," Madame said, not giving Abdul the opening he required to save his soul. "So I'm not sure whether I have anything new to say," she continued. "I've been misquoted before, you know. Some man from the *New Yorker*, or was it *Vanity Fair*? He came here, all friendly to me, and went away writing terrible things about me. You are not like that, I hope."

This wasn't a question. Madame, I realised, was a forceful woman. And I suppose she had to be to have survived here, on her own, for forty years. She had come to the cottage in 1956, buying it from an Italian who had pioneered the growth of pyrethrum in the area. She had divorced her husband, Kenneth, a big game hunter turned film maker – in fact, she said proudly, he shot the first colour films of wildlife back in the fifties on 16mm Kodachrome, in the days when Armand and Michaela Denis were introducing America and Europe to Africa in black and white – and now she was running an English-style garden centre in the heart of the equatorial rainforest, growing flowers and supplying Kigali's hotels, restaurants and embassies.

She rang the bell again. The soup dishes were cleared away and a plate of steaks was laid on the table. Abdul poked at the meat, which covered the willow-pattern plate. Madame's face enquired.

"It's not pork, is it?" he said.

"No," she said.

"Thank you, Madame Carr," he said, his knife flashing across the fat of the fillet. "You have made me a very, very, happy man," and he smiled at her.

"I don't think McGuire was the killer," Madame pronounced. "He was a pretty worthless young man, when I knew him. But I don't think he had a motive for killing her."

"We saw the Procureur, Bushishi," I said.

"Now, did you?" said Madame, as though we were talking about a summer acquaintance we both knew from the Hamptons. "And what did he have to tell you?"

"He said that whoever killed her had a key to her door."

"I don't see why they, or he, would have needed one. Her doors were always unlocked. Her bedroom door was unlocked. Her front door was unlocked."

"Did you see the body?" asked Abdul.

"No. I saw it when it was brought down from the mountain. It was wrapped in sacking, in burlap sacks. It was put into the back of Kathleen Austin's car, and we drove to the hotel in Ruhengeri, the Mohubura, and ate lunch there with the body in the back of the car. You know she had a lot of trouble with the body. I asked Kathleen what she was going to do with it, and she said she'd take it to the morgue, but the morgue had no ice, so she took it to the brewery and when the people came to work the next day, they refused to work there with it. You have to be buried in Rwanda within twenty-four hours of death otherwise there are bad omens and all sorts of terrible things will happen, so she had to take it to the embassy and then the coffin was too small and they had to make a new one for her. It was a mess. And then, at the funeral, which I attended, there was Dian in this coffin, surrounded by all sorts of people who either didn't know her or who actively hated her. There was the big man from the American Embassy who had a son called Twiga – he was six foot seven or eight – and he was asking questions and taking photographs. It wasn't right."

"Was the prefect there?"

"Yes, Protais was there."

"Zed?"

"Yes, Protais or Zed. I have always known him as Protais. I like Protais. I don't find him a liar."

"Why do you say that, Madame?"

"Oh, so many people in this country attack him and his brothers and his brother-in-law. Anyway, at the funeral I said to Protais that it was strange to have a Protestant service when Dian was a Catholic. He agreed, so he gave a benediction. In Latin. It was very moving."

"What about these stories?"

"No one I've ever met has doubted the integrity of the President's family. I love the President. He's really one of the great Africans. I like his wife, Agathe. She's not beautiful, but she dresses beautifully. They've been here so many times. Of course, this is his home area. You know, my houseboy is the President's first cousin. He had no shoes and no shorts when he first came here and he said he would write to Juvenal [the President] and ask him if he would meet me. It could only happen in Africa."

"So you like Protais and the President and Agathe and Seraphin and Sagatwa?" I said.

"Yes, they are good people. Look at what the President and his family have done for this country." She paused. "Well, to tell you the truth, I'm not too happy about one of Protais's brothers."

"Which one?"

"Seraphin."

"Why?"

"He came here with his wife one day. I was having people to tea and he wanted flowers. I told him he would have to wait until my guests had gone. He made a fuss. He insisted on taking the flowers there and then. He said he wanted the flowers that were growing in front of the house. He said he didn't want to wait. 'I'm the President's brother-in-law,' he said."

"So what did you do?"

"There was nothing I could do. He had already told the houseboy to pick those flowers. Not only that, he told him to dig up some plants that he had taken a fancy to."

"So, you like Protais, but not his brother. Who else do you like?"

"The man in charge, the officer, in charge of the investigation. He was a nice man, a thoroughly nice man."

"And who was that?" asked Abdul.

"Captain Karangwa, I think."

"What was so nice about him?"

"A charming man, a gentleman. He told me that there was a hair in Dian's hand. He said it was a secret. He said it was a European hair."

"When did he say this?"

"The day after the killing, I think. When they brought the body down the mountain. No later than that."

"So he had made his mind up already," murmured Abdul.

Madame carried on with her story, oblivious of the aside. "I planned to go up to Karisoke as soon as I heard about the murder, but I never made it to the top. Protais had arranged for a jeep to take me to the bottom of the mountain. He had filled it with food and drink and he had ordered the soldiers who were escorting me to carry me up if necessary. He wanted me to be there to tell the US Embassy officials not to move the body so that everything could be done according to Rwandan regulations. He wanted to make sure the body was buried according to Rwandan law, within twenty-four hours."

"There and then, on the mountain."

"Yes, that is what she wanted."

So Protais was anxious for the body to be buried as soon as it could be. He was concerned that American Embassy people did not move it. He did not want it brought down the mountain. Was he using another American, the highly respected Madame Carr, to fight his corner against the Americans? It would certainly suit his purposes, I thought, if the body had been buried that day.

"Was it a good investigation?" asked Abdul.

"Good?"

"Competent?" I said.

"Well, they were really stupid with the way they treated the trackers."

"Why?"

"Because they were the best trackers in Rwanda. And they arrested them all. They should have been sent out to track the killers. Instead they were all put in prison."

"Did you know Rwelekana?"

"I have letter after letter from Dian saying how she liked him. She kept saying he was the best tracker she had ever had. I don't think he killed her. And I figured out that if the Rwandans knew that McGuire was the killer, then they would have kept Rwelekana alive to testify. But if he knew that someone else was the killer, a Rwandan, for instance, then they would have had to have him killed."

I told Madame about Haguma and asked her if she thought he had been poisoned.

"I don't know about this man, but I tell you that poisoning is big here."

"How widespread?"

"My night watchman was poisoned by his wife. It took three weeks for him to die."

"Are you sure?"

"Sure. You bet. I watched him die. He got thinner and thinner. He even said he was being poisoned. We called in a witch doctor but he said it was too late."

"Any other examples?"

"Since I've been here, I've heard of over a hundred people who have been poisoned. It's weird, but it would have been much easier to have poisoned Dian. No one would have known. They might have suspected, but no one could have been sure. You know there is a woman who lives near here who got rich curing poison cases. People will pay anything for a cure. And they would go see her and come back well. The doctors in Ruhengeri, the French, heard about her and one went to see her to discover her secret. He pretended not to be a doctor, but she saw through his disguise, or his story, and chased him away. My man, Sembagare – he's the character in the film about Dian, you know, her right-hand man – was afraid to drive one of the villagers to see this woman because the man was so weak with poison and Sembagare thought he would die before he got to her house. Anyway, I insisted he take him, and six weeks later that man walked back here. He was fit again. He had lost a lot of weight but she saved him."

"How does she do it?"

"It's a good thing we have finished eating," Madame pronounced with a degree of relish. "She makes the patient, the victim, vomit, and then she analyses the contents of the stomach and from this she can discover just what poison has been used. And then she can find the appropriate antidote. It's very simple, really."

"Pity Mrs Haguma hadn't known about this woman," said

Abdul. And that reminded me. She was another one we had to find.

Kigali: November 1992

AS SOON as Abdul set eyes on the translator that Enno had finally found for us, he nudged me and said, "This one. Look at him."

I looked. Enno was proudly and proprietorially introducing him to us in the bedroom at the Milles Collines.

"Hello, Albert," I said, staring down at the mini-person who, pencil in hand, had swung around in his chair to face us, leaving for a moment the pile of papers from the dossier that he was going through.

"So? What's the matter?" I whispered to Abdul.

"Well, look at him. That's what's the matter."

I began to scrutinise Albert. He was small. His face was semi-scrub, and his body was slight. He had long arms, probably out of proportion with the rest of his body, extremely short legs, and he spoke with a lisp. And in Rwanda, none of this was unusual.

"Donation," Abdul whispered. "He's got a donation."

"How do you know?"

"Well, look at him. He's thin and he looks ill."

Enno had missed out on this semblance of medical textbook talk, but it didn't matter. Why spoil his mood?

"I found him," he said, much like any proud new owner of a handyman, "in the human rights organisation." He paused and then added, clearly even more impressed by what he was about to reveal, "Albert is a musician."

"There," said Abdul, fingers extended, like a mongoose poised above a cobra's neck. "What did I say? Speaks English, plays music, thin; donation it is."

"By that reckoning, Abdul, half of our pop stars have got a donation." I smiled to myself.

"Sorree," said Abdul, shaking Albert by the hand, "but I know about you music men. You have all the girls chasing you."

Albert, like Enno, unaware of Abdul's observation, took his

hand, pumped it, and smiled. "Yes. I rike the girls. I pray music in many rands."

Whatever he played, and however well he played, I was concerned that, like many Africans, he could not cope with ls and rs. If he had a problem speaking the language, how would he cope with putting it down on paper? We left him and Enno in the room grappling with his lisp and the dossier and went in search of Haguma's widow.

We found her, not by going back to the school she taught in, nor to the hospital where she worked, but, by chance, in her brother-in-law's office in the UNDP HQ.

Agnes Haguma was a neat-looking woman, sitting next to me on the wrong side of the desk from Cyridion, her brother-in-law. She wore, outside that relentless Rwandan capacity to suffer, a pale cardigan with a pendant hanging down over her chest. Her grey skirt was straight and covered her knees. She looked frightened. Her head rested on her chest so that the pendant, at times, was obscured by her chin. She told me that she married Haguma in July 1986 and that they had three children, two boys aged five and three, and a girl of two. Her husband was a fit man, always healthy. He never suffered from malaria, nor any other illness. Of course, she was worried when he became ill in that first week of October. He came home to her on Tuesday, October 6, and it was clear that he was unwell. But he never told her he was ill. All he would say was that he thought he had eaten badly or drunk bad beer.

"Why do you think he died?" I asked.

She shrugged. The head lolled once again.

"Natural causes?" Abdul said, gently.

Agnes Haguma shook her head slowly but firmly. Again she looked down. "He died. That's all," she said. And, after a silence, "I do not know if there was any reason why people should want to kill him."

I asked her what her husband was doing when they married in 1986.

She thought for a moment and replied, "He was working for the SFC."

I looked to Cyridion.

"The Fichier Centrale. It's the security services."

I asked her if her husband ever talked about the prisoner Rwelekana or about Fossey.

"We saw the film. People said that Rwelekana died when my husband was in charge of the prison where he was kept. But I never heard any accusations against my husband."

"You are a nurse?" said Abdul.

She nodded.

"Then you must have had some idea of the seriousness of your husband's illness?"

"Not really. I thought it was just sickness. I didn't really begin to worry until the Wednesday night. I didn't think he was going to die until the Thursday morning. About two hours before . . ." The voice faded, the memory pincered by all those what-might-have-beens.

"What did your husband say to you?" I paused. "At the end?"

Silence. "He said that he thought he might have been poisoned."

"Did he say by whom? Did he say why?"

"No." She shook her head.

I told her I was very, very sorry.

She thanked me and shook hands with Abdul first and then with me.

Abdul told her he was sorry too.

"*C'est normal,*" she said.

As we left Cyridion's office, she turned her head away from our goodbyes. She sat in her chair, looking down at her knees.

Back at the Milles Collines, Albert was steaming through the depositions. He was hunched over the makeshift desk, pencil in hand, dictionary in the other, scribbling away. Concentration was sweating out of the back of his neck. Enno was reading the autopsy report on Rwelekana. And, sitting next to him, sipping a Mitsig, was Charles.

He, too, was poring over a document. It was the photocopied picture of Rwelekana, hanging in his cell in the Gikondo Brigades. On the floor, by his chair, were the photocopies we had taken of the death certificate and the autopsy report. Charles turned the picture this way and that. He was, he said, trying to work out where the picture had been taken from, at what angle and whether he could see if Rwelekana was sitting down.

"I called Charles. I knew you would want him to see the dossier," Enno explained.

He was right, I had wanted Charles to see the dossier. I wanted him to read the report marked "SECRET" that I had found in the dossier, the report compiled and signed by Karangwa.

"Look at his neck," said Charles, pointing to the picture of Rwelekana. "The neck is forward. I have a book on hanging, and this never occurs. He must have been sitting down." He glanced through the rest of the findings listed on the autopsy report, screwed up his nose and tossed the report to me. "Not worth the paper it's written on," he said.

Charles, of course, would say that. He was an amateur, but not only that – he had a compelling reason to dismiss the report.

While we argued over the veracity and accuracy of the report, Abdul was calling doctor after doctor listed in the Kigali directory. There was no listing for Dr Venuste, but Abdul was convinced that a fellow member of the profession would know him, if he was still alive. He had no luck. Venuste was not known in Kigali. And then Abdul remembered his doctor, the woman we had met in Nairobi at the Rwandan Embassy, the ugly one who had approached us as long-lost friends the day we were sitting outside the General Hospital waiting for Haguma's wife.

"She gave me her number. Maybe she knows him."

She answered his call. He was yabbering away to her in Swahili, making her feel, I thought from the tone he employed and the gestures he was making which were as near to tuning as I have seen off the disco floor, that she was Rwanda's answer to Sharon Stone. The voice wheedled away for a few minutes and then he turned to me, thumb up, and smiled, and crashed the phone back down on its stand.

"Kigali Nights for me tonight, Nick," he said. "She knows Venuste. She works with him in the hospital."

"Which one?" It couldn't be the military one, or could it?

"The General Hospital. The same one where Haguma's wife works, where this one works," he said, still smiling, jerking his thumb to the telephone.

"Is he there now?"

"Yes. In a staff meeting. We'll go, yes?"

Of course, Dr Venuste was not there. The meeting had ended and he had gone home, via his wife's office. She worked in the

Nyamirambo district. We drove, and waited outside the shop where she worked. It was raining and this made it difficult to see who was coming and going what with the spray kicked up by the passing traffic and the clouds of condensation that had misted up all the windows in the Peugeot. Abdul still hadn't been able to fix them and we had to sit in the car with the doors open. We waited half an hour, and then Abdul told me that there was a price to be paid for the doctor's information.

"What? Venuste's information? Hell, I don't mind paying him," I said.

"No, not that doctor. The other one. The very ugly one."

"What deal have you done?"

"I told her you would take her dancing. I told her you had selected her."

"No way, Abdul. You can do that. You're the one going to Kigali Nights tonight."

We gave up the vigil and asked where the doctor lived. His house was a few streets away near the stadium. He wasn't in. Nor was his wife. I scrawled a note and gave it to his *zamu*.

As it happened Kigali Nights was off. The predators lurking in the shadows of its dance floor saw neither of us that night. Nor did the lady doctor have the opportunity to fill her capacious pockets, or for that matter any other part of her sparse body. Just as we were leaving the hotel to honour Abdul's arrangements, we were called back into the foyer by the midget doorman Zo-Zo. This time, he didn't ask if we required change, a taxi, or a girl. He simply said there was a phone call for me. It was Dr Venuste. He had finally arrived at his house and found the note I had left for him.

"What do you want?" he said. The voice was harsh and anxious. "Your message says it is urgent."

"It is, Doctor. But I can't speak about it on the telephone. Can I come and see you?"

"It is late."

"Well, tomorrow morning in your office at the hospital then?"

"No, come to the house. You know where I live. Come now."

The rain is still teemimg down when we pull up outside his house. Abdul toot-toots for the *zamu* to open the gates. I step out of the car once Abdul has parked inside the compound, and disappear down a drain. There is water up to my knees. I pull myself out and limp over to greet the doctor who is standing outside his front door, waiting for us to emerge from the Peugeot.

I shake the drain water out of my trousers and squelch across the grass and mud into his house. He has seen me fall, but there isn't a hint of a smile on his face. Instead he apologises for the bad weather, and invites us to sit down. No one is talking. He is waiting for us to make the first move. The only sound in the room is the blab of a black and white television which flickers hopefully for a few seconds and then dies away as he dials down the sound.

Dr Venuste has been a doctor for fourteen years. I estimate his age at mid forties. He has led a particularly quiet life for a doctor. And he wants to continue that way. That is why he is not at all happy to see us. More than that he makes it perfectly clear that he is not at all happy to talk to us.

I tell him that I am trying to find out who killed Dian Fossey. He says nothing. I tell him that I have been given access to the Fossey dossier, the entire dossier. I make sure I stress the word entire. He says nothing. I tell him that his name is mentioned in the dossier. He says something. He asks me where his name is mentioned.

"In relation to the death and autopsy of Rwelekana."

"Who?"

"You must know the name," says Abdul, careful not to repeat it.

"Yes, but it was a long time ago, many years. Why should I remember this name?"

"Because you performed an autopsy on this man."

"Yes, but it is just another case. In my time, there have been many cases."

"Not like this one," I say.

He says nothing.

"How many times have you had to deal with a suicide?" I ask him.

"Suicide is not the way in Rwanda."

"And suicide by hanging?" says Abdul.

"Once or twice. Maybe a woman patient of mine has hanged herself because she is unhappy with her husband. It is rare."

"And suicide by hanging in a prison cell?" I ask.

"Why are you asking me this? I am a doctor and I have a duty not to disclose these things."

"This man is dead. Your duty is not to him any more."

"And nor is my duty to you. Who are you anyway?"

Dr Venuste is nervous of us, of this conversation, of the whole subject. He is building up his defences. He is trying, desperately, not to talk, but there is something within him, something I can instinctively sense, that is compelling him, much against his own better judgment, to keep opening his mouth.

I tell the doctor who I am, who Abdul is.

"You are American," he says, staring at us. Now his hands are wrestling with each other. He cannot keep still. He is desperate to get out of his chair. I can smell the sweetness of the after-work beer that has staled on his breath. "You are CIA."

We laugh. The doctor doesn't. He is quite serious. I reassure the doctor that we are neither American, nor its agents. I tell him that the case of Rwelekana is one that he cannot honestly invoke medical ethics to shield behind. I reach into my briefcase and fish out the picture of Rwelekana, and with it, the report of his autopsy, the report signed by Dr Venuste.

"I do not know who this is," he says after he has looked at the picture. He dismisses the picture with a flap of the hand.

"It's Rwelekana, the man you performed an autopsy on."

"What if it is?"

"And here's the report," I say, handing it to him.

He receives it in his hand as if it is coated with plutonium. He can't wait to pass it back. "I will comment only on the report that I wrote," he says finally.

That is something. I look at Abdul. He looks as if we have won a victory. A small victory.

Then, before we have time to ask him about the report, he shakes his head and exhales noisily, and says, "This has bad memories for me. This case is a bad memory."

"But you said that you had no memory at all of the case. You told us this when we first came into this room."

He says nothing.

"When did you see the man, Rwelekana, first?" I ask.

"I can't remember. At night, I believe."

"It was in the morning that he was brought to the hospital," says Abdul, reading from the report.

"Yes, that is correct. I was on duty at the hospital."

"Which hospital?"

"I refer you to the report."

"The Kigali General Hospital?" tries Abdul, reading the name from the report.

"Yes. It was my luck, my bad luck, to be on duty."

"Why do you say bad luck? After all, wasn't this just another case? You said so yourself."

"No, it wasn't another case. It was a case I wish I had never had anything to do with."

"Did you see the dead man in the cell of the Gikondo Brigades?"

"No. He was brought into the hospital. I've told you already. I was on duty. They brought him in. I examined the corpse. I performed an autopsy and I made a report. That is all."

"So why was it such an unpleasant experience?" I ask.

"Why is it an unpleasant experience?" corrects Abdul.

"I refer you to my report."

"That is no answer, Doctor," I say.

"A few weeks later . . ." He begins to speak and then he stops.

Abdul says nothing. I say nothing. We wait.

He starts up again. "A few weeks later . . . I was called to the President's office. It was a very bad experience for me. Look." He pauses. There is an edge now in his voice. His hands are waving at us now, his chest is heaving. He thrusts his right hand into the open neck of his collar as if he is going to throttle himself. "Look, I did my job. I want to wash my hands of it."

"Of what?"

He sighs. The hands wave again. "Of this. Of this case. Of your questions. I am a Rwandan and this is Rwandan hospitality, but why should I answer any more of your questions?" The voice is raised now, hovering between hoarseness and loss of control. "I did my job," he repeats, more to himself than to us.

"Why did the President's office want you?"

He looks at me and shrugs. "I do not know."

"What did they ask you?" says Abdul.

"They asked me a lot of questions about the autopsy. They interrogated me. It was a bad time for me."

"Was the President there?"

He laughs. "No. They came for me here and took me to the President's office."

"Did you know why?"

"No. Why should I question it? Maybe they were going to make me Minister of Health."

Now we are laughing, forcing it out, desperately trying to calm him, to massage his ego, to cap his well of intensity.

"Let's go through the report," I suggest. "'His body was brought into the hospital. I examined the corpse. There were marks of a cord around his neck.'"

"Does this mean," Abdul asks, "that these marks were from a rope or a shirt or something else?"

"This is a question I won't answer."

"Are you frightened to talk to us?" I say.

"Maybe I am. Maybe I am not. In my opinion, I am not. But this case is a case of many issues. It is," he says, "not a good case to recall."

I can see now that he is going to say little more than he has already said. I get up to go. Abdul shifts himself in his seat too. My feet are still wet and my socks carry the odour of the drains.

"I would ask you," Dr Venuste puts to us, "to forget about what I have told you tonight."

"You have told us nothing, Doctor," says Abdul.

"Nothing that we did not already know," I add.

"No, please forget what I told you about me going to the President's office. I gave them assurances."

"What assurances?"

"That is all I can say."

In the Peugeot, driving through Myrambo and back to the Milles Collines, Abdul recalled the last statement of Dr Venuste. "He said that he gave assurances. And then he said that is all he could say. What do you make of that?"

"I don't know, Abdul."

"I'll tell you what I make of it. That Rwelekana was no suicide case. That's for sure. And that doctor is a very frightened man."

"What do you think he will do?"

"About us?"

"Yes."

"I don't know. But he could tell the President's office that we called on him."

"Or worse. They could tell the Réseau."

"I wouldn't worry, Nick. It amounts to the same thing."

But I was worried. I was worried about why this Dr Venuste had agreed to see us. He had spent the evening on the defensive. He had made it more than clear that he was a reluctant host. He had ended the evening by realising he had said too much. But why, in the first place, had he allowed us into his house? It would have been simpler for him to have said no to us on the phone. And then I remembered he had taken quite a few hours to answer my message. Had he taken advice? Had he contacted someone? Someone in the President's office? Or the Réseau? Had he been told to see us? To find out what we knew?

It was then, sitting in the front seat of that broken-down old Peugeot, watching the rhythm of the windscreen wipers as they flicked away the Kigali rains, that my stomach began to tell me what my brain already knew, but wasn't yet prepared to admit – even to Abdul. I was beginning to get seriously scared.

Chez Lando, Kigali: November 1992

CHARLES had left a message for us when we reached the Milles Collines: he wanted us to meet him at Chez Lando. I called him there and recognised the urgency, the insistence in his voice. He had, he said, found something in the dossier. He needed to talk.

He was not, thankfully, sitting in the nightclub. He was outside, huddled in the quiet of the garden, under one of the straw shelters from which the last drops of the day's rain were fitfully dripping on to the vast metal plate that was littered with the remains of his *poulet et frites* supper. He was leafing through a set of papers, the papers I'd wanted him to see. He handed the first four pages over to me. Stamped on the top of each page was the word "SECRET".

"Karangwa wrote this," said Charles, pointing to the papers I was holding, "on January 1, 1986. At least that is the date that is stamped on it." He leant across the bench table and pointed out the date to me. "This probably means that the document was received in Kigali on January 1, which means he wrote it either on December 31, or even before. My guess is that he wrote it as quickly as he could."

"So what?" said Abdul, who was itching to get to the disco floor around the corner from the garden-restaurant.

"So," said Charles, "it means that within forty-eight hours or so of the murder, Karangwa had made up his mind who was responsible; he wrote that hairs had been found in her hand and that one of them belonged to a white person. Karangwa says that the hair must be examined because it could come from an assailant."

"Well, that's quite a reasonable assumption," I said.

"I'll tell you what I think is curious," said Abdul. "Nick, you saw Kathleen Austin and she told you that she took the hairs from the hand, but did she say that the hairs were from a different person at that stage?"

"No."

"Because Ros Carr told us only the other day that Karangwa had said to her when she saw him at the bottom of the mountain that he had a secret. He had found a hair belonging to a white person. Do you remember?"

I did. I turned out my pockets and found the note I had made of Karangwa's conversation with Ros Carr.

"They met on December 28, and, yes, here it is, he told her he had found a blond hair and she should not tell anyone about it."

"And what did Kathleen Austin tell you?" asked Charles.

"She said that the first anyone had heard of hair which belonged to anyone other than Dian was when the report came back from Paris and that was several months later."

Kathleen Austin had no doubts. She took the hairs from Dian's hands and from her head. I told Charles and Abdul what she had told me. She said that it was dark by the time she reached the cabin and she, along with Dr Bertrand, examined the body by lantern. It was obvious, even in this poor light, that there was hair in Dian's clenched fists. She said that she and the doctor left the room, and then decided to go back into the bedroom to take a sample of the hair. She took the hair from both hands and cut some off the head of Dian and sealed the samples in three envelopes which she labelled "left hand, right hand, and head".

"Did she notice the hair in the hands was different from Dian's?" said Abdul.

"She said that the hair was certainly not negroid. But she also said that it was bloodstained and in that light there was no way that she could have known it belonged to anyone else. She said that the first she heard that it belonged to someone else was when the Paris report came back to the authorities in Kigali. She said also that when she removed the hair from the envelopes at the embassy some days later when the Rwandans wanted their sample, even in that light, and under those circumstances, there was no way you could tell if the hair was from a different person."

"But was there any discussion between her and Karangwa and Bushishi about the provenance of the hair?" said Charles. "Or any speculation?"

"She said there wasn't. I've spoken to her a number of times about this and she is quite adamant."

"What sort of person is she, Nick? CIA?"

"I don't think so, Abdul. She is administrative, a bureaucrat. She is paid to get things right. She is a stickler for detail."

"This means –" But Abdul broke in before Charles could finish what he was going to say.

"Could mean," said Abdul.

Charles ignored the interruption. "This means that as early as December 28, the day after the murder, the first day of the investigation, Karangwa had decided that the murderer or murderers were not Rwandan. One of them was '*un sujet blond*', and the hair belonged to someone other than Dian. In other words a European. And this had to be McGuire."

He paused and removed his spectacles and wiped his forehead with his handkerchief. Charles had a seemingly infinite supply of them. And never once did I see him using them to blow his nose.

"Look at the last page, Nick, and you will see what Karangwa has concluded."

I turned the pages of the report and started to read Karangwa's conclusion. Charles was right. Karangwa was not at all reluctant to make clear his suspicions.

He wrote that the Service de Renseignements – the secret service whose chief, of course, was Augustine – were watching four people. They were Amy Webber, the American who had once worked with Dian and had fallen out with her, and who now lived in Kigali where she had just had a baby; Jean van der Becke, the head of the rival Mountain Gorilla Project, and another enemy of Dian's; McGuire; and Dr Bertrand, the young Frenchman who was working in Ruhengeri hospital and who had not performed an autopsy on Dian.

After McGuire's name he had written in brackets: *"Chercheur Américain assassin probable de Dian à l'aide de Rwelekana."*

The complete scenario, according to Karangwa, was this: a massive conspiracy existed, a plot cooked up by Mrs Webber and van der Becke, whose aim was to rid themselves of Fossey. McGuire and Rwelekana carried out the plan and Dr Bertrand provided the polish by refusing to perform an autopsy. Karangwa went on to say that what was certain was that the motive for the murder was not theft and therefore no Rwandan could have been involved, other than Rwelekana. Nothing of value was touched, and this therefore excludes murder by any Rwandan wanting to enrich himself.

It was clear from the tone of the report that Karangwa was looking for an early resolution to the affair. He wanted to clean it up as quickly as he could, and it was with this sentiment that he concluded his report.

But was he under orders? Was he told to find a scapegoat? Did he really find the hair, the one belonging, as he says, to *"un sujet blond"*, in Dian's clenched fist? Or did he pick up the hair elsewhere in her room?

"Well, that means that Bushishi has got it wrong," said Abdul. "He told us that he gave Kathleen Austin the hair. Or," he paused, "he is lying."

"So, why, if Kathleen is adamant that no mention was made of hair belonging to anyone else, or any other white subject, does Karangwa speculate about this in his report?" I asked.

"And why," said Charles, "does he tell Ros Carr that he has found the hair of a white person and it is a secret? No mention was made at that time of hair belonging to anyone other than Dian. Yet, a few hours later, at the foot of the mountain, when Karangwa met Ros Carr, he told her, 'in secret' that he had found a hair belonging to a white person and that it wasn't Dian's hair."

"Was there anyone else there whose hair it could have been?"

I turned to Abdul. "What do you mean?"

"What I mean is this. Was the hair that Karangwa says he found the hair that was sent to Paris? Was this the hair that was not sent to Washington? And would Karangwa tell us?"

"I do not think you will be able to see him," said Charles. "He is a very powerful man here in Kigali. He runs the internal security."

"Theo said he was a friend. Ask him to fix it," suggested Abdul. He got up, twisted his trousers around his stomach and said, "Come on, let's dance."

"You know, Abdul," I said on the way back to the Milles Collines, "that hair, the one Karangwa said he had found, or at any rate the one he mentions in the report belonging to the *sujet blanc*?"

"Look, Nick, let's not talk about hair any more. I'm up to here with hair. For all you know it is a spaghetti."

"Exactly, well not exactly spaghetti," I said. Spaghetti was Abdul-speak for pubic hair. "But maybe that hair belonged to one of the other Europeans in the room. It could have fallen out of the doctor's head, or Amy Webber's or Kathleen Austin's. It could have been picked up and kept by Karangwa."

"Exactly," said Abdul.

Karangwa did agree to see us. The next morning we drove towards the airport, passed through a roadblock and entered the Brigades, the military area that was off-limits to the average citizen of Kigali. In front of us, a troop of gendarmes, equipped with steel helmets, batons and riot shields were disgorging from a couple of trucks, parked by the side of the road. A French officer was watching them intently.

"Expecting trouble?"

"Or training to make trouble," said Abdul.

We had to leave the Peugeot outside the gendarmerie HQ. The guard phoned to say we had arrived. He was not, this guard, one of nature's gossips. His Kalashnikov did his talking. We followed its muzzle, stepped inside the wire and found the inner guard-house.

For such a powerful man, Karangwa's command post was minuscule. Maybe the office looked smaller because there was a bed jammed between the desk and the wall which seemed to swallow up most of the space in the room. Karangwa sat behind the desk and glanced at us briefly as we shuffled in to the office and waited for seats to be brought for us. He gave every indication that he was irritated that morning, whether by us, or because he had too much work in front of him, I couldn't tell. He kept looking at his watch, and drumming his Biro on the desk.

I began asking him questions. How long had he been in Ruhengeri? 1983 to 1989. Did he know Dian? Only to see in the town. Where was the body? On the floor.

And then he interrupted me, and said, "Let me tell you the story, let me tell you what happened. I'll tell you my way."

Karangwa may have been accustomed to interrogations, but he was clearly not used to being interrogated himself; he was accustomed to being in control.

"I was the commandant of the Ruhengeri gendarmerie and it was at my HQ in the town that I heard that Dian had been killed. I went immediately to Karisoke. I saw her body in her bedroom. She was lying near the bed on the floor. A hole had been cut into the wall. A panel had been removed. This hole led straight into her bedroom. There was a pistol in her hand. Like this." His hand vanished beneath the desk and reappeared. In its grip was an automatic. He slapped the butt and a magazine slid out. He pointed the pistol at me. "Yes, very like this one."

"In which hand was the pistol?"

"I can't remember. I examined her pistol and I found that she had tried to fire it, but the bullet had jammed. She was trying to put the wrong magazine into the gun. We went to see a student, the American, McGuire, who was working in her research station. He slept in a house not far from her cabin.

"The Procureur, Bushishi, spent the night in her cabin with a couple of gendarmes and the next morning we began the investigation. First we arrested everyone who worked at Karisoke. We brought a French doctor to the camp to examine the body. There was hair in her hand, though I am not sure which one. The doctor took a sample of this hair and also a sample of her head hair. At the same time we searched McGuire's house and we found there under the mat documents that belonged to Dian. This happened on the first day of the investigation."

"Are you sure?"

"Yes. We took the documents to Bushishi."

"What were these documents?"

"A daily journal kept by Dian. It was very big. It had eighteen years of entries in it. It was handwritten. A red book."

Precisely what I had seen in the Procureur's office in Ruhengeri, and the same evidence that Bushishi told me had been seized on February 3, 1986. Had Karangwa's memory failed him or was he lying?

"We also searched Rwelekana's house and we found clothes belonging to him were stained with blood. We sent these for analysis and had these stains compared with samples of Dian's blood. The blood matched. The hair came from a white man."

"White man?"

"Yes. McGuire."

"But the lab report does not say that. It says that the hair was not hers and was Caucasian."

Karangwa shrugged. "We concluded," he said, "that Rwelekana and McGuire had killed her. When we wanted to arrest Wayne McGuire, we informed the US Embassy and then McGuire fled the country. We sent out an international warrant for his arrest and extradition, but there was no agreement between us and the USA so we never got him back to stand trial."

"Where was Rwelekana at this time?" asked Abdul.

"At what time?"

"At the time you received the lab report from Paris."

"In the Ruhengeri prison, but we transferred him to Kigali and he was put into a cell at the Gikondo Brigades. The day after he committed suicide. He took off his shirt and hanged himself."

"Why," I asked, "was he transferred to the Brigades?"

"Because he had to give many explanations in Kigali."

"What do you mean?"

"I mean he was to be interrogated there."

"But surely there was no need of further interrogation. Didn't you already have all the evidence you needed from the lab report?" I said.

"And wasn't the Procureur of Ruhengeri in charge of the investigation?" said Abdul.

"Generally we transfer prisoners to Kigali, especially where they are accused of serious crimes."

"Generally, do they survive?" murmured Abdul.

Karangwa said nothing. But the coal black eyes drilled into Abdul.

"Why were the men, the men who worked with Dian, tortured?" I asked.

"No. They were not tortured. That is impossible."

"So why did they tell us that they had been tortured?" said Abdul.

"I don't know. You tell me," Karangwa replied, glancing at his watch and giving it more attention than us.

I asked Karangwa if he could tell me about the incident Dian wrote about in one of her last letters, the incident where a commando of gendarmes intercepted a gorilla trafficker and shot him dead.

"I remember it," said Karangwa. "The gorilla was an infant and had been smuggled into Rwanda from Uganda. I was in charge of the operation to catch him. We tried to arrest him and he resisted. He was killed. We recovered the gorilla but it died shortly afterwards. I remember there were ten men in the gang and they were armed with bows and arrows."

"Who was this man who was killed?" asked Abdul.

"I don't know, but he was the dealer, I believe. Now, gentlemen, I have no more time for you. I think you should see Bushishi and you should read the dossier. The full story is in it."

"We have," I said.

"Seen Bushishi?"

"Both."

"And the dossier?"

I nodded.

Karangwa squeezed past his desk and opened the door to let us out of the room. The last I saw of him he was smiling.

"He didn't tell us much, did he?" I said to Abdul, as we walked past the armed sentries and through the chain-link fence towards the car.

"No. But there's one thing we can be sure of. For a top policeman who is recalling a highly sensitive case, and remember, Nick, this was probably the most sensitive and important investigation of his career up to that time, Karangwa's got a very bad memory."

"Or," I said, "it is highly selective."

Kigali: November 1992

ZED was in town. He had been seen in the city. Theo called me with the news. He said that if I was going to see him, it had to be now.

"Where is he?"

"He's been in Gisenye. You have heard about the blockades on the Ruhengeri–Gisenye road?"

"What blockades?"

"The farmers there are stopping beer lorries getting through. The brewery is in Gisenye and they are preventing beer lorries from bringing beer to Kigali."

"Why?"

"Because they want compensation. The new road has taken their land and they say this is the only way they can make their point."

"What has this got to do with Zed?"

"He has a house near Gisenye and he was caught in the blockade. He joined the protesters and brought them food and drink and gave them his support."

"A man of the people," I said.

"Not really," said Theo. "He's doing it to destabilise the country."

"But how can stopping beer destabilise Rwanda?"

"Easily," explained Theo. "No beer in Kigali and the people get upset."

"But there is beer here in Kigali."

"Yes, I know, but the price has doubled."

I told Theo it was a re-run of that summer's French lorry drivers' dispute.

He agreed. "Yes, someone sees those demos on CNN and the next thing they copy them. Even here in Rwanda."

"So Zed's here. He got through the blockade then. How do I go about fixing a meeting?"

"You will have to see him through his brother."

"Sagatwa?" I didn't relish the thought of going through Sagatwa. Enno had described the security chief, Zed's brother, as having the blackest, coldest eyes he had ever seen.

"No, Seraphin. Call him at La Centrale – that's the name of his company." Theo gave me the number and wished me luck.

I called Seraphin. He said there was no problem. He would come to the Milles Collines and pick me up.

While I wait, I go through the dossier with Albert and Abdul. They are already reading Bushishi's report marked for the attention of the Minister of Justice. It was dated May 9, 1986 and was stamped "CONFIDENTIEL".

Abdul is laughing. "You won't believe this, Nick," he says. "Bushishi writes that van der Becke from the other gorilla project is saying that Dian killed herself. He says that she refused to have watchmen or guards, she wanted to live alone and for years the Rwandan government had done nothing about her security, and that it was sufficient for a doctor to use his expertise and authorise her burial in Karisoke."

"Some suicide," says Albert.

"What else does Bushishi say?" I ask.

"He describes the cabin. I'll read it for you." Albert starts to translate.

"The house where Fossey lived is situated 300 metres from the other houses where the guards live. The house was being guarded by the park rangers. They had been told to move nothing, touch nothing and to wait for someone from the American Embassy. The track which led to the house gives direct access to the back of the house. You enter it by the kitchen door which you go through to reach the sitting room.

"He says he noticed a hole in the wall at the left-hand corner of the house. And this hole gave direct access to the bedroom. The house was constructed of wooden beams and galvanised panels. There are six rooms, a sitting room, a bedroom, two rooms for visitors, a pantry and a kitchen. In order to make the hole in the wall, the criminals cut through the panel with a sharp object and made a hole which was large enough to allow a man to penetrate inside the house."

"Hold it a minute."

Albert stops the translation.

"Abdul," I say, "what did Bushishi say about the hole in the wall?"

"He said that the assassins entered with keys and then made the hole."

"So why is he saying here that they entered by the hole?"

"Because that was what he thought when he wrote this report."

Albert looks at me and I nod and he continues.

"'We enter through the kitchen. There all seemed normal. Nothing had been moved. But in the sitting room the desk drawers were hanging out of the desk; papers were in disorder; some objects had been moved, someone had been searching the room. The door of this room which leads to the front of the house was open, like all the doors inside the house. Several parcels were badly arranged beneath the Christmas tree. In the bedroom, everything was in a mess. The hole in the panel was at the bottom of the victim's bed. The bed was half made; the covers and the blankets were stained with blood. The body of the victim was at the side of the bed – the right side – lying on its back. You could see wounds on the face and head caused by a sharp object like a *panga*. The head was half hidden by a small bedside cupboard under which she was lying. This cupboard was marked with the blow of a *panga*. It had been struck with force. At the side of the cupboard there were four *pangas* on which there was blood which seemed to have squirted from the body. But one of the four *pangas* seems to have been used to crack the head of the victim because it is stained with blood and hair. A pistol without its magazine is visible beneath the bed; the magazine has been thrown by its side and a bullet was found near the body. The rest of the room is in such a mess that it is difficult to place where some of the objects would be before the crime. The cupboards are open, trunks and cases have been forced, but, curiously, nothing seems to have been taken. You could say that the attackers were interested in something other than money or other objects of value.'"

"Okay, Albert, stop there," I say. "Does Bushishi say what they were looking for?"

He reads on. "Yes, he says here that they were probably looking for documents which they couldn't identify at the moment and this was the motive."

"What does he say about Kathleen Austin?"

We wait until he finds the reference.

"He says that she arrived and then she looked at the body and then the doctor examines it and says that Dian was killed by the machetes or *pangas*, what you call them? And then he examined her fists and saw there was hair in them."

"What does he write?" I ask. "His precise words."

"'We were surprised to find hair belonging to a white person.'"

"Exactly the same words as Karangwa used," says Abdul. "And I bet he goes on to say that the doctor said they were Dian's hair and he says that the hairs could be from one of the assassins."

"Yes. That's it," says Albert.

"What else?"

"He goes on to say that Rwelekana was interrogated – it was on December 30, and that they discovered bloodstains on his boots, so they go to the house and find his clothes and on them there are more stains. He then says that while he is waiting for the results of the forensic tests, he will give his reasons for the basis of his suspicions."

"Go on then. What are they?"

"Where McGuire is concerned, he says that Dian never allowed him to see her research work."

"How does he know that?" Abdul asks.

"He says that McGuire wrote a letter to a man called David on February 2, 1986. It was intercepted in the Post Office at Ruhengeri and is in the dossier."

Abdul begins to riffle through the pile of papers.

"And," says Albert, "the documents which were found in his house were the ones he never had access to while Dian was alive."

"Well," I say, "we've seen them and they are innocuous."

"He says in the dossier that he asked McGuire how he got these documents and Wayne's reply is that Dian gave them to him before her death, so Bushishi is saying that the letter he wrote to his friend David in February contradicts this. He says it is certain that these documents were never in McGuire's house before her death."

"That would never stand up to an argument in court," I say.

"Then he talks about the hair. He says that these hairs belong without mistake to a white man."

"He says that?"

He nods. "Yes, he says that, and he goes on to say McGuire is the only white man to have stayed the night at the camp at Karisoke." He puts down the paper on the bed in the room and says, "*Voilà!* There you have the case."

"And whatever McGuire did after that, he is guilty," says Abdul.

"Yes."

"Then he describes how McGuire allegedly broke into Dian's house by forcing a window and took the documents. The guards spotted him."

"And a few days later, they search his house and find three keys which open Dian's door?" I ask.

"Yes."

"So why would he want to enter her house through the window to steal these documents when he could have entered with the keys all the time?"

"It doesn't make sense," says Abdul.

"And that is the case against McGuire and Rwelekana," says Albert.

Abdul passes over a copy of McGuire's letter to the American, David, the one that Bushishi had intercepted at the Ruhengeri Post Office.

"McGuire says that he was having trouble with Dian as most of the other researchers at Karisoke had experienced. All she was interested in was the daily reports and the number of days he spent in the field. What irritated her was to hear brief reports on the activities at the centre. She told me not to busy myself with the system of the gorillas which she said she would show me how to set out, and then he says in brackets, that this was what he wanted to do – i.e. get access to the daily reports of the trackers. But she never kept this promise."

"So is that the same as saying that she denied him access to certain papers?" says Albert.

"I suppose it is," I say.

"At least she is treating him no worse than she treated everybody else," says Abdul. "What about Dian's letters?" he says.

"Well, we know about her letter about the gold. What we have in the dossier is a massive amount of evidence she had compiled in the months before she died which shows how widespread the traffick in gorillas really is."

It was true. There was a dossier within the dossier which named over seventy men who she claimed were involved in trafficking. It was a comprehensive document giving names, addresses, and details of the part each *braconnier* played in the trafficking. Some merely kept weapons, others made them, and others actually captured or killed gorillas. Dealers were pinpointed too. There was one whom Abdul was especially interested in, a Mahindi, as Dian described him. This Indian Dian had said was from Bujumbura, the capital of Burundi. He had made many visits to the Ruhengeri and Kinigi areas in his Volkswagen Combi. The vehicle was grey and had tinted windows.

"Why tinted windows?" says Albert.

"So no one can look inside. No one could look inside and see what he was carrying," says Abdul.

"And why would that be? Gorillas?"

"How did you know about gorillas, Albert?" I ask him.

"Because now, it is so obvious and anyway you might be able to trace that vehicle."

"How?"

"Get Theo to check Burundi-registered vehicles crossing the border at Butare during the time that Dian was writing about. I'd say 1980 to 1985."

Abdul picks up the phone and dials Theo to give him instructions. He puts down the phone and says that Theo would try and get us an answer by the next afternoon.

"I might be able to find this man, the Mahindi, through my friend," says Albert.

"What friend?"

"He is someone I know in Kigali. He told me that he once went to Ruhengeri and brought an infant gorilla back to his house in Kigali. He kept it there for three days."

I can't believe what Albert is telling us. "Why didn't you say this before?"

"I didn't realise that this is what you were looking for and when I heard you discussing *braconniers*. . . I thought you were looking for a murderer. I'll try and see if I can find him."

Seraphin was jangling the keys of his Mercedes as he watched me walk from the lift and over to him at the hotel's reception desk. I shook his hand, taking in the broad, easy smile, the green check sports jacket and slacks, and polished black shoes with shiny buckles. There was a badge on his left lapel which served to display his allegiance. Centred in it was a portrait of his brother-in-law,

Monsieur le Président. The hair was grey, and trained to cover the shiny spots on his forehead where recession had eaten into the body. He seemed calm and his handshake transmitted his confidence. He was dressed like an angel, like his name, but I couldn't see the wings, and it was difficult to reconcile this image with the darker picture of a man said to be one of the most remorseless killers in the country, a man alleged to be at the heart of *des escadrons de la mort*. Nor was there any sign of the charmless martinet that Ros Carr had described, the man who insisted on having her flower-beds dug up, the man who felt it was necessary to remind her of just who he and his brother-in-law were.

The Mercedes was kitted out with a flimsy aerial that trailed in the wind as we drove through the city to his office near Chez Lando. Inside there was a mobile phone, not the yuppy sort, all black and compact and businesslike, but a cruder Third World-first version complete with battery-charger and python-thick cable. He drove towards the airport, past Chez Lando, taking the road for the Meridien Hotel, and then steered the car off the road, bumping the Mercedes through potholes that oozed with red water and clay and parked inside the red brick walled compound of La Centrale. He led me up one flight of stairs, along a corridor and through a door marked DIRECTION.

Was this an example of a thriving import-export business? Hardly. There seemed to be almost no activity. One or two employees looked out from their desks through open office doors, a man lurked at the head of the stairs, and said good morning, but no phones were ringing, no word-processors whirring, no faxes buzzing.

Seraphin's outfit may have come from a glossy mail-order house, but his office was a mess. Papers were strewn over the desk and the small low-legged table that squatted in the middle of the room. The one area of tranquillity and order was the shrine beneath the window. On it plaster saints mingled casually with a Madonna. There were two pictures on the walls, one of the President, and one of the Pope meeting the President.

A large file caught my eye. It was perched at the top of the pile of rubbish on the desk. I picked it up, about to ask Seraphin if he used it to buy his clothes. I saw from the cover and the title "Best Friends" it was a catalogue, the sort of thing the aspiring middle classes send off for to Fortnum or Harrods, and leave lying around their sitting rooms for every visitor to chance upon. I opened it and saw, instead of pages packed with pictures of designer fashion or cans of jellied Christmas turkey and seasoned duck, a series of letters and memos to a lawyer in Brussels. This innocuous-looking glossy was the legal arsenal that held the ammunition that was going to be aimed at those human rights activists in Brussels who had made the death-squad allegations. He saw I was interested, and I realised then that he had meant me to see it.

"Yes, we are having some problems. These people come to our country and they listen to lots of lies about us. They never seek to check their stories. We do not control death squads. It is not the Rwandan way."

"But people die here. They are murdered or die suddenly."

"Like who?"

"Like Haguma."

"He died of natural causes."

"They say he was poisoned."

Seraphin laughed. "They say that in many cases."

"But people do get killed."

"Yes, and these people, these human rights people, they have put my family in danger too."

"How?"

"By charging us with being killers they have made us into targets."

"Have you ever had an attempt on your life?"

"Yes, two, I think."

"You think!"

"Yes, I have evidence, but I can prove nothing, therefore I will not tell you what I learnt. I am not like these other people in this country who will tell you what they hear, not what they know."

"But what about your family?"

"I can tell you about that. In fact I will show you when we have finished here. It happened only a few days ago. My wife's shop was grenaded."

"Was anyone hurt?"

"Yes, three people. My wife was lucky."

"She was there?"

"Oh, yes. This happened at about four in the afternoon."

Seraphin was sitting behind his desk now, looking over the pile of papers and files and books, trying, I guessed, to look down at me, and control the conversation. But it was difficult for him as he was neither a tall nor imposing man.

"Here," he said, handing me a fax. "Look at this. It will give you an idea of what these human rights people are like."

I studied the fax. It had come from Brussels and was a complete run-down on the programme of the human rights delegation. It detailed the days, the times, the venues of their meetings. It reported who they had seen, whether the meeting had taken place in a hotel, a restaurant or even a hotel bedroom. It also reported that the mission had been lent a car belonging to one of the leaders of an opposition party.

Why had he shown it to me? I guessed he wanted me to have no doubt that everyone I was seeing, and everything I did was being noted too. It was time to attack. I asked him about Dian.

"She was a great asset to Rwanda. We valued her as we would value a gold mine. These gorillas that she protected represented an extremely valuable source of wealth and uniqueness."

Now there was a statement that was capable of being read two ways. I decided to give Seraphin the benefit.

"So why, if she was so highly thought of, did she have so much trouble getting a visa?"

"This is a very interesting question," said Seraphin, smiling at me from over the bumf-strewn desk. "I was asking this question only the other day, not about Dian . . ." and he laughed lightly, "but on behalf of businessmen who want to come and work here, and they can only have six months. That's the rule, even if they are coming here on a regular basis."

"Sorry, Seraphin, but you are wrong. I checked it already and the law states that missionaries can get a visa for two years, volunteers one year, businessmen one year and tourists six months."

"Who told you that?"

"The Ministry of Immigration. I needed to know because I was concerned about why Dian had so much bother over the years."

Seraphin smiled again. "I will look into it, but if you are right, then it is good news for me."

"You were involved in the Gorilla Fair. Can you tell me about the part you played in it?"

"I knew the man who organised it, Monsieur Barry," admitted Seraphin. "He was so plausible, he came to Rwanda, announced he wanted to set up the fair and help the country. I did all I could to help him. I even paid for a room for him to work in at the Milles Collines. But when he left here, he was telling everyone that I was a bad person."

"Why?"

"Because he had cheated us and we had found him out. He went straight to our opponents inside the country and told them."

"What sort of man was he?"

"A charming man, *le petit monsieur*," said Seraphin, smiling at me as if the charm of the man he was describing would rub off on himself. "The kind of guy who is good at manipulating good-hearted people."

"Like you?"

"Yes. And the President's wife."

"How did Monsieur Barry manipulate Agathe?"

"Oh, he charmed her. He charmed her children. He became the friend of the family. He said he knew the whole world. He showed us pictures of himself with presidents and famous people. He comes to Kigali, rings someone, tells them he is with Seraphin, or Agathe, and then they agree to see him. That sort of person."

"But he was speaking the truth, Seraphin."

"No."

"But he was with you, he was with the President's wife. That was not a lie."

"He told everyone who was invited to Rwanda that we, the Rwandan government, would pick up the bills. Then he told us that these people were paying their own way. It was a mess."

"So why wasn't he prosecuted?"

"Because he escaped from the country."

"You are not very good at keeping your alleged killers here, are you?"

"I do not understand you."

"Wayne McGuire."

Seraphin looked blankly at me. "Why not let me show you the shop where my wife was working when the grenade was thrown at her?"

I got up to go, walked over to the bookcase and withdrew from it a thick leather-bound volume. Proverbs of Rwanda. There must have been thousands of them. I looked up *vérité* and asked Seraphin to translate a few. "This one, Seraphin, what does it say?"

He fingered the line and read; "All truth is not good to say."

The shop, Le Petit Lapin, did have some of its windows broken, and there were bloodstains outside on the pavement and the scars of shrapnel on a concrete wall some yards away from the building. There was no doubt that someone had hurled a grenade, but whether they hurled it at the shop was debatable. What Seraphin omitted to tell me was that at the time the grenade was thrown, a political demonstration was taking place in the same road as the shop and that a group of CDR agitators – the government's street thugs – were involved in violent scenes with opposition party supporters. Who threw the grenade? Was it aimed at the shop? Was it thrown from the street? Was it thrown from inside the shop? Nothing was clear. Only that someone had thrown it.

Seraphin dropped me back at the Milles Collines and invited me for dinner that night. "I'll pick you up at 6.30," he said. "And you can meet my brother tomorrow. At 9.30. His office."

I was one night away from Zed.

Kigali: November 1992

ABDUL was eating *un sandwich cannibal* at the side of the swimming pool of the Milles Collines and watching the French Foreign Legion playing water polo. "If that's the way they behave when they are being friendly, God help you if they catch you on the street," he said.

I sat next to him, wondering who had christened the glistening shreds of meat and gristle that were forcing their way out of their toasted wrapping, and told him about Seraphin and the dinner he had invited me to that night.

Abdul said nothing. He was concentrating on driving a wooden toothpick into the back of his mouth.

I gave up. "What's that like?" I asked, pointing to the remains of the cannibal.

"Disgusting. You have to wait an hour for them to bring it and when it comes, it might as well eat you. At least that would be more honest. I need a curry."

I asked him what Albert was doing.

"He's up there," he said, jerking his head towards the multi-storeyed layers of cubes, each with their own balcony, that represented Kigali's contribution to Corbusian art form. "He's going through the dossier. You can't stop him. We spent the morning reading the depositions. Wayne McGuire's and Rwelekana's. I tell you that Rwelekana told the truth right from the beginning."

I went back to the room with him to read the interviews, more concerned about whether I should go alone to Seraphin's that night or take Abdul.

Albert was first to offer advice. He was against me going for dinner at all with Seraphin. Especially if he was taking me to his house. "He will poison you. Go to lestaurant."

I laughed. "He would be foolish to try it." And anyway, it would be good to see how he lived, what sort of house he had, meet his wife. It's not often you get the chance to dine with one of the top men in the Réseau.

"Then I come with you," said Abdul. "I stay in this hotel room all day, all yesterday. I need to go out."

"What about poison?"

"Bloody fuck poison."

"I won't eat anything, and no, Abdul, you can't come. I'll tell you what is said when I'm back. Now, what does poor old Rwelekana have to say?"

Albert passed me the depositions he had translated.

"By the way," I said, "how's the guy who kept the infant gorilla in his house?"

"I rooking for him. He is out of town just yet."

The deposition I had in my hand was dated August 19, 1986. It consisted of a question and answer session conducted by Bushishi at the Ruhengeri prison. It was the last interview Rwelekana was ever to give.

The Rwandan tracker answers the questions with dignity and with consistency. Never once does his story change, never once do the denials soften, never once does he take the opportunity to incriminate another. And this in the face of the devastating news from Paris that Bushishi has just broken to him, the news that the bloodstains on his clothing match the blood group of Dian.

"Do you still deny?" demands Bushishi.

"All the proofs are against me," says Rwelekana, "but I didn't commit the murder."

"Did you not think there would be specialists who could find out what you had done?"

"I only know that I have done nothing."

"How do you explain the relation between the bloodstains found on the torch and on your clothes?"

"I don't know. I only admit that the stains on my clothes were from bananas."

"But the specialist found they were bloodstains. How can you still deny this?"

"How can I accept something I did not do?"

"The source of the blood is clear. The blood came from Dian who you killed."

"The day you showed me the clothes was the day Dian was buried. Probably someone else tried to frame me."

"Do you accept that explanation yourself?"

"Do I have to accept something that I didn't do?"

"Why did we find hair in Dian's fists? Hair belonging to a white. Who is that man?"

"I don't know."

"We think you do know who it is, because Dian's blood would not be on your clothes if you were not with the white man."

"I don't know who the white man is because I did not leave my home."

"We know the white man is Wayne McGuire, because he was the only white man in the camp."

"I don't know Wayne. I don't even know what his face looks like. He does not know me either. I left Dian before he arrived in Karisoke."

"Then make us understand how you came to be stained with Dian's blood, while the white man's hair remained in Dian's fist."

"I have explained everything concerning the blood, unless someone else tried to involve me with Dian's death, because you showed me my clothes with the blood on them the day Dian's body came from Ruhengeri to be buried in Karisoke."

"Do you mean it is us who put the blood on your clothes?"

"I mean that someone did."

"Do you suspect anyone of doing this?"

"I know of nobody."

"Do you think we would be wrong to charge you now we have the proof?"

"You would be wrong and only God can make you pay."

"Is there anything else you would like to say on behalf of your defence?"

"I ask you to enquire more deeply and free me."

A last will and testament? Three days later Rwelekana was dead.

I finished reading out the deposition, and sat in silence in the room.

Abdul was the first to break it. "He is a brave man. He kept to his story to the end."

"And Bushishi must have been thinking he was on to a pushover now he had the evidence from Paris."

"Yes, even with that evidence, he refused to be browbeaten," said Abdul. "And remember he had been tortured." He paused, scratching his head and then he pushed his hand down to his trouser belt and squeezed the spare tyre around his waist. "What I don't understand is why he never accused McGuire. It would have been much easier for him to have pointed the finger at McGuire. He could have blamed him for everything. Especially after McGuire had left the country."

"Bushishi offered him the chance and he refused to take it."

"So that means that someone put blood on his clothes," said Abdul. "And found hair. And planted them. Who?"

"Bushishi?" I suggested.

"No. I don't think so," said Abdul.

"Why?"

"Because when we saw him he was convinced that McGuire and Rwelekana had done the murder, yet he told us that he did not believe Dian had been killed with *pangas* and he did not believe the killers had entered through the hole."

"So?"

"So, you are very stupid sometimes. Why should he introduce into the case an element of doubt and say he does not believe two vital points of the evidence when he is party to a frame-up all along the way?"

Abdul was right. I asked Albert what he thought.

"I use my instincts," he said. "I think he is an honest man."

"And remember if you are going to frame two people, then you have to start cooking the evidence straight after the murder," said Abdul.

"Like killing a chicken and immediately making up the curry mix," I said.

"And," Abdul continued, "if you have a conspiracy, then you keep it to as few people as you can possibly manage."

"So who were the conspirators?" I asked.

"Well, one of them has to be Karangwa."

"Because," I turned towards Albert, "you think that he was the man there who could do all these things."

"Yes, Nick, he was in the perfect position. The chief of the police."

"No, you are both wrong. It doesn't have to be Karangwa." Abdul spread his hands in front of his chest. "It could be Colonel Rwangasore."

"Yes, it could be. Pity he's dead."

"And why is he dead?" asked Albert.

"Because he was going to tell the truth about what happened," I said. "Which leads us back to Zed."

Kigali: November 1992

SERAPHIN'S beach-boy bottom was all I could see in the corner of the room. His head had vanished into the depths of his cocktail cabinet and would be there for some time if Abdul and I kept vetoing each drink suggestion he made. I was sitting at the end of one of the three wall-to-wall settees that lined his sitting room, feeling I was in the furniture department at Heal's. A relative of Seraphin's sat about ten yards away from me, stroking the arm-rest at his side of the settee. Furniture was the one thing in common that Rwanda shared with Romford. When they made it big in either place, transference of the entire contents of the local furniture showroom into their own front room was priority.

"Primus?" he invited. I shook my head, and then realised he couldn't see me because his head and half of his body was still immersed in the cabinet. I said, "No." Primus was what had finished off Haguma. Once more Seraphin dived into the cabinet which was parked next to his household shrine. Would he keep poison so close to God? Maybe it was more potent if it sat alongside his collection of pious plasters. Seraphin's head re-emerged. "Whisky?" Johnnie Walker Red Label and the bottle was half full. I thought of Abdul. There was never a time when he could resist Johnnie Walker. Besides ingesting Loch Ness amounts, Abdul knew much about its history. He talked of Johnnie Walker as if it was a dear old friend. He knew where it came from (Nigeria), when it was bottled (Look at the serial number, Nick) and how long it had been in the country (ditto). But would the numbers on the back of the label tell him if Mr Walker had been poisoned? I shook my head and waited for Seraphin to pull out something else. This time it was a bottle that had been tortured into the shape of a rhino, the sort you can buy at the Jomo Kenyatta duty-free shop in Nairobi; it contained a Kenyan version of whisky. More important the bottle was sealed. I said yes. Seraphin plonked down the rhino so it sat squat on the table, eyeing the Johnnie Walker. He picked up the Primus, tore off the top and poured out a glass for himself. I pretended to sip at the rhino liqueur, licking the glass, but not swallowing any of the brownish treacle that was sticking around the edges of the glass. I was waiting to gulp back my glass, but Seraphin was eyeing me and my reluctantce to let any of the liquid enter my body. He put his glass down on the table in front of him and began to make small talk.

"I built it myself," Seraphim said. "When I was a bachelor. Twenty years ago." Indeed it was a fine house, tucked neatly against the steep side of one of Kigali's many *collines*. I asked him how many children he had, and patted them as they peeked their heads into the room.

We'd been there half an hour by now and my brain had sent out no signals of impending bodily collapse. The extremities of my body had not turned ice cold. Nor was my breathing laboured. Just as well, because Seraphin's wife had brought snacks, Rwandan cheese that tasted of cheddar, and then a plate of grilled *chèvre*. We ate with our fingers and wiped away the grease with paper napkins.

As Seraphin chewed away with both hands at the heart of the *chèvre*, nipping with his sharp little teeth at the texture of the meat, he railed at the enemies of the state. "They lie," he spat, between each bite, "they accuse," between each wipe of the lips, "they invent," between each gulp of Primus.

"You told me this morning," I said, in an attempt to stem this gush, "that you had been targeted at least twice. Why won't you give me the details?"

"Because, as I told you this morning, I cannot prove it. I have evidence, yes, but I am not like the opposition people. I am a responsible man."

How could he say this?

"You are making very serious allegations. You should back them up, I said."

Seraphin spread his hands wide as if to say all right, I agree. "The first attempt was a car accident. The next with poison and the last was to be by shooting." He smiled again.

"Go on, then. Tell us what happened."

"We had informers working for us. They warned me in each case. I had arranged to go to a restaurant in town for a drink. I was told a car would crash into mine on the way there. I didn't go. Second, I was about to make a trip to Europe. I was told a Rwandan in Brussels had planned to drop a substance on to my head . . ."

"A brick?"

Seraphin laughed. "No, not a brick. It was some sort of poison that my body would absorb through my hair."

"What did you do?" I asked. "Wear a hat?"

This time he didn't laugh. "No, I cancelled my trip. I took this seriously."

"And the third occasion?"

"It would have happened here. Some men were planning to break in here to my house and shoot me here." He stood up and pointed to his chest and then waved his hands as if he was inviting the room itself to be his witness.

"Do you have security here?" I asked him.

"No, only bows and arrows. And," he paused, and turned around dramatically so he was looking at the altarpiece behind him, "and God."

"You showed me your wife's shop this morning."

"Yes, where the grenade was thrown."

"Why didn't you tell me there was a demo going on at the time in that same street?"

"Didn't I? What relevance does that have? What is relevant is that I know my wife was the target."

"But the grenade didn't explode that near her shop."

"God saw to that."

"Or the CDR," I muttered into my rhino liqueur.

Seraphin leant across the table towards me, trying to pick up what I had said, and as he did, we heard the gates clanging open and the sound of a car gliding down his drive. Seraphin broke off, straightened himself and marched out of the room on to the patio. He reappeared a few minutes later with a hulking gorilla of a man who was wearing a brown suit and what looked to be a Hitler moustache and whose solid black frame shut out the darkness behind him and dimmed the jaundiced African lights in the sitting room.

I knew Seraphin was somewhere in the room, but I couldn't see him. This newcomer, this stranger, was towering above me, forcing his shovel of a right hand to me. I grasped it. The left hand was gripping my shoulder. The eyes, one severely bloodshot, laser-drilled mine, forcing my eyeballs right back into my head. At least that was what it felt like. Then there were the lips, which were clenching his teeth to such an extent that I was beginning to think that everything inside, his tongue, his saliva, his gums, his gold fillings, even the rotten bits left over from his lunch, the scraps beyond the range of his toothpick, would fall out, and land on me. I wondered too if the moustache was real. For a second I considered whether to reach up and tug it, but I couldn't move my hands away from the clingfilm grip. In any case, you don't count seconds when something like this is happening to you. All I could manage was to hold on and try not to unlock my eyes from his.

He didn't speak to me and I didn't speak to him. And then the duelling was over and he relaxed and forced out a smile and the grip on my hand relented. "*Enchanté*," he said, sliding out every syllable and adding a few more.

Zed. This was Zed. Zed. Zed at the end of my arm, hanging on to me, looming before me, touching me with his eyes and his fist. And, behind him, the insignificant fixer, the slighter, lighter brother Seraphin, swinging his arms, redundant now that Zed had already introduced himself.

So here we were, in Seraphin's furniture store, face to face at last. And as I looked across at him, making himself comfortable, noticing the relative, and then ignoring him, reaching for a beer, settling his bulk into the settee, I realised the two of them, the two brothers, had planned this all along. The meeting tomorrow – that was never on. Neither could wait for that. They wanted to surprise, retain the initiative, dominate me psychologically. All along, tonight, this cosy dinner planned by Seraphin, with its dishes of Rwandan cheese, and giggling faces of children, and grilled *chèvre* and now chicken, had been a charade.

I had been set up. I had been mugged.

Seraphin sat back, sipping his beer. He had completed his night's work. The stage was Zed's. I was relieved, to tell you the truth. Not because I had wanted to meet Zed on terms dictated by him, but because Seraphin's conversation, or lack of it, had been driving me to sleep.

"It is a paradox," Zed was saying as he, too, chopped and chewed and sucked and licked at his chicken leg. This was his favourite phrase. "It is a paradox." Whatever I asked him, this formed the start of his answer, four words that provided him with time to load his Kalashnikov and aim it at my head. We were talking about trafficking, a subject that Seraphin had earlier in the evening declared that he, a successful businessman, an African businessman, knew absolutely nothing about, which indeed did seem to me to define a paradox.

Zed had taken up the charge and was proceeding to deny any involvement in trafficking. In tungsten, wolfram, drugs, currency. Zed was clean. Zed was indignant.

"Many people," he began, and the small eyes pinpointed me, as if I was a cardboard duck waiting to be blown off my perch at the end of a shooting gallery. "Many people are telling stories about me." He stopped and twisted in his chair. He was choosing his words carefully, speaking slowly, emphasising each point that was vital to his argument, addressing Abdul and me as if we constituted a crowd who had come to hear him speak at a political rally. The voice was strong and deep and potent. That was when he was talking to us. Silence was just as valuable to him. He knew too that silence, as well as words, carried power.

"These storms that surround me are built out of *nothing*." The word "nothing" crashed down on to us. "I was accused of being caught in Nairobi airport with currency which I had not declared. I have *never* been there. *Never*. I always travel through Brussels and Paris."

"Perhaps the people, they are jealous of you. You are a rich man, yes?"

Zed ignored Abdul's interruption. He leaned towards Seraphin's wife who had joined us on one of the sofas. His eyes glinted and the lips broke into a smile. Was this the Zed who was said to have collected and discarded so many mistresses?

"My parents were affluent. I did not start from nothing. They gave me a start. They were not peasants. In 1957 my father bought a Chevrolet truck. An eight-tonner. He built his fortune little by little. And all this happened before the general came to power. People speak about me and my brothers. But they never speak about other people being as successful as us. It is a paradox."

"But you owe your position as prefect to your brother-in-law?"

"It is true. But what people do *not* say is that I was already a diplomat in Brussels before this and I had been an MP."

"You admit, then," I said, "that you owed your position as prefect to your brother."

Zed stared at me. And said nothing. Was he tired of the subject? Had his reservoir of justifications dried up on him? It was a case of next question. I was about to oblige, but then Zed said, "I owned a Mercedes, a new one, and several houses before the President came to power. I had a Volvo, too, and four houses."

"So you were a rich man?"

Seraphin the stage manager now became the prompter. "No one is rich in Rwanda. Not by Western standards."

"When I became the prefect, naturally I had to give up all my business interests. I had to devote myself to the job."

"What did you do?"

"I concentrated on developing the region for the people who lived there. Here is a paradox. My business stagnated. My prefecture was one of the successes of the country."

Could this have been because the President came from the north, from the region which Zed controlled? Or was it a coincidence that so much money poured into the Ruhengeri area, the presidential power base nicknamed the Akazu, the President's hut?

"When did you stop being the prefect?" I asked him.

"In 1989. Since then, I have held no official position."

"What did you do?"

"I borrowed 60 million Rwandan francs and set up a fleet of trucks. But the people I did business with, my partners, embezzled the money. I have sued them."

This, of course, was Zed's version of his short-lived dealings with Nurildeen, who had told me how he had been cheated by Zed, and how his accountant had been killed.

"What about Dian? Did you know her?"

His voice dropped, forcing me to lean towards him to catch what he was saying. As he spoke, I could see small white beads of Primus glisten on his homage-to-Hitler.

"The news was very dramatic. That morning, the morning she died, I went up to Karisoke with Captain Karangwa. He was then the commandant of the gendarmerie in Ruhengeri. We organised ourselves to climb the mountain." Zed stopped. He had dried up. He took another gulp of Primus. "I don't feel like going on. I don't feel that I can tell you anything."

"Why?"

Zed ignored me. "But if I can help, perhaps provide you with something positive . . ."

I nodded.

"I often saw her in Ruhengeri. She would come down from the mountain to the town and we would greet each other. We valued her presence in Rwanda because the gorillas that she protected constituted a wealth for us. They are a rare species. And just as she was helping to preserve this species, so I as the prefect wanted to preserve her life. We knew she was not on good terms with her fellow researchers." He paused and looked at me hard. "Was it this that ended her life?" He paused again. "Or was it the *braconniers*?"

"If it was the *braconniers*," I said, "then why was nothing stolen?"

Zed shook his head. "She once took a small boy, a poacher's child. She held him to ransom. This was a good enough reason for her to be killed by them?"

"But that happened years before she was murdered," I argued.

"We could say that the Batwa, the pygmy people, wanted to get rid of Dian, but I do not believe this."

"Why?"

"Because the Batwa do not attack the Hutu. And I don't believe it was Hutu either. However, someone from the area could have played a part in the murder."

"I don't understand what you say about Batwa and Hutu. After all, Dian was white. What would stop a Batwa killing a white?"

"They don't. They don't kill Hutu either. But if a Hutu was involved in the killing, it would be unlikely that he would do it with the help of a Batwa. No, whoever did this, knew her habits. He, or they, broke in, they removed the panel, they knew the panel was next to her bed."

"Do you believe the American McGuire and the Rwandan Rwelekana killed Dian?" I asked.

"I have a number of question marks." Zed flung out his right hand and pulled at his index finger. "First," he said, "McGuire was not on good relations with Dian. After the murder there were rumours that he was the culprit. When it was decided to arrest him, it was found he was not in Karisoke. He had left the area and, indeed, the country. No one knew how he went. Now if he was innocent how come he fled the country?"

"Perhaps he was frightened."

"Of what?"

"Of not being given a fair trial," I said.

Zed smiled. "I was not happy about McGuire's exit. I knew there were shortcomings in the investigation."

"Such as what?"

"We were not so efficient."

"When?"

"When McGuire left. He should have been followed."

I decided not to let Zed know that I had seen Augustin and that I had heard how efficient he had been when he had brought back one of the Lizinde coup plotters from Kampala in a chest.

"There were problems too when the Rwandan was found dead. We were surprised to learn of his death. And we regretted it. He had been in Ruhengeri and he was being questioned there and then it was decided to transfer him to Kigali for further questioning."

"Did you agree to him being moved?" I asked.

"We wished to interview him in Ruhengeri."

"Well, he didn't say much, did he? He stuck to his story. He died denying he was the killer."

Zed said nothing. "Second," he said, "Dian was a US citizen. We had to respect this. It was up to the US to decide whether there would be an autopsy."

"The embassy says no. The embassy says it was up to her relatives."

"Third, the French doctor who came to see the body was her friend. It was he who established the cause of death. It was he who said there was no reason to perform an autopsy."

"Do you think she was killed by blows from a *panga*?" I asked.

"This is what the doctor said."

"But, you?" I pressed. "What do you think?"

"I think several *pangas* killed her."

"And the fact there was no blood on the walls and ceiling?"

"That is true. What I can assure you is that Dian fought for her life. Captain Karangwa saw hairs in her hand."

"Karangwa?"

Zed nodded. "These hairs were taken from her body and sent to France. You know, of course, the result of the examination?"

I nodded.

He continued: "We believed that she had taken her own hair from her head when she was hit. But we took samples of this, and we proved the hair to be from another white person."

Zed wasn't expressing the same sentiments as Karangwa had in his report of January 1, 1986.

"You were at the funeral, I hear," I said.

"Yes, I spoke. I regretted in the name of Rwanda, my country, and my prefecture, and in the name of all who lived there, the infamous death of this woman who had given her life for nature and for Rwanda."

The voice boomed now across the room, the chest was full, and the eyes on fire. Zed was no longer sitting in his brother's best room, sipping beer and lecturing us, he was back seven years, up on that mountainside, standing beneath the sad Hagenia, looking down on the fresh mound of brown, thick wet earth that was covering Dian's grave. Around him stood Ros Carr, weeping, and next to her were the bleak faces of Dian's men, the trackers who had worked there with her for years, and next to them were the Americans, the embassy people, wishing it was all over and they could write off the whole sad episode and stumble back down to Kinigi and drive home to Kigali. Among them stood Dian's enemies, out of place, embarrassed, masking their pleasure.

"I spoke about the friendly relations between the United States and Rwanda, and I said that in my opinion I hoped that this unexpected death would not interrupt the programme. This blood, I said, bought for the protection of the gorillas, would be a lasting tribute. It would encourage us to keep up the fight, her fight that she had fought for so many years."

The reprise of the oration was over. We sat there quietly giving him the chance to catch his breath.

Zed was relishing the evening. He had dominated me ever since he had looked me in the eye. But it wasn't to last. It was then, when I raised the subject of gold trafficking, that he lost his nerve.

"I never heard about it," said this master of blandness. "I knew coffee was being smuggled across the border from Zaire, but gold?" He shook his head. I caught Seraphin aping his elder brother's action.

I told him about Dian's letter, the letter she had written one month before her death, the letter that recounted the capture of the "oldtimer".

Zed laughed. "You are saying you have evidence that gold was smuggled across the Virungas from Zaire and into Rwanda that way. That would be stupid." Zed looked to his left, at Seraphin. Seraphin laughed on cue. "It would be easier to bring it in by road. Or plane. Why trek all that distance over the mountains, weighed down with gold? It does not make sense."

I let him finish. "I do not have evidence of that," I said.

Zed was still smiling.

"But I have evidence that Dian knew there was a gold trafficking trade, an illicit trade, being carried on between Walikale and Rwanda. She had names, rendezvous, routes, everything."

"How do you know this?" Zed had jerked himself forward now.

"It's in the letter."

"What letter?" Had he been listening to me?

"The letter she wrote that I have a copy of. The one I've told you about. It is in London."

"And what names and places does she write about?"

"Oh, people and places. You know, the gold dealers in Walikale were working with people this side of the border. This oldtimer's letter told her the whole story."

"And you have this letter?" He didn't wait for my reply. He hunched towards me now with both hands clasped together tight, as if he was crushing a nutshell; this was not the Zed who a few minutes ago was eulogising Dian, filling the room with the bombast of farewell. This man's nerve was on hold. The tension had taken grip of his hands and his voice. What was he so concerned about? Zed rose from his seat. The evening was over. We shook hands.

"Nine thirty tomorrow," I said.

"I cannot be there. I have to go to Butare." He pointed to his bloodshot eye. "There is a specialist I must see there."

I didn't really care. Instinctively, I knew I had nailed him.

Abdul didn't share my elation. "You don't nail a man like Zed," he told me back in the Milles Collines. "He nails you."

Kigali: November 1992

THE PHONE call came just before midnight. A man's voice.

"Leave. Leave now."

"Who's speaking?"

No name. "I am with human rights. You must go." A pause. "Quickly."

"Why? Where are you calling from? Who are you?"

"Brussels. You must go. You know why. We have discussed it. You are in trouble. You must go."

"But I can't get out. There's no plane till Friday."

"Then go by car. Drive to Burundi."

That was it. I listened hard and heard nothing. The conversation was over. I put the phone down, conscious that I was avoiding looking down at the mouthpiece the way they do in the films. Whoever he was, he was panicking. Or was he trying to panic me? Who was he? Abdul was awake now, sitting on the side of his bed, rubbing his eyes, and waiting for me to speak.

"We've got to go." I told him about the phone call.

Abdul dismissed it with a choke. "This place gets crazier."

And then the phone rang again. It was the same voice. "I have called another person in Brussels. There is news from Colonel Charles. He has written an open letter to the human rights people in Kigali."

"What does it say?"

"His letter affects you. Directly. You must leave."

"What does the letter say?"

"He is linking gorilla trafficking with the man."

"What man?"

"I can't say his name. But you can guess."

The phone died. I replaced the receiver.

"Charles has gone public. He's said that Zed is trafficking in gorillas."

"Has he the evidence?" asked Abdul.

"I doubt it."

"So we have got to leave. Can we afford to rent a car?"

I shook my head. "We'll have to wait."

Abdul nodded. "Friday. Kenya Airways."

That gave us forty-eight hours in Kigali. Two days to find a proof against Zed. I doubted if we could do it.

"We don't have to go," said Abdul. "This man in Brussels is going mad. Fuck Brussels."

He climbed back into bed, pulled the sheet over his body and addressed the curtained window-doors. "This whole country, you know, these people are all the same. They are paranoid. They kill each other, or they die and then people say they have been killed. Poison! Everyone is a poisoner. No one screams. Women don't feel pain. No one trusts anyone. Everyone talks about everyone else. There is no such thing as a secret."

He was right. Rwanda was ready for a session with a psychiatrist. The appointment had already been made – we didn't know it then but the doctor was waiting. And the doctor was impatient.

By six the next morning, Kigali was displaying all the symptoms of dementia that Abdul had identified the previous night. There were people on the streets, men with drums and whistles, women in oversized dresses the colour of a rich sunset, shouting and yelling. From the hotel balcony window, I could see army lorries and police Land-Rovers, with grim cargoes of steel-helmeted gendarmes stooping behind plastic see-through riot shields, possibly the same men we had seen training the morning of our meeting with Karangwa, pelting past the hotel, making for the *centre ville*. And then there was the throb and tramp of marching men. And chants that became audible as the crowd increased in size and ranged nearer to the hotel. "Go now!" "Resign!" "Stop the killing!" "End corruption!" All to the insistent imperative of the drummers and whistles.

At *le rond-point*, the dual roundabout system that marks the centre of the city, I watched a dozen ragged protesters who could have been no more than twelve or thirteen leap out of the back of a Hyundai pick-up with all the freshness of that morning. They skipped down the hill towards *le rond-point*, their arms tucked in front of their bodies. It was the only way, without plastic bags or sacks, that they could carry the stones they were about to throw. Two of them dashed to the side of the road where the hotel garden sweeps down and wrenched the branches off the nearest and weakest tree they could find.

La manifestation had begun, and these raggy-trousered thugs were determined not to miss it. Tension had been rising in the city for the past week. There had been an upsurge in grenade-chucking, and men who had publicly opposed the regime had been killed or had vanished. *La manifestation* had been organised by the main opposition party to demonstrate the people's displeasure at the way the government and the President were allowing the country to collapse into lawlessness. Twenty thousand people were said to be on the streets, all of them converging on *le rond-point* before marching to a rally at the soccer-cum-civil-centre stadium in Myrambo.

Another pick-up, a red Toyota, lurched towards me, as if the driver was desperately trying not to be sucked back into the screaming, waving, chanting maelstrom of people at the roundabouts. Standing, leaning against the cab, a gendarme nursed another, quieter kind of Kalashnikov on his shoulder. His weapon didn't shoot high velocity bullets, but it was as pernicious as a canister of CS gas. He pointed the lens of his video camera in my direction. I smiled and wondered whether I would now be barred from attending soccer matches in the city. Hi-tech crowd control had come to Kigali. Next to the cameraman stood a stills photographer in plain clothes. His camera dangled disconsolately around his waist, slapping his chest as the Toyota gathered speed and disappeared at the top of the hill. He too realised that his days of single-frame static surveillance had been superseded.

"Hello, Mr Gordon." I didn't know who he was, this man with dark shades and a navy blazer, who was shaking my hand, and saying, *"c'est terrible."*

Where had we met before? I couldn't work it out. I turned to Abdul who never forgot a face. He shook his head. We moved on, nearer to the rock-throwing. There was a white Peugeot parked as near as a vehicle could approach the roundabout. Sitting inside, watching impassively as the events unfolded, Abdul pointed out, was someone we had met, someone we did know. It was the Belgian colonel we had been introduced to in Butare a week or so before.

A man carrying a cheap cardboard suitcase stumbled up the hill towards us. Behind him the mob didn't notice that they were now one person less. Blood, thick and dark red, streamed down his face. It matched the red and black beret that he was wearing.

"They are," he said, "beating their enemies."

"Now who would have thought of that," muttered Abdul. "Let's go." I could see he was nervous, that he did not want to involve himself in the riot, that in his view looking was the same as taking part. But I said we'd wait a few more minutes.

"Who," I asked the man with the suitcase and the bloody face, "did that to you?"

"Someone who doesn't like my party," he said, touching his beret.

"The CDR?"

He nodded.

The crowd were dispersing now, making their way to the stadium about three kilometres away. Even so, those who loitered at the twin roundabouts, picking their way through the mess of rocks and sticks that had been scattered across the tarmac, managed to raise a jeer as a government helicopter clattered overhead. Inside the stadium, a Millwall-sized crowd flaunting a disproportionately sized hate complex was chanting:

The President's a Band-it,
The President's a Band-it,
The President's a kill-er,
Get Rid Of Him.

The rhythm of the slogan was now developing into a warcry which threatened to drown out the speeches. I watched from the edge of the pitch, kicking my feet against the remains of a termite mound whose inhabitants, oblivious to the cheers and the chants and the whistling and the Dalek voices of the politicians, were endeavouring to repair it. There were others here too not listening to the speeches. A man was standing with his back to the crowd, taking photos. And dancing in front of me were masked boys with wooden sticks which they had fashioned into replica assault rifles.

I spotted Charles and was about to wave to him but I couldn't move my arm. Abdul was shaking his head and pinning me back. "Don't!" he warned. "It is better that you are not seen with him."

Abdul was right. After that letter, it would be foolish to acknowledge publicly that we knew each other. We slunk out of the stadium, two away supporters whose team had no hope of winning and drove back into the *centre ville*.

The government was expecting trouble. Of that there was no doubt. At each intersection groups of soldiers and gendarmes leant on their Kalashnikovs and waited and watched. Nearer the *centre ville* a lorry-load of riot police were parked up a side avenue.

"This will die down this afternoon. You can be sure," predicted Abdul.

"Why?"

"The rain. It will rain. And everyone will go home." In a way he was right. It did rain, and Kigali sheltered indoors. But that night there were explosions across the city. Not just grenades, but mines.

Albert was smiling. It was Friday now, and we had just decided that we would ignore the Brussels phone call and head for Ruhengeri. We would stay until the next plane for Nairobi on Tuesday. That would give him time to complete the translations.

He was pleased with himself for other reasons. He had, he explained with a sense of superiority, spent the time when we were looking at *la manifestation* profitably. Had not been frivolous with his time. After all, he reminded us, we were paying for it.

"Well," advised Abdul, "why don't you stop wasting it, and tell us what you have accomplished."

Albert told us he had contacted the Procureur of Ruhengeri in a bid to trace the Mahindi who Dian had discovered was a big player in gorilla trafficking. The Procureur had said he would check his files and that morning he had called back.

"There is a man who could be this Mahindi. But he is not from Bujumbura. He is an Arab."

"What is his name?" asked Abdul.

"Hamud Ahmed."

"And he is not from Bujumbura?"

"No."

"So what makes the Procureur think he is the same man?"

"Because he drives a VW Combi."

"With tinted windows?" asked Abdul.

"Yes."

I asked Abdul if Theo had found a trace of the VW crossing the border.

"No. He said the records weren't in Butare. He was looking in Kigali this morning. We should know soon."

"And what about the other man, Albert? Have you found him yet?"

"What other man?" Albert looked up from his pile of translations. He scratched his head and shook it and translated the neon that was flashing up on my face. "I'll call now."

"He's getting thinner, Nick," whispered Abdul. "He'd better hurry with those translations."

I could see Albert was smiling as he put the phone down. "It is," he said, "a precious track that I am finding. My friend says he will talk to you. He says that he knows this man Hamud Ahmed. He says that this Arab is the Mahindi and that he is close with Zed."

It was coming together. I knew that if we could prove that Zed was a trafficker, then we could prove he was an enemy of Dian's.

I called Theo to tell him we were going to Ruhengeri.

"When?"

"Today. Now."

"Don't move. I am coming round. I have some urgent news."

He rang off. We waited.

I thought Theo was going to tell me he had found the Mahindi from Burundi. But I was wrong. There was no trace of him crossing the border. I wasn't that disappointed. We still had the lead in Ruhengeri.

"That's why I come here," said Theo. "You must not go to Ruhengeri."

"Why?"

"Because it is too dangerous."

"For us?" asked Abdul.

"Yes. I cannot guarantee your safety. You go to Ruhengeri and you could be killed."

"Who will kill us?"

"The Réseau. I have heard more stories about you. You are said to be CIA agents."

"Yes, we know that," I said, "but that was going the rounds a couple of weeks ago."

Theo nodded. "But the stories are circulating again. I am certain they are being put out by the Réseau. They now say that you are here for two reasons. The first is to destabilise the country."

"You see, Nick," said Abdul, "I told you that we were crazy to go to the demonstration. They probably thought we had organised it." He sat on the side of the bed, his head in his hands.

"And the second reason?"

"You are here to collect information for the human rights commission."

I'd heard that before as well.

"So, if we go to Ruhengeri, we could be in trouble."

"Yes. It is much simpler for them to deal with you there than if you stay in this hotel."

"What you mean deal with?" I asked.

"Kill you. Both of you," said Theo.

Albert looked at me. "You want me to continue with the translations? You will wait for them?"

"Fuck wait," said Abdul. "You want to go to Ruhengeri, we stay. You want to read translations, we stay, you want to fuck, we stay. You want to live, we go."

We went to the airport.

There was a spare seat to my right at the back of the plane. We must have been halfway to Bujumbura when a grey-haired, well-groomed man in his mid fifties asked me in French that had been seasoned under the tropics if the seat was free.

I invited him to join us. "Where are you from?" I asked him.

He leaned towards me, still trying to fire his lighter. "Napoli."

London: December 1992

"NORMALLY," said Dr West, "they write the report first, and then they do the autopsy."

Dr West was telling me about the African way of covering up violent death. It was hardly scientific, but it was a subject with which he was familiar. He had just returned from Nairobi where he had been investigating the circumstances of the murder of Kenyan cabinet minister Robert Ouko. "We have problems on that score," he said. "There have been threats. I don't know if I will be going back. I suppose it all depends if Moi wins the election. Now let's look at this report."

He lit up a cigarette and blew smoke across the desk in his office in Guy's Hospital Medical School. I waited for his opinion, certain he would say that everything was in order. He fingered the flimsy piece of paper which I suspected had laundered the death of Rwelekana, pigeon-holed it and consigned it to the archives, took a drag, and said, "I suppose I must have seen 200 cases of hanging. In only three of them was death due to a broken neck. Here we have the doctor saying that Rwelekana died from a broken neck."

"So that is unusual?"

"Very. Death by a broken neck happens in a judicial execution. Not when someone hangs himself. And this man is said to have hanged himself."

I nodded. "So what do you die from if you hang yourself?"

"You would asphyxiate. You would lose consciousness very quickly. The pressure on your neck arteries would cut off the oxygen supply to the brain – and this could happen within seconds – and you would die, sometimes almost instantly." As he described the last moments of life of the hanging man, he put hands on to his neck and gently squeezed his carotid arteries. "Anyway, for the doctor to have come to this conclusion, he would have had to have opened up the body. Do you know if he did this?"

I shook my head.

"Well, in this case it does not make much difference whether he did open him up or not."

"Why?"

"Because if he had opened him up, and he discovered that the man had a broken neck, then we have a most unusual cause of death, which would suggest that the man did not commit suicide."

"And if he had not opened him up?"

"Then we have an autopsy that isn't worth the paper it is written on." He paused. "If he has not done an internal examination, then he's making an assumption. If it's not an assumption, then this man didn't hang himself."

"What about the line which says that there are no other visible signs of traumatism on the body? I suppose he means marks or bruises."

"Well, there wouldn't be, would there? I mean the guy was black, yes?"

I nodded.

"So bruises would not show. The only way he could tell if there was bruising would be if he had opened up the body and examined the tissues beneath the surface. You can see if damage has occurred if you do this."

"Which means it is unlikely that he made a proper autopsy," I suggested.

"The other factor is the time of death. Here," and Dr West put his finger on the line which referred to rigor mortis, "he writes that there was no rigor mortis and 'therefore the time of death is recent'." West stubbed out his cigarette. "So if there was no rigor mortis, then how could there be an oedema of the penis?"

"Yes, I was going to ask you about that," I said. "I understand that often men who are found hanging have an erection or ejaculate."

"Sometimes. You can get a semi-erection, you can get an ejaculation. Sometimes the penis looks engorged. But if there is no rigor mortis, then there can be no oedema. Oedema implies a build-up of fluid between the skin and the blood vessels which would cause an erection. You would have to hang for a long time to get any significant oedema of the penis. And if, as the doctor says, there was no rigor mortis and the death was recent, then how can there be any oedema?"

"So why did he say there was?"

"Because I would guess this man had been whacked in the penis area."

I asked Dr West what his judgment was.

"I think the poor man was hanged. I don't think he hanged himself."

I walked out of his office, between mouldering corridors, and out into cold winter evening air that was bedding itself down in the quadrangle that contained the medical school. I was elated. At last, we had something concrete. Rwelekana had been murdered. It was a cornerstone upon which we could build. Why had he been murdered? Who had killed him? Why was Dr Venuste so scared? Why had he been interrogated at the President's office? Why had Haguma been poisoned? Why had Rwangasore been poisoned? Why had Wayne McGuire been allowed to escape? Why was the US State Department so reluctant to release the documents about the murder and the investigation?

There was another why awaiting me when I came home. I had been sent a fax from Albert. The building containing the court records in Ruhengeri had been burnt to the ground. Why? Was it an accident? Or was there someone who wanted to destroy evidence? The fire, though, had come too late to prevent me from reading the file on Fossey.

There was something else too. Albert had found a couple of people in Kigali and Ruhengeri who had dealt in the gorilla trade. They were, he said, willing to talk, and they both had connections with Zed.

I knew then that I would have to go back, but, this time, alone – Abdul had found employment. He was back in the Sudan with the UN.

Kigali: February 1993

IF THE Milles Collines was World Bank, attaché cases at dawn and black-tie receptions for the diplomatic corps, the Hotel Isimbi in downtown Kigali, just opposite one of the opposition party headquarters, was more bum-bags all day long and missionaries from Wolverhampton.

"You can spend fifteen nights here for the price of one at the Milles Collines," explained Albert as we sat, he waiting for Primus, me trying not to smoke, in the hotel's basement bar. It was true. I was pleased with the lodgings he had found for me, though I didn't know then, as I sat in the dimly lit, low-ceilinged bar that there would be no water, hot or cold, by the time I woke up next morning, and that my sleep would, in any case, be a very short one, because half of Kigali would be arriving in the next few hours with the intention of partying there until the next morning.

I asked Albert what the news was. He put down the copy of the newspaper he was reading. I could see there were pages and pages, lists of names, almost as if the university exam results had been printed. I asked him what these names meant.

"They are the people who have been killed in the past two weeks."

"Where?"

"All over the country, but mostly in the north. Ruhengeri and Gisenye."

"Who killed them?"

"The MRND. The CDR."

He meant the government. "Why?"

"It's the same story as before. These people opposed the President. So they die." He reached across for the Primus and sipped the froth at the top of the glass.

"What are the names with figures following them?"

"They are people who paid to live. They gave a thousand francs or so and they bought their lives with it."

A thousand francs. Less than ten dollars. Seven pounds and if you didn't have it, then there was no way you could bargain.

"I escaped myself," he said. "I was in a car and we were forced to swerve off the road. The woman who was with me, she was the driver, was really badly cut."

"And you think this was an attempt to kill you?"

"I'm sure of it. I was on a precious track, a track for you, and I am certain that they wanted to eliminate me."

I smiled. Albert saw me. He looked away, and down at his beer.

"'Owmuch'saphowncalltowEngland, mate?"

Leaning over me was a dark, Nigel-Mansell-moustached, tall man in shorts.

"Pardon?"

"A phone call to England. Yow're from England?"

"Yes. But I don't know how much it is. I haven't rung England."

"Ow. Oithoughtyew'ad."

"No."

"I'm told it's cheaper here. I'm from the Midlands," he said, tapping himself on the chest as if there was a possibility I might confuse him with someone else in the room, and then he held out his hand. "Wolverhampton. To be precise. I'm John. Pleased to meet you."

I shook his hand. He turned to go. "What are you doing in Kigali?" I asked.

"Oh. Spreading the word of the Lord." He smiled and left the room, ducking his head as if the ceiling was about to plane off the top of his haircut.

"I have got some people for you to see," said Albert, not at all concerned by the visitation. "The man who kept the baby gorillas in his home here."

I nodded.

"And there's a man from Gitarama I want you to see. He knows something about the death of Rwelekana, I think."

"Where is he?"

"I don't know. I had arranged that he should come to Kigali today to see you. I may have missed him. I was waiting for you for so long at the airport . . ."

"Okay," I said, "he'll turn up."

"Then there's the man from Kinigi who deals in gorillas, the man who deals with the Mahindi from Bujumbura."

"The Mahindi that Dian spoke about?"

"Yes, the one with the VW."

"Yes."

"Well, I can't find him. I think he is not in Kigali."

"Where is he?"

"Ruhengeri."

"So we go there tomorrow and find him."

Albert shook his head.

"Why not?"

"It is dangerous. You have no idea. So many people got killed there in the last two weeks."

"Okay. We'll go early and come back before dark."

"Oh, hello, speak French, do you?"

The Wolverhampton wanderer had returned. This time he was not alone. By his side, holding out his hand and his heart to me – if you considered the generous expression that had paralysed his face below the nose as being reflective of the man inside – was a shorter, swarthier, and hairier version of John.

"I'm Alan," he said. "I'm spreading the word of the Lord. We're rumour-mongers . . . God's rumour-mongers, aren't we, John?"

John laughed. Alan laughed.

I asked him why he wanted to know if I spoke French.

"Because I'd like some soup."

"Nothing to do with the word then?" I asked.

"Oh, no. We have a man who tells us what they are saying."

"But aren't they all Catholics?"

"Yeah. I suppose they are, really." He tossed his head back. "I'm a convert. You know that. Would you guess it, ever?"

I looked at Alan.

"Go on, look at me. Now would you know that I was a son of a sikh, would you?"

"Sorry. You were what?"

"Son of a sikh."

"Were you? So how can you be a missionary?"

"Easy, that. I converted, I heard the Lord and the Lord told me that a son of a sikh I should not be, so I came to Africa. Here, what's this soup?"

His finger, which had led the blessing of multitudes, prodded the plastic-backed menu card of the Hotel Isimbi. "*Soupe de poison*" it said, with another "s" added above the word as a charitable afterthought. I told him.

The waiter came.

His finger drilled the menu. "Er, waiter, er poison soup, fish, I mean," he said. "And I'd like the chicken, the *poulette*, the breast, plenty of breast," he said, scooping his hands in front of his chest, increasing the size and shape of his pecs into Page Three proportions. The waiter got the message.

Ruhengeri: February 1993

THE COURT-HOUSE may have been burnt down, but the Fossey dossier was still intact, saved, maybe, by the Procureur's manifest inability to maintain a tidy desk. I handed over a bottle of Scotch, the one I had promised him when I saw him in November, and asked him if I could see the pictures inside the dossier once more.

"Of course," he said. He dug inside a precipice of papers on the desk, causing a momentary landslide, and then, as if he had suddenly remembered where he had filed the dossier, swung around on the heel of his limpy leg, and reached across the room, past me and Albert, and fished from the shelf the familiar yellow and blue files.

I flicked through the files of pictures, debating whether it was worth risking stealing some of them. I discarded the idea quickly. I was sure he would not notice. I doubted if he would check, but what was I going to say if and when I was searched and these exhibits were found on me? They were hardly passable as holiday snaps.

I asked if there were any duplicates. He fished around and gave me one which showed Rwelekana's cell. It was taken the morning he died.

"Why don't you come back and copy the pictures with a good camera?" said Albert. "I can get you one."

The Procureur agreed. Monday morning, 8.30.

Sitting in the car with us is the man who Albert tells me has kept gorillas in his house in Kigali. His name is Patrice and he is from Kinigi, twenty kilometres off the tarmac road, and nestling in the armpit of the Vulcans. It is Patrice who is going to show us where Buroko lives. Buroko is the man who worked for Zed, a man also from Kinigi, a man who like Patrice has been involved in the trafficking of gorillas. But, as the car turns off the wide main street of Ruhengeri, and zigzags between potholes, it is clear that Patrice is having trouble pinpointing Buroko's house.

"It is not *his* house we are looking for," he says.

"Then whose house is it?" I say, trying to retain my faith in Albert's "precious track" on which the car's suspension is at that moment of revelation from Patrice receiving a severe test.

"His brother's," says Albert, twisting his head around from the front seat. "We must first find the brother and then once we have located him, we can ask where Buroko is."

This was not easy. Ruhengeri may look to be a simple one-street town, but turn off its broad way and you are enmeshed in Africa's byways, as run-down and remote and complex as all the bends in the Nile. We stopped to ask for Buroko at corners, at potholes, at dusty side-street bars which proclaimed that although Guinness was good for you, it was not to be had inside; we accosted strangers, and washerwomen, boys pushing wooden barrows loaded with plastic containers of water, and then we drank down in one milky tea just the wrong side of warm that had lain around for too many minutes in a chipped Thermos and ate an omelette. It was breakfast and though we were hungry it was not satisfying. It was breakfast without Buroko.

Patrice is thirty-seven. He is a musician. He plays the guitar with the Rwandan national ballet. He has played in France and Italy and Belgium, but now, because of the war and the troubles of the government, Patrice's fingers are silent. There is no music in Rwanda. He is not working. Nor is he acting as temporary landlord for baby gorillas.

Patrice is mopping up energetically the excess grease that has allowed his omelette to double-axel around his plate. He is embarrassed about not being able to find Buroko. When he is satisfied that there is no hidden molecule of nourishment to be extracted from the plate, he starts to tell me about his time as a trafficker.

"I did it because I was hungry. I needed the money," he says, looking up at me as if I was his judge.

"They all say that," I tell Albert. "How much did they pay you?"

"About 15,000 Rwandan francs."

I work that out to be $80. "How did you in particular get involved?"

He looks at me as if I have hit him with a frying pan. "Uhh?"

"Why you?"

"Oh, it could have been me, or my friend, or my brother, or my uncle. Only they weren't asked because they were of no use to the traffickers. They would have done it, I am certain, but they didn't have a place to keep a gorilla in Kigali. I had a place in Kigali, and when the men who were paying me found out where I lived, they made it worth my while."

"Where did you keep these gorillas? In your bedroom?"

"No." Patrice wrinkles his eyes at the absurdity of my suggestion. "In a house, a small hut next to my house."

"So you lived in a nice house? A big house?"

"Yes."

"How could you afford it?"

"His house is not so big," says Albert. "You have seen houses in Kigali. You have been to Seraphin's house, and I tell you that Patrice's place is a tenth of the size. No one is rich who is a musician. I should know."

"Who asked you to keep gorillas?"

"Men from Zaire."

"Where did you meet them?"

"In Kigali. They knew me from people in Kinigi, then they looked for me in the city."

"When was this?"

"In 1988. That was the first time that I did it. The men from Zaire came to a commune near Gisenye, a place where I have relatives. They would ask if anyone had people, relatives, living in Kigali who would help them. My people gave them my name, so they came to Kigali looking for me. I listened to what they said and went to the commune near Gisenye. I saw the gorillas there."

He pauses and hold his hands apart. Between his fingers there is a space of between six to nine inches. He wraps his leather jacket into a ball, as tight as he can make it, and cradles it in his arms, rocking the jacket to sleep. He is cuddling it and smiling down as if those babies were in his arms here in this on-street breakfast bar in Ruhengeri.

"Did you bring the babies back with you to Kigali?"

He shakes his head. "No, the deal fell through."

"Why?"

"The people who were going to buy the gorillas backed out."

"Who were they? Do you know?"

"I think they were diplomats. But I never heard which embassy they were from."

"What happened to the gorillas?"

Patrice shrugs his shoulders.

"Did they die? I mean," I say, "they could hardly be put back in the forest, could they?"

Both Patrice and Albert find this thought amusing. I wait until the grins vanish.

"So what happened then?"

"When?"

"When did you next see a baby gorilla?"

"Oh, then. When I was told to be at my house in Kigali and expect someone to bring me a gorilla."

"Who told you to stay in Kigali and wait?"

"The same people. They were involved in trafficking between Gisenye and here and Kigali. They brought it –"

"What is it?"

"A baby gorilla."

"How did they come?"

"By road."

"But wasn't that risky?"

"In those days, this was before the war, there were no road-blocks."

"How old was it?"

"About one month. I fed it on bananas and milk. I kept it with me for two days."

"Where?"

"In a room where there were no windows, where people could not see it or smell it."

"Smell it?"

Patrice laughs. He wrinkles his nose. "They are smelly animals. Babies would be smelly too if they lived like gorillas. I kept it in a basket and when you were in my house, you could not smell it because it was outside in a hut."

"What were you paid?"

"Two hundred thousand francs."

About $1,200. Ten years' salary. Two days' work. I wonder how many bananas the baby ate.

"What were the villagers paid?"

"Between 30,000 and 50,000 francs."

And these were the people taking the risk.

"So if they were on the 30–50,000-franc scale and you were

earning about four times as much, how much would the people who received the gorilla from you be paying for it?"

Patrice blows out his cheeks. "I'd say at least 5 million francs. You see, it can be sold over and over again before it gets to its eventual destination."

"Were you ever involved in other kinds of traffic?"

"Gold, cannabis, cocaine, mercury."

"Tell me about gold."

"I'd cross the border, go into Zaire, go to Bukavu and meet gold dealers and buy what could I afford and bring it back here."

"Where did these people come from?"

"Walikale."

"How much did you buy?"

"*Itora.*" His brows plough up his forehead. He is trying to remember, working out an average. I wait. "It all depends," he finally says. "Maybe about a hundred grammes."

"And who did you sell it to?"

"Mostly airline people. And some traders in Kigali. Arabs, Mahindi."

"And drugs?"

"I bought cannabis. They grow it here. And cocaine. You can find it in this area. I bought about four bottles."

"Bottles?"

"Yes, that is what they sell the cannabis in."

"It's in liquid form?"

"No. They measure it in bottles."

"What sort of bottles?"

"Johnnie Walker. Scotch. Whisky bottles."

"So how much for a bottle of Red Label?"

"One hundred thousand francs." Patrice looks around. I realise he is still hungry. "But," he said, "in Nairobi, you would get much more. Much more."

"So who is this man Buroko?"

"He is involved in the trade. He works for his boss."

"Who is his boss?"

"The man who was once the prefect here."

I say nothing.

Eventually Patrice murmurs, "Mr Zed."

"How do you know all this?"

"Through the drivers, the men who work for Mr Zed. He has a

big transport business here. He employs lots of men. One driver of a car which belonged to the director of the prison here in Ruhengeri told me that if I wanted to get into the gorilla trade then I should have a chat with Mr Buroko."

"Would this be a normal sort of conversation?" I turn to Albert, but he does not answer. He does not appear to be listening. He is looking past us, across our faces, out into the alleyway that leads on to the main street, and the main street in this town, if I believe Albert, leads to trouble.

"Nothing is a secret here," says Patrice. "And no one really thinks that gorilla trafficking is a crime. It was a way of making money, making the most out of what was in short supply."

He's right. I look over at Albert; his eyes are fixed on a group of young men who are hipswinging in our direction.

"Those men. They are CDR." Albert is up and walking towards the car.

I'm in the car with him now, and we are continuing the trawl for Buroko. "So?"

"So, when the CDR come out off the big street, and into that restaurant, I don't like it. Remember we are strangers here. Strangers get killed in Rwanda."

"You mean," I say, "everyone should remain in their place? Stay at home?"

"Exactly, Nick."

Kigali: February 1993

HALF of Lac Kivu was gushing along the corridor, hurtling lemming-like past the door of my room in the Hotel Isimbi, and without hesitation hurling itself two floors down the stairwell until it was blotted up by street dust.

It wasn't the noise of the torrent that had woken me, but the parrakeet which lived in one of the houses opposite the hotel. Since dawn this creature had maintained a jaunty and optimistic one-way conversation with itself, an act as invasive and irritating as the lightening of the day that accompanied it. Of course as I became inured to the squawk and talk I realised that I wasn't noticing it, and when I grasped this, I knew some other sound had hijacked my perception. At first I thought it was rain, but the missionary with the moustache disabused me of this idea immediately I poked my head out of the door.

"Oh! Sorry, Nick. You are Nick? I'm a devil, shouldn't say it, should I, I'm bad at a name. We met yesterday." He stopped first to gather breath and then to allow me the time to recall our conversation, as if I could have forgotten. "Yeah, Nick." He stopped again. He dodged the water. He stared at me staring at the river that was sourcing from his bedroom door. "Forgot to turn off my tap, you know. I wanted a bath, you know, but I came downstairs and forgot . . ." He rubbed his hands together and watched one of the Isimbi's boys direct the stream towards the stairs. "Always busy, you know."

I said nothing. I had endured another sleepless night and now realised why there was no water to fill my bath.

"Every day it's the same, you know."

"Sorry," I said.

He raised his voice as if I was deaf or foreign. "I said every day it's the same. We do the Lord's bidding." He put his hands together as if in prayer and mimed kneeling. "Not just weekends you know."

I nodded.

"I mean," he went on, "you might think that just because we are spreading the word of the Lord, we work just Sundays. You know."

I didn't as a matter of fact. It was Sunday now. Why weren't this man and his friend converting the misguided?

"Not so," he declared. "Not so. The Lord's work is done every day, you know." He slid, against the current, back to his room.

I surfed down the stairs and out into the street in search of Buroko. He wasn't in Kigali. Patrice could not find him. Neither could Albert. We drove out of the city, towards the airport. Albert sent Patrice to ask. Some minutes went by. He climbed back into the car. He told Albert that Buroko was on a safari.

"Where?"

A shrug. A pause. "Could be he's anywhere. Out of the country even," said Patrice.

We stopped at the nearest garage. This time Albert vanished, leaving Patrice in the car with me. He was gone about five minutes. When he came back, he told the driver to go off the road and follow the track to a Third World version of a lorry park. We parked outside the perimeter fence. Albert vanished again.

"Bad news," he said, shaking his head as he slammed the car door shut after him. "Buroko is out of Kigali. I don't know where."

"So maybe we can still find him," I said.

Albert patted his chest twice as if to say "enough". "We will not be seeing him, I think. He is working for Mr Zed."

"But we knew that, Albert. What difference does that make?"

"A lot, Nick."

"Go on."

"When I saw him a couple of weeks ago, when I was with Patrice, we had a big problem getting him to talk. The only reason he did was because we found his weak point."

"And what was that? Money? Women?"

"No. None of these. It was Mr Zed."

"Zed?"

"Yes. You see, Buroko eventually told us that he had fallen out with Mr Zed and he was no longer working for him."

"So he talked?"

"Yes. In the end he talked."

"And now he has his job back with Zed?"

"Yes. So he won't talk. And he's not even in the country to talk to."

"Where is he?"

"He could be anywhere. Mombasa? Nairobi? Bujumbura? Dar es Salaam? Anywhere. Driving a lorry for Zed."

"Why do you think he got his job back?"

"Because maybe he went to see Mr Zed and told him that some people had been asking questions."

I sat back in the car, screwing up my eyes to keep out the sun. It was going wrong: no Buroko, no connection. I said nothing. No one talked. I wondered what I could do next. Albert's "precious track" was leading nowhere.

"I have a copying camera," said Albert. "We'll go to Ruhengeri tomorrow and copy the pictures."

"No," I countered, "we'll go today."

Albert did not like it. He argued against going. But he wouldn't say why. "It's a feeling I have. It is difficult for me to explain it but there are bad things going on in Ruhengeri."

"What?"

"Killings. People are being killed. Can't you understand?"

I was getting tired of this. Paranoia. Rwanda. Lockjaw. "Look, Albert, we'll stay at the hotel. A tourist hotel. Do you think they are going to come in and kill us in our beds?"

"I think."

There was another silence.

"All right," he said at last, "I'll come. But I must not stay in Ruhengeri. Nor you. We will stay in a mission near Gisenye and we can get up early and be in Ruhengeri for breakfast."

I agreed. I didn't know it then but it was the best decision I have ever taken in my life.

"Tell me about Buroko," I said to Albert as we sat in the back of the Peugeot that was taking us through Ruhengeri that Sunday afternoon, and beyond to Gisenye. "What did he look like?"

"He was about forty, I'd say."

"Tall?"

Albert nodded. "About your size."

I laughed. I am no giant unless I stand next to Albert.

"And he was strong-looking. He had clear skin. Hutu."

"What else?"

"He didn't smoke."

I groaned; I'd given up. I hadn't even thought about a cigarette until then.

"Anything else? I mean what was he wearing?"

"Brown."

"Sorry, Albert?"

"Brown. His trousers were brown and his shirt was black with a flower pattern on it. Large white flowers. And he had plastic sandals. Brown again."

"Who was with you?"

"Patrice."

"Go on."

"We went to his home in Kinigi. He was outside his house cutting firewood. Chopping away."

"What sort of house did he have?"

"The usual. One level. Tin roof. He is married. He had two children but maybe he has more."

"Maybe? What do you mean maybe?"

"I mean I only saw two children."

I laughed. "Good, Albert, that is good. You tell me only what you see or hear."

"I could tell he was suspicious of us. He asked us why do we come to him."

"What did he say to you?"

"He said, 'I don't know you.' And then he stared at Patrice and said; 'But I do know you.'"

"So what did you say?"

"Nothing. I let Patrice do the talking. He told Buroko that we had things to talk about, that I was from Kigali and that we wanted his advice."

"And then?"

"We went for a drink. To a local bar."

"What sort of bar?" I'd been to Kinigi and it wasn't exactly Las Vegas.

"You know the place," said Albert. "There is maybe one place that can call itself a bar and then there are houses which cater for the drinker. This bar had no name. We'd call it a *buvette*. Not even a *boîte*."

"Were there other people there?"

Albert nodded. "In fact, Buroko did not want to drink in the same room as them and he didn't want to drink the same beer as them. They were on local beer. He wanted Primus. He asked if we could go in another room."

"Did you?"

"Yes. I had introduced myself by now. I told Buroko that I was out of a job, I needed money, and I had a connection with a man in Europe." Me. "He said that he recognised me. He knew me as a musician and wanted to know what a musician was doing in Kinigi. I told him that I was here because I had no work. It was then he said he had no work. He said he'd been fired. I asked him why. He said he had had problems with his boss. He said his boss had accused him of not taking care of the lorries and also of smuggling."

"Did he say the name of his boss?"

"He said he worked for Zed."

"How relaxed was he by this time?"

"Do you mean how many beers had he drunk?"

I laughed.

"We had five or six that afternoon. He drank most of them. He told us how he first met Zed. It was in 1978 and he was a young man and he went for work to Zed's house and was taken on as a houseboy. Zed liked him and trusted him and said he could learn to drive. Then he got a licence for Buroko and he was driving Zed's lorries."

"What do you mean: Zed got a licence for Buroko?"

"I mean he never took a test, a driving test."

"Do you have driving tests here?"

"Yes, of course, but there are ways of getting a licence without passing the test."

"So Zed must have thought a lot of this Buroko?"

"A lot. Enough to give him a job, give him a licence, a lorry cab and a regular income."

"So what happened then?"

"By now he was on his second or third Primus and his mouth really started to open. He had lost all the reserve, the suspicion of us strangers, and then I decided I would get the subject of the conversation around to gorillas."

"What did you say?"

"I told him that I had been in Europe as a musician and I had made good contacts there and that people were asking me if it was still possible to obtain gorillas in Rwanda."

"What was his reaction?"

"He said nothing. So I asked him if it was possible." Albert sighed. He was getting tired and we were nearing Ruhengeri.

"I'm sorry, Albert, but I have to get you to recall this as if I was there myself. I have to have the detail."

"Anyway," said Albert, "he talked about the roadblocks and explained how difficult it was to traffick now there were so many checkpoints."

"End of conversation?" I suggested.

"No. Far from it. Buroko saw that the more he talked the more Primus was coming his way and what did he have to lose now he no longer was working for Mr Zed? Nothing. So I asked him what it was like before the war. Before 1990. He said it was possible, but even if there were to be peace tomorrow it would be difficult for the likes of us to break into the gorilla business."

"Why?"

"Because it was a business that was run by important people."

"He said 'important people'?"

"Yes. So I said to him that there was a rumour that his boss was one of those 'important people'. I was laughing, trying to make him relax."

"What did he say?"

"He said 'yes'. He said that his boss was a very clever businessman who did not show anyone exactly what the nature of his business really was."

"So why did people think that Zed was involved?"

"I asked him this, too. You see, Nick, I am one ahead of you too." Albert wiped the perspiration off his brow. "He said that was the trouble. His boss, Zed, had to rely on other people in this sort of business. I asked him who. He said that there was an Arab who would come regularly. I asked him from where. He said Bujumbura."

"Did you ask his name?"

Albert waved my question away. "He said his name was Nur al Nasr. Oh, I said, I've heard a story about a man from Bujumbura, a man with a VW Combi. And he said, 'It's the same man. I know him. But he was no more coming since some years.'"

"Was he excited talking about this man?" I know I was. It had to be the Mahindi who Dian had talked about.

"Not in the least. The opposite, I'd say. More matter-of-fact. His mood changed whenever he talked about Zed. As soon as the name was mentioned he'd become very angry."

"How did he know this man from Bujumbura? I mean did he really know him, did he do business with him?"

"He said these people from Bujumbura –"

"Hold on, Albert. You said people. What do you mean people? I thought we were talking about one man from Bujumbura."

"No. There were others besides Nur al Nasr. He said these people from Bujumbura went to see Zed. They made a deal with Zed there and then, and then Mr Zed sent for him – Buroko – and he took them to the forest to contact the poachers. Men like Mporanzi, for example. Buroko said he was given money by Zed to dispense to the men in the forest who would capture the gorillas."

"What happened after the gorillas were captured and sold to the Mahindi?"

"They were taken out of the country. In the case of Nur al Nasr, they went into Burundi and then –"

"How did they cross the border?"

"The customs at Butare were bribed. And from Bujumbura they went down Lake Tanganyika to Zambia. He said they went to a place called Kitwe Moliro. There white men from South Africa or Namibia took them."

"Were there any other routes out of Rwanda?"

"Through Uganda. Through a place called Cynnika."

"Anything else?"

"It was curious, this, but he said that Zed never paid him extra for what he was doing."

"Do you believe that?"

"I don't know. Maybe Zed thought that he had given this man enough already. Anyway he said that after he was fired Zed persecuted him. He was so worried that he left his home for three months. He went into hiding. He was that frightened."

"And now he is all friendly again. Working for the man he was frightened of!"

"Why?" asked Albert.

"I don't know. Maybe he's a damn good driver, or maybe he's just indispensable company. Like you, Albert."

I left Albert to work out Zed's motives for re-employing Buroko and stared out of the window at the wide main street of Ruhengeri. It was Sunday afternoon around five o'clock. In twenty-four hours this town would be the scene of a bloodbath. And another four days would pass before they even began to think of removing the bodies from this same street. Beyond the town, to the north, in the purple mist that cloaked the volcanoes, men were checking M-16s, Kalashnikovs, grenades, mortars, field telephones; they were patching their boots (if they had them), and they were listening, taking in their orders, and looking, peering down from the mountains, as far as they could see, focusing their field glasses or screwing up their eyes, and trying to make out the tin roofs of Ruhengeri that were winking back at them. Because that was their target.

We drove past the Muhabura Hotel, past the court-house where

I thought I would be seeing the Procureur the next morning, past the hospital which, like the hotel, was about to enjoy its last night on earth in its present form, past the prefecture, and out of town, towards Gisenye.

"Seems crazy," I muttered.

"What?"

"To have to drive another fifty miles or so when we could be sleeping right next to the court-house."

"It's not crazy."

"Oh really? What is it then?"

"Wise."

"Why?"

"I know Rwanda. You don't."

I said nothing. I was sick of Albert and his paranoia.

Kigali: February 1993

I NEVER saw Ruhengeri again. During the following days I pieced together what happened there but I never kept my appointment with the Procureur and I never pointed Albert's copying camera at the Fossey file. There wasn't a court-house to photograph, so I was told, let alone any pictures after the rebels, the FPR, had finished occupying the town. Nor would the Muhabura Hotel have offered me a safe haven. Parts of it were destroyed and people who were staying there, Canadian and US tourists, survived by taking cover in their bathrooms. For sixty-two hours they lay on the cold tiles, and waited for the shooting to finish. Sunday evening supper at the Muhabura ended with cheese and biscuits. By Wednesday they were still trying to chew the crumbs.

The road to Ruhengeri from Gisenye had been cut by the rebels. There was no passage back to the city. Nor were there telephone links and the only way out of Gisenye and back to Kigali was by air. It took us twenty-four hours. Albert wore a smug "now-am-I-paranoid?" expression for the next three days.

In Kigali the track had grown cold. There was no one else to see. Only the man from Gitarama and he was in hiding. According to Albert he was being hunted down not only by government hit men, but also by a prominent member of the judiciary, someone Albert said I knew.

"Who?"

"You have had breakfast with him."

"Tell me."

"Nkubito. The Procureur Général of Kigali."

I remembered the man whose eggs order the waiter at the Milles Collines kept getting wrong. The man who had investigated the death of Rwelekana. "He's big in human rights, isn't he?"

"He is now," laughed Albert.

"So what was he up to before?"

"Well, according to an article his little speciality was to persuade people to make false depositions."

"How?"

"In murder enquiries. What would happen is this. The government wants to remove someone. Most probably someone who is an opponent of the President. This man is found dead. Murdered. There is a big reaction. People start talking. The word gets about that this is a dirty business. So the government orders a judicial enquiry. Someone is accused of the murder. He is put in prison and interrogated. During the interrogation he admits to knowing a lot more about the crime than he has admitted before. He even implicates others in the crime, and what is more, those co-accused are without fail big opponents of this regime."

"What you are saying then is that magistrates, judges, I mean, are actually part of a conspiracy to ensure that anyone the regime does not like can be accused and convicted?"

Albert nodded. "If the judges are involved, then what on earth has the government got to worry about?"

"And Nkubito was doing this sort of thing?"

"According to the man from Gitarama."

Albert showed me the article. It was over four pages long and every name that was printed was in capital letters. I recognised a few of them. Colonel Rwangasore, Colonel Charles, but there was one in lower case. Rwelekana.

"Why is Rwelekana's name mentioned?"

Albert snatched the paper off me. "I hadn't noticed that before. You see they have made an error. His name is not in capitals."

"Never mind that," I said, "what does it say?"

"It says that Rwelekana was taken from the prison in Ruhengeri by Rwangasore and murdered in Kigali's Gikondo Brigade."

"What would the man from Gitarama know about that?"

"He was in prison in Ruhengeri. That's how he knows."

I knew then that I had to see him; I reckoned he was my last chance.

But the man from Gitarama did not come easily. He was frightened. The bout of killing in Ruhengeri over the past two weeks and the frenzy over the last three days had scared anyone who was known to hold critical views about the government. The man from Gitarama was probably in a more vulnerable position than most dissidents. He had gone public and had accused a top judge in print of being involved in corruption.

Albert set out to look for him, but each day he returned to the hotel and shook his head. He wasn't in Kigali. Charles had not seen him, though Colonel Anselm, the officer whose wife worked with Haguma's brother-in-law, had. This track, though, was not a precious one. There was no sign either in Gitarama. Albert had left phone messages with a friend of the man's but they had not been acknowledged.

"Maybe he does not want to see you," said Albert.

"Why?"

"Maybe he thinks you are working for the government."

"Well it's up to you to tell him I am not."

I was losing Albert. To tell you the truth I was tired of him and his "precious tracks" which were increasingly turning out as cul-de-sacs. I decided I would leave at the end of the week. I had come so far, but still there was a chasm of fact to be bridged, and I doubted if it was possible to see the people and obtain the information that would lead me across that bridge.

I lay back on the hard mattress in the Hotel des Diplomates – I had decided to change yet again, this time for security reasons – and tried to imagine Dian in the last year of her life. Who would have benefited from her death?

It was a dreadful year for her. There had been an increase in the mortality rate of her gorillas; an increase in poaching, mitigated only by the confession she had extracted from Sebahutu, the veteran poacher who had given her all the names, and the information about the Mahindi from Bujumbura. But it seemed what really was wearing her down were the campaigns that were being waged by those who worked with her – the scientists – and those who she worked with, the Rwandan authorities. The battleground was her territory: the volcanoes. The area of contention: gorillas and their exploitation. First there was the security of the area. It was clear she was worried about that. And second there was the plan to encourage more tourists to come and view the gorillas. Tourism meant foreign currency meant wealth. To Dian, an explosion in tourism spelt the end of everything she had been working for.

I paced the room. What if Dian had not received her visa? She would have been forced to relinquish control of Karisoke to someone else and to leave the country. She would have done this only under great protest and I am certain that once back in America she would have done everything within her power to return, much like a monarch who has been cheated of her birthright.

So who would have gained from her removal from Rwanda?

1 Poachers. They would have had an easier life without Fossey terrorising them. But nothing was stolen, and would poachers ignore money, or firearms, or ammunition? And would poachers, assuming they killed Dian with *pangas*, leave their weapons behind? And would poachers, assuming they used *pangas* to kill Dian, use weapons they found in the house? Would you go to someone's house in the middle of the night with the intention to kill, but not to rob, without taking a weapon along?

2 Her colleagues. The only white scientist at Karisoke was Wayne McGuire. Why would he kill Dian? Because he hated her, because he loved her, because he coveted her research notes, because he wanted to take over at Karisoke, because he wanted to be the leading primatologist in the world. So he goes to her house, unarmed, enters through the front door, which was rarely locked, takes a *panga* from the wall and proceeds to slice Dian to death. Then he cuts a hole in the wall to foster the impression that someone broke in, and he goes back to bed. He takes nothing. He does not take the notes he believes will make him the number one apeman of all time. While he is killing Dian, she grabs his hair, one strand which is found in her fist and which is sent to Paris by Bushishi, and which, along with his desire to pirate her notes, provides the strongest part of the evidence with which Bushishi condemns him. Oh, and on the way to Dian's hut, McGuire teams

up with Rwelekana, a man he has never met before, and informs him of what he is about to do, and asks Rwelekana to join him in his criminal enterprise. The Rwandan, who does not speak English, and who cannot communicate with the American in Kinyarwandan, Swahili or French because the American can speak none of these languages well enough to invite a stranger to conspire to commit homicide, readily falls in with the American and they both kill Dian. Afterwards, when Rwelekana is in prison, he refuses to incriminate the American, though this could have saved his life. He refuses to budge one millimetre from his story, and that story is that he is innocent.

And what of McGuire's alleged motive? Bushishi says McGuire was jealous of Dian and wanted her notes and wanted her job. Fine, but she had made no notes, nothing of significance, for years. The plain fact was she was too ill to study gorillas. Not only that, the notes found in McGuire's house, the papers that so excited Bushishi, contained no astonishing discoveries. I have read them. They are banal, day-to-day reports. Ah, but what about the keys that Bushishi says were in McGuire's possession, the keys found in his house underneath the rug? Bushishi argues that these keys allowed McGuire to enter Fossey's house. But he also admits the keys did not fit any of the locks on the doors that gave entry into the house proper. They were keys only to the outhouses. So how could McGuire have used them to enter the house?

No, I thought that McGuire could only have killed Dian if he was insane. But would a madman have remained, as McGuire remained, at his post for over another six months? It would be far more likely for McGuire to have cracked, to have broken down, to have confessed, or to have killed himself in remorse. Especially so, when you consider the shadow of the forensic report hanging over him. He knew it was coming from Paris, and there is no reason to believe that he did not know hair, a white man's hair, had been found in Dian's clenched fist. To be guilty of murder, and to stay at the scene of the crime would have been a foolhardy act. To stay in such a hostile environemnt as Karisoke, hostile enough without the added nightmare of a murder investigation going on around him, and increasingly pointing towards him, would have been the act of a lunatic. And then there was the uncontrollable factor in the investigation. McGuire's alleged accomplice, Rwelekana, had been in custody in Ruhengeri jail since the day after the murder. What was to stop Rwelekana confessing? What was to stop Rwelekana blaming McGuire? McGuire could not have been confident in Rwelekana's ability to keep silent. If the two had conspired together, then it would have been far more likely for McGuire to have fled the country in the knowledge that his co-assassin was in prison and was facing daily pressure from his interrogators. He did none of these things. He hung in and tried to carry on with Dian's work.

Even in death, McGuire held Dian in awe. He respected her, he looked up to her, he feared her. Would he have dared to come close enough to this figure whom he would normally shrink from, close enough to touch her, close enough to kill her? There were easier ways of killing Dian. For Wayne, the rifle. He did have one, which he kept in his room. For the Rwandans, poison.

3 The Rwandan authorities. They wanted Dian out of the country. Why? And who wanted her to leave? Or did they want her to leave? After all she had been given a visa, not for three months, but for two years just before she was to die. And who had authorised her visa but Augustin, the chief of the Sûreté. Surely, the Rwandans could argue that they cooperated with Dian and had overruled bureaucratic practice to keep her in the country. She had spent, I knew, the last few months of her life despairing of getting a visa, and then this. Two years. Did it make sense?

I began to think about it. Really think. I tried to put myself in the place of Augustin, and then it became clear. How could he refuse her a visa? Now that would have looked bad. Imagine it. No, Augustin had no choice. And, by granting the visa, and being so efficient, so cordial about it, he contrived to persuade Dian that the country, the government, the President were on her side and that her real enemies were maybe the lowlier of the bureaucrats and the scientists with whom she had always been in conflict. So why did the Rwandan authorities want Dian out of the country?

Because they believed she knew too much. Dian had arrested and interrogated one of the country's most notorious poachers in the spring of 1985. She had sent copies of her report which named almost one hundred poachers, gave details of their armouries, and outlined their modus operandi, to the authorities in Ruhengeri. She made it clear that she expected no favours to be given to these men, and when nothing drastic was done, she made her displeasure clear to those authorities. She had met the President that year too and she told him how worried she was about the security in the park. He reassured her that something would be done. Nothing was. Then there was the letter she wrote to Ian Redmond. It was dated November 24, 1985. It was the letter which told of her arrest of the "oldtimer", the gold smuggler with the Walikale link, the man I told Zed about that night at Seraphim's. The man who made Zed lose his composure.

Dian had, I had been told, a great capacity for bluffing, for persuading people that she knew more than she really did. It was a trick that served her well when she dealt with scientists, and it served her equally when she dealt with the authorities. It could be, I thought, that it was a trick which might have contributed to her downfall. It could be that the traffickers, or those organising the traffick in gorillas and drugs and gold suspected that Dian was aware of their involvement and they could not risk this knowledge being passed on, say to people outside the country.

Then there was Dian's stated opposition to the expansion of tourism in the park, an area which was close to the heart and pocket of the President and his family. Tourism meant foreign currency, people eating at the Tam Tam, staying at the Ribero or the Hotel President, dancing at Kigali Nights, paying hundreds of dollars to the ORPTN (the Director of Parks was a presidential appointment) to view the gorillas. So the absence of Dian would certainly have been welcomed by anyone who had an interest in promoting tourism.

And then there was the trade in gorillas. This was big business for Zed. Buroko had told Albert of the link between his boss Zed and the Mahindi from Bujumbura. Dian knew about the Mahindi's visits to the Kinigi area and had gone so far as to inform the authorities in Ruhengeri of her discovery. It is inconceivable that the news of her knowledge of the Mahindi's activities had not got back to Zed. As far as he knew, she possessed information about him, which, if made public, especially outside Rwanda, could be extremely damaging, not only to Zed himself, but also to his close relatives.

You get a good price for a gorilla – zoos were paying up to $20,000 for a healthy male specimen, not too old and still capable of reproducing. But there were not enough gorillas to make a fortune. And, for Zed, there was that damn Fossey woman guarding them in her crazy way. She lost them, to be sure, but when she did, she raised such a row that gorilla trafficking just didn't seem worth the hassle. Besides, she had the President's ear. He approved of what she was doing, and obviously, the more gorillas there were in Rwanda, the more the tourist trade could be encouraged, and that meant more hotels, more hard currency, and more loot for the Akazu. Zed could live with Fossey, but he needed other outlets to make his money. Occasionally a gorilla deal would be pulled off, but generally he steered clear of the woman. She was trouble.

But there came a time when he couldn't avoid clashing with her. It was 1985, the autumn, and an infant gorilla had been snatched from across the border in Uganda's Impenetrable Forest. The infant had been smuggled into Rwanda and there had been an almighty mistake. The police had been informed of the place where the gorilla was to be handed over. They had set up an ambush. The dealer was shot dead in the fire-fight. Worse, the gorilla never recovered from its ordeal. Fossey was making noises now. She wanted the gorilla back. And not even Zed could breathe life back into a dead infant. Fossey was threatening him. Apparently she knew what had been going on in the Virungas, her territory. She had intercepted one of his couriers, one of the old boys, who he used to bring messages from Zaire, letters that set up meeting places and deals with the gold dealers of Walikale across the border. She knew too much, and she was threatening to tell the President and the Americans. She had to be stopped. What made the situation worse was that that idiot Augustin had given her a visa for two years. He thought it would please the President. The fool! If only he had delayed it, she would probably have had to leave the country. Zed knew the Americans wanted her out. Not only the embassy but also her own colleagues at Karisoke. She was trouble for them too.

Okay, so he hadn't planned actually to kill her. The men were under orders to rough her up, take her notes, but they had panicked, gone too far. They had removed the side panel after the killing to make it look as if she had been a victim of thieves, and then the idiots had not stolen anything. Now Zed had to pre-empt the explosion that he knew was going to come from the President. To kill a foreigner was madness, but to kill a famous foreigner, that was careless. Agathe, his sister, the President's wife, had got him out of awkward situations before, but this time she could do nothing. The President was so furious that he had taken his anger out on her and she had had to seek the protection of the Papal Nuncio.

Zed had to move quickly, deflect the blame, limit the damage, find a scapegoat, a fall-guy. But first he made sure that he attended the funeral. He climbed up that mountain to Karisoke and gave a funeral oration that, if it didn't impress the trackers who had worked with Fossey, certainly touched a nerve with the American preacher, Dr Wallace. He wasn't sure about the Americans, the embassy people. But then they couldn't even organise the coffin properly. It was too small for Fossey. He had smiled at that. They had not allowed for rigor mortis to set in, and their estimate of six foot was not enough. They had had to have the coffin taken apart and remade before they could bury the woman. Then there were the men, Fossey's men, to deal with. With the help of Colonel Rwangasore, they were quarantined. Then they were tortured to see how much they knew. They were lucky, only one knew a semblance of the truth. Rwelekana. He was dealt with in the Gikondo. There was of course Magayani. They planted the items of Fossey's on him and had him eliminated too.

But Zed knew he had still to wrap up the case. He would have to involve the American. He, too, had seen what had happened. He would have to be dealt with. But how? It was here he had his stroke of genius. He got someone to send a sample of the American's hair to Paris. That would effectively seal the fate of the American. Or would it? Zed pictured the American in the witness box telling all that he had seen that night. No, it was a better solution to allow the American to flee the country.

Were these reasons, taken either singly or together, enough to kill Dian? I wasn't sure, and then I thought of the conspiracy that would have to have been put into motion if what I was suggesting was true. And if this were done, who did it? Bushishi?

He had the opportunity, but I don't believe he did. Why? Because Bushishi was the only official involved in the investigation who cast any doubt on the official explanation of the murder. He would hardly have told me that in his opinion Dian was strangled and not killed with a *panga* if he was part of a conspiracy to frame McGuire. It would have been much more likely for Bushishi to have agreed with the authorised version. Why introduce an element of doubt into a case you know not to be watertight?

What about Karangwa? Karangwa told me he could not remember much about the investigation. He told me that he had found documents in McGuire's house. This was untrue. Karangwa wrote a report marked secret which was dated January 2, 1986. In this he makes it clear that he suspects McGuire and Rwelekana, and it is only a few days after the murder. He also states that he was in Dian's bedroom when it was noticed that there was hair in her clenched fists. This, according to Philippe Bertrand, whom I had met in London after Christmas, was not correct. The French doctor told me that Karangwa was not in the room and could not have known about the hair in Dian's hand, nor the fact that it looked like the hair of a white person. Bertrand assured me that when he saw the hair he told Bushishi and Kathleen Austin that this could be a vital discovery and they should keep it a secret as the provenance of the hair could well lead to the discovery of the assassin.

How did Karangwa know about the discovery of the hair? The simple answer is that Bushishi told him. After all, they were colleagues. But when did Bushishi tell him? By January 2? Certainly, because, by that time, Karangwa had filed his report and said that he knew about the hair because he was there in Dian's bedroom with Kathleen Austin and Bushishi and Bertrand the moment it was discovered. We know this to be untrue, but we also know that Karangwa told Ros Carr, when he met her at the foot of the mountain the day after the body was discovered, that he had a secret, a clue to the identity of the killer, and that it concerned the discovery of a hair.

So Karangwa lied in his secret report about knowing about the discovery of the hair. Could he have planted it? Possibly. He had the opportunity. But did he have the brains to think of planting it? And if he did plant it, where did he get it from?

Did he pull it from McGuire's head? Hardly likely. Did he pick it up from McGuire's pillow? Possibly. Could he have found the hair in Dian's bedroom? Certainly, because Dian did cut McGuire's hair shortly before she died. McGuire always claimed that this really happened and said, by way of explanation, that Dian had kept the hair as a sort of *sumu*, a way of controlling him. During the making of the inventory of Dian's effects, an envelope containing hair was found. McGuire's name was on the envelope. Was he telling the truth? Did Dian cut his hair? I had thought it unlikely

– haircutting in the bush, and not professionally in the barber's shop, is a curiously intimate process – and I doubted whether such a relationship existed between Dian and McGuire. But I was wrong. Philippe Bertrand confirmed that she did indeed cut his hair.

Outside my room, I could hear the clacking of an army helicopter. It was landing in the next block to the hotel. I suspected it was carrying the wounded back to the hospital from the battlefield at Ruhengeri. I leaned over the railing of my balconette and looked down at the two men who were methodically scything the top off the Bermuda grass lawns with slow and easy strokes. Backwards and forwards, backwards and forwards, no hurry, no worry. I wondered if they would finish the lawn before I left the country. Two days to go. And still I had not found the evidence I needed.

I thought again about the person who could have framed McGuire, the one who could have faked the evidence. It had to be Augustin. Karangwa would have had to move fast to have put hair in Dian's fist, and anyway, what if there were hairs there all the time? All Augustin had to do was insert white male hair in the Paris envelope. This was plausible. What wasn't was the idea that the hair in Dian's hand had not been planted, because if it wasn't McGuire's hair, then whose was it?

I went to bed thinking about it and when I woke up I realised that none of this business of the hair mattered any more. I doubted whether any court of law, outside Rwanda, would accept the forensic evidence in this case anyway. Everyone who had claimed to have handled the hair was telling a different story. Kathleen Austin, Matthieu Bushishi, Philippe Bertrand, Karangwa, Augustin. Not only that, there were two reports which drew conflicting conclusions. Forget the hair. The hair did not provide compelling evidence.

Kigali: February 1993

ONE DAY left in Kigali. How many times could I pace this room in twenty-four hours? Twenty-four hours to crack a murder. I couldn't stay any longer. I didn't want to stay any longer. The plane took off for Nairobi the next afternoon and I would have to be at the airport at midday. I wasn't sorry. I thought of packing; it's strange, but what is a pain before a journey is a pleasure at the end. I put it off and lay back on the bed and counted the divides in the ceiling plankery. Fourteen. And then, for some reason I will never be able to explain, I closed my eyes and saw shadowed in his pith helmet, standing on the edge of Rwanda, the face of Stanley, the great Stanley who had never crossed over the borders into Rwanda, but instead had contented himself with campfire stories of the snake-tongued Arab merchant Hamid Ibrahim with his florid tales of dwarfs with ears that touched the ground, useful appendages because at night they could be doubled as duvets. I wondered what tog they would have earned had a British Standards Institution inspector been accompanying Stanley. I lay back and thought of Stanley raping the continent. He hadn't penetrated Rwanda. And neither had I. I had accumulated as much evidence as I could, but was I any nearer the truth than I was to finding Hamid Ibrahim's Disnoid-eared dwarfs?

It was past lunch, getting towards three, and I was thinking of desperate measures. A bath? Yes, a bath. Running the water. That would take ten minutes, and I could lose another ten wallowing inside it. Yes, a bath would chip away at the flagging remains of daylight, but a bath was meant to be relaxing, and did I need languidity?

I didn't so much as dip a toe in that water. I had no chance. There were people moving around outside the room. Muttering. Shuffling. I forgot about packing and afternoon shadows, bath taps and H. M. Stanley. I opened the door.

Albert stands there, unable to shift the grin from his face. Alongside him, looking down the corridor, looking everywhere but at me, is an altogether more collected man. I have never seen him before, but from the victory signals radiating from Albert's face, I know his identity.

"I found him. This is him," says Albert, pushing his plunder past me and into the room with all the brusque swagger of a Fleet Street cheque-book specialist. Albert displays such little regard for his charge that I am certain he is frightened that the man will change his mind and vanish back to Gitarama before some spy sees the three of us together. I shake hands with the man from

Gitarama and wave him towards one of the easy chairs, though why they were called easy I don't know, for they have no arms and the seat is so low that it is difficult to remain upright. I suspect it is because they were easier to make than chairs with arms. Anyway they were just the job for an interrogation. I clear a space for Albert to sit in the other, matching chair by flinging my suitcase on to the floor and I turn and fish from my briefcase my reporter's notebook.

Albert is telling me about how lucky he was to find the man and how difficult it was to persuade him to come to see me. "He changes his address every night. He never sleeps in the same house twice. He is convinced he is a target for the death squads."

I ask him to tell me his name.

"Boniface," he says, "but you are not going to use it. Are you?"

"No."

Boniface leans forward and takes a sharp look under the bed. He gets up, and stands at the end of the bed I am sitting on. He bends forward and lifts up the bedcover and examines the carpet.

"What is he looking for?"

"A bug," says Albert.

I smile at Boniface. "No tape. No bug. No microphone. Just this," I say, waving in front of him the reporter's notebook.

"He thinks that you are a government spy and you are going to trap him," explains Albert. "He doesn't like this hotel. The last time he was arrested it happened here."

"In this hotel, you mean?"

Albert nods. "I didn't dare tell him where we were meeting you until we were practically standing in reception."

Boniface begins to tell me his story. It is long, and convoluted, beginning in Bujumbura where he worked as a taximan-spy.

"I was recruited by Burundi intelligence in 1982. They asked me to work with the PF, the frontier police. I was responsible to Colonel Ndabanezi and my job was to inform on people. I was a taxi driver so I was in a good position to hear gossip and to talk to people, ask them questions. The Burundi people were pleased with the intelligence I was gathering for them and then I joined the Rwandan secret police. This was two years later. There was a big conference due to be held in Burundi with many heads of state invited and I was asked to report on it."

So what has this got to do with Dian, with Rwelekana? I say

nothing. Let him talk. I have waited long enough to hear him.

"But," he continues, "everything went wrong for me. I was working for two masters. The Rwandans were trying to obtain documents. I was able to channel the papers they wanted to see to them. In 1986 there was a diplomatic incident. The embassy in Bujumbura was under siege –"

He stops. It is almost as if he anticipates the knock on the door that fills the silence. He is jumpy. It is only a waiter bringing Primus and water.

He returns to his past, full of names, dates. He is confident and comfortable in his past. It is a meandering and complicated story of intrigue and double-dealing played out by the rival intelligence services of two nations which share a border and little else but a violent antipathy nurtured on the blood of generations. He tells me that the intelligence operation mounted by the Rwandans inside Burundi ended in disaster and public humiliation. He was the man who had laced together the contacts. He was the man who was blamed.

"Were you recalled to Kigali?" I asked.

"No. There was no way I would come back at first because I knew the intelligence people here would want to interrogate me. I stayed where I was, but in March 1986 I had to return to my home."

"Why?"

"Because my father had died. I wanted to bury him."

"What happened?"

"I was here at this hotel. I had a room here and they came for me and arrested me. The man in reception got me arrested. He called the Sûreté. They always are doing that. They get paid."

"They took you away?"

He nods. "I was accused of spying for Burundi. That was on April 15, 1986. I was taken to the jail in the President's office and kept there for twenty-one days and then I was taken to the Central Prison in Kigali. I was then transferred to the special prison in Ruhengeri."

"When was this?"

"July 8, 1986."

He has a *Mastermind* memory. I ask him how he manages to pin down all the dates and names and places.

"It is not something I was born with. It is not a talent of God. I was trained. I was a spy. I was taught how to hold things in my brain. Details are like precious stones. I was told always to keep them, hide them. Details are worth money."

I leave him to rest for a few minutes, and wait while he finishes his Primus.

"When I reached Ruhengeri prison, I was received by Major Lizinde [later to be sprung from the prison and now an FPR general based in Kampala], Captain Muvunanuambo and Commander Bisuroko [now the leader of rebel forces in Rwanda]. The next day I was transferred into a cell. In it was Rwelekana. I was to spend eighteen days with him."

"What was he wearing?"

"Red shoes made of leather, a prison tunic, the pink tunic, and trousers. This was two months after they had introduced the pink uniform for prisoners. Before everyone wore black. The man who escorted me to this cell was the adjutant principal of the prison. Munyeshuri. He was a ballistics expert."

"What did you talk to Rwelekana about?"

"When you go into a cell, the psychology of the situation is simple. You have no choice but to discuss your case. I told him my problem, why I was there; that was what interested me most of all. Me."

"And what did he tell you?"

"He was the same. He told me his problems. It was curious, but we seemed to be having the same sort of trouble."

"In what way?"

"Well, because I was not sure who was in control of me. Was it Burundi intelligence or Rwandan intelligence? I did not know who my master really was."

"Why was Rwelekana's problem like yours?"

"He too said he did not know who was controlling him. He was scared that he would be killed at any time."

"What did he mean when he said he did not know who was controlling him?"

"He was being visited by very high-up people."

"Where?"

"In the prison."

"How could you know that?"

"Because Rwelekana would be taken from his cell and when he returned he would tell me."

"Who came to see him?"

"Silas Habirayamana and Joseph Ruzindna. They were the chief in charge of the prison and his deputy. They were trying to make him sign false depositions."

"Why?"

"Because they wanted him to accuse the American of the crime."

"Which American?"

"Wayne."

"Who sent them to do this?"

"He told me that the prefect sent them."

"You mean Zed?"

"Yes. Mr Zed."

"Why was Zed involved?"

"When Rwelekana returned to the cell he asked me what should he do. He told me this was happening to him. I asked him why they were asking him to make up these depositions, and he said it was because –" He stops talking in mid flow. He cuts off the words as quickly as a light is extinguished. He is looking hard at Albert and then at me.

I wait.

"He is worried about what you are asking him. He does not entirely trust you."

I look straight at Boniface. I tell him that what he has told me is valuable, but that I need to know as much as he knows. I need the whole picture. "Tell him that I shall protect him."

But before Albert can offer the reassurance, a sheaf of ageing paper is pulled out of Boniface's wallet. He has three letters in his hand. He passes them to me. They are addressed to him, posted in Paris and London, written by officials of Amnesty International.

"I need a passport. I need to be able to leave this country. I cannot at the moment."

"Amnesty helped you before?"

"Yes."

I tell him I will speak to the Amnesty people when I am back in London. (I did but they said they could do something for Boniface only if he was in prison, which, I thought, sounded like a line from *Catch-22*.)

We go back to the point he broke off. "You were telling me what Rwelekana was saying . . ."

"Yes. He said that Mr Zed was in complicity with Agathe."

"Agathe?"

"The wife of the President. The sister of Zed," says Albert.

"Why should she be involved?"

"Gorillas," says Boniface. "Zed and Agathe were trafficking in gorillas. They were involved also with Mr Karekezi who was intelligence director of Ruhengeri at the time and Jeremy Sukiranya, the director of the prison. All of them were involved in transferring gorillas out of the country. Rwelekana knew this because when he was arrested they made him understand that if he made false depositions, false accusations, he would be released after some time in jail."

"Being told to make false depositions and knowing the wife and brother-in-law of the President were involved are two different things. Where is the link between them?"

"Because they told him. They told him that there were people who were very powerful who wanted him to say these things in his deposition. They believed that Rwelekana was a stupid peasant who would either be impressed or frightened and that by mentioning these names he would do as he was told."

"What sort of man was he?"

"He wasn't stupid. He was intelligent with a serious side to him. He was about thirty. A tall man. Strong-looking. And stout with it."

"Was he despairing about his case?"

"He did despair. He was offered this one chance to save himself. If he took it, then he would be released, he said, after a certain time in prison."

"What chance?"

"The one I told you about. The one where he had to make false depositions."

"Yes, but why was he killed in the August? It was a long time after Dian was killed. Was he killed then because McGuire had fled the country?"

"I don't know. That could be true. But I think it was because the Americans had decided to send someone from the embassy to question him."

"How do you know this?"

"He told me. He was taken from his cell and when he came back he said he had been summoned to the office of the director of the prison. He told me that an American was coming to interrogate him. And he had to make a deposition in defence of the Rwandan government, so he had to accuse Wayne McGuire of the murder. He had to accuse an American of murdering a fellow American citizen."

"Did he ever see the American?"

"No. He was dead before they came."

"So you believe that he was killed because he refused to tell the Americans what the Rwandans wanted them to hear?"

"Yes."

"Dian was killed because she knew about Zed and his sister's gorilla business?"

"Yes."

"Who killed Dian? I mean, who actually did it?"

"In late 1984, Dian Fossey had met the President, and she complained to him about the lack of security in the Karisoke area. She told him about the increase in poaching activities. The President told her that she had nothing to be concerned about. He promised that he would raise the question of security with the prefect of Ruhengeri."

"Zed?"

"Yes. It was at this point, when the President returned to Kigali and discussed his meeting with Dian with his wife and Zed, that a decision was taken to kill her."

"But she was given a visa after all this, after the decision was taken. Why?"

"To throw people, throw her, off the scent. They wanted to make her believe she was being protected."

"How was she killed?"

"She was cut with *pangas* because they wanted people to think it was poachers."

"What about the fact that Bushishi believes she was strangled and hit afterwards?"

"That could be so. Rwelekana never told me."

"Who killed her?"

"Rwelekana did not kill her. He told me that the people who killed her were themselves killed immediately afterwards."

"Where?"

"In the prison in Ruhengeri. They have special cells there for the internees. These people were kept in these special cells and killed. There were four of them. Two were civilians. Two were ex-military."

"Names?"

"I never was told their names."

"How were they killed?"

"The director, Sukiranya, came and took them from their cells and brought them to another cell. This was in the charge of an adjutant whose name was Gakuba. They were brought into this cell and beaten to death by Gakuba."

"What with? What were they beaten with?"

"A hammer. The executioner was Gakuba and he killed them in front of the director of the prison. This was done in the evening around six. The bodies went back to the cells and from there to be buried."

"Did you see them?"

"No. We couldn't see them. We saw the blankets they were concealed in. Lizinde saw them."

I ask him who gave the orders to kill Dian.

He is frightened again. He still thinks I have a hidden recorder in the room. "Those four people. The ones who killed Dian. They were working for Agathe."

The room is quite dark now. Boniface has pulled the curtain across the windows that lead out on to the balcony. I can hear a mosquito somewhere to my right; it is then I notice the swelling on my elbow. I start to scratch.

"Agathe considered that Dian was working against her interests."

"What interests?"

"Gorilla trafficking, smuggling, tourism."

"How did she organise the killing?"

"She put her brother in charge. Mr Zed was in contact with many people who could have done the job."

"But why," I ask, "did they kill her? Why not frighten her, or get her kicked out of the country?"

"Rwelekana said that they did not make a choice of killing or expulsion. If this occurred to them, they rejected expulsion because they thought that once out of the country Dian would make a huge row, and she might name them as being responsible for the deaths of many gorillas. So they had no choice. They made sure she had the visa as I told you already and then the murderers went up to her house and, according to Rwelekana, knocked on the door. There was no response. So they were forced to enter the house by another way."

"By cutting the panel?"

"He never told me. He did not know."

"By the roof?"

"No, he never said. I told you. He did not know."

"So Rwelekana told you all this. Did he tell anyone else?"

"He told two of Lizinde's men. They were in jail with us, but they are both dead. They were executed before Rwelekana was killed."

"And you?"

"I told a Catholic bishop. He was visiting."

"Who else would know the truth?"

"There is an Army Captain who knows the truth."

He pauses; I stare at him. "Who?"

"Kayumba. Kayumba from Bayumba."

I try not to laugh. "Why would he know the truth?"

"Because he was part of the plot. It was his job to visit Rwelekana and coach him in his depositions."

"Tell him what to say?"

"Yes."

"How would he do this?"

"We would see him in the prison and then Rwelekana would be taken from his cell and then he would come back and tell us what Kayumba wanted with him."

"Who else?"

"Colonel Rwangasore."

The colonel I had so narrowly missed on my first day in Rwanda, the ghost I had mistaken Charles for that afternoon at the Milles Collines.

"He was the commandant in Ruhengeri in 1986 and 1987. He was the man who took Rwelekana from Ruhengeri prison to the Gikondo Brigades in Kigali."

"What happened there?"

"I only know what I have been told. I was not in the prison then. But I have no doubt that Rwelekana was executed there by Haguma."

I hand to Boniface the stats of the photographs I have found in the dossier. He bends forward to look at them.

"*Vite!*" he shouts to Albert who is in the bathroom, peeing out the Primus he has drunk that afternoon. "Look!" And he points to the Polaroid picture of Dian's gun, the picture with CIA written in Biro on it. "They made a rumour that she worked for the CIA. I think this inscription on the gun was put there by Augustin's men."

I ask him if Rwelekana had told him how McGuire was framed.

"He said nothing about that. All he told me was that she was killed because of the complicity of those people I mentioned to you."

"What about gorilla smuggling?"

"Rwelekana said that from about 1984 Dian knew who was taking the baby gorillas from the volcanoes. She knew that the President knew also. She was a witness who nobody wanted."

I thought about Dian seeing the President, telling him all her worries, and not realising that the man from whom she was seeking help was in fact her judge.

"All the depositions say that whoever killed Dian knew the layout of Karisoke, knew exactly where her hut was. So how did the people who killed her, these four men, know where to look for her?"

"The intelligence services were involved. Mr Karekezi, the intelligence officer, would have known the exact layout of Karisoke. He could have briefed the killers."

"What about the blood on Rwelekana's boots?" I ask.

"He always denied that there was human blood on his boots. He told me it was bedbugs."

Albert can hardly contain himself. He has mortared himself off his chair. "That is what Rwelekana said to Bushishi. He always denied it was human blood on his boots. He always said that the blood had come from the bedbugs he had crushed in his cell."

There is no doubt in either of our minds now that Boniface and Rwelekana did share a cell. The only way Boniface could have known about the bedbugs was either by reading the depositions which was impossible or hearing it from the mouth of Rwelekana.

"When did you hear about Rwelekana's death?"

"About two days after it happened. I was not surprised. I felt it was a montage."

"And Haguma?"

"He was a man involved in so many killings."

"And Rwangasore?"

"He was just one of a number of killers. He was part of the *escadrons des morts*. He and Kayumba planned Dian's death. He and Kayumba worked out the detail of it. Zed told him to organise it and Agathe told Zed."

"Do you think Kayumba will survive?"

"They tried to demote him not so long ago. They did not succeed. He has been buying arms from South Africa for the President so he knows a lot. But that may not save him."

Outside it was fizzing black, like a tropical cocktail. The night had settled firmly upon the complacency of the dusk.

Boniface rose. He held out his hand. "Talk to Amnesty. I need a passport." He shook my hand. I never saw him again.

I looked at my watch. Eight o'clock. One more night in Rwanda. Only now I had a notebook to hide, a notebook as lethal as a used hypodermic. I wanted to get out fast.

I wanted to climb once more to Karisoke, to look again at Fossey's grave, to talk aloud beneath that Hagenia tree, to tell her the truth. Because up there, in that alpine meadow, squelched beneath that Hagenia tree, and surrounded by all those graves, the truth had been brushed aside, ignored, conveniently forgotten by the people who believed that the survival of the gorillas was more vital than discovering the truth about the murder of the woman without whom there would have been no species for them to protect. I wanted to talk aloud beside that grave and tell her about the country's big brother and the big sister who coveted money and power, and who had killed to hide the truth. I wanted to tell her about Rwelekana, and Rwangasore, and Haguma, all dead, all three of them. I wanted to tell her about her friends, and those she didn't know, those who had risked their lives to help me find the truth.

But I couldn't tell her any of these things. There was a war raging in the volcanoes. Karisoke was empty. Only the gorillas were left now.